Social Work with Children and Families

Third Edition

MAUREEN O'LOUGHLIN AND STEVE O'LOUGHLIN

Series Editors: Jonathan Parker and Greta Bradley

Los Angeles | London | New Delhi
Singapore | Washington DC

Learning Matters
An imprint of SAGE Publications Ltd
1 Oliver's Yard
55 City Road
London EC1Y 1SP

SAGE Publications Inc.
2455 Teller Road
Thousand Oaks, California 91320

SAGE Publications India Pvt Ltd 150
B 1/I 1 Mohan Cooperative Industrial Area
Mathura Road
New Delhi 110 044

SAGE Publications Asia-Pacific Pte Ltd
3 Chuch Street
#10–04 Samsung Hub
Singapore 049483

Editor: Luke Block
Production Controller: Chris Marke
Project Management: Deer Park Productions,
Tavistock, Devon
Marketing Manager: Tamara Navaratnam
Cover Design: Code 5 Design Associates
Typeset by: Pantek Media, Maidstone, Kent
Printed by: MPG Books Group, Bodmin, Cornwall

MIX
Paper from
responsible sources
FSC
www.fsc.org
FSC® C018575

First published in 2005 by Learning Matters Ltd
Reprinted in 2006.
Reprinted in 2007.
Second edition published in 2008.
Third edition published in 2012.

British Library Cataloguing in Publication Data

A catalogue record for this book is available from
the British Library.

ISBN: 978 0 85725 939 4
ISBN: 978 1 44625 707 4 (hbk)

PCF Diagram used with permission of the College
of Social Work.

**Edith Rigby
Library & Learning Centre**
Tel: 01772 225298

**PRESTON
COLLEGE**

Please return or renew on or before the date shown below.
Fines will be charged on overdue items.

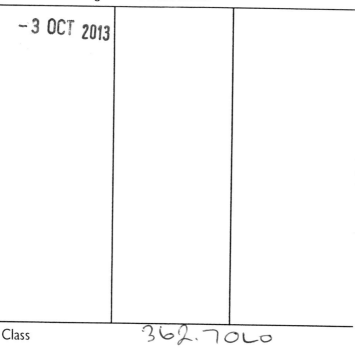

−3 OCT 2013

Class 362.7OLO

Barcode 096447

29-HF-1006-PW-0(

Contents

This book is dedicated to all the children, young people, families and students we have all worked with and who have taught us so much.

About the editors and contributors

The editors

Maureen O'Loughlin is an Independent Social Work Consultant who has substantial experience working with children and families as a social worker and a Guardian *ad Litem*. Formerly an academic she undertook independent assessments for court proceedings in a variety of areas for a number of years. She continues her interest in adoption and fostering through chairing adoption and fostering panels for local authorities and the Independent Reviewing Mechanism.

Steve O'Loughlin also works as an Independent Social Work Consultant. He currently acts as a tutor for qualifying students. He is an experienced fostering and adoption worker and undertakes independent assessments. He acts as an advocate for carers and young people. Steve is committed to Black issues and to furthering the interests of Black and Minority Ethnic children and families.

The contributors

Julie Bywater is a Senior Lecturer and Programme Leader for the MA in Social Work at the University of Chester. She teaches on both the BA and MA qualifying social work programmes, and is committed to working closely and collaboratively with students, with the aim of students becoming research-minded, critically reflective practitioners. She is the co-author of the text, *Sexuality and Social Work* with Rhiannon Jones (2007, Learning Matters) and is currently undertaking a PhD.

Jackie Hughes is a Senior Lecturer at the University of Huddersfield where she is Course Leader for the MSc in Health and Social Care. She has been a practising social worker and involved in social work education for many years. She worked with the Joseph Rowntree Foundation on housing issues for families with disabled children, and with the National Development Team on short breaks for children with learning disabilities and complex health needs.

Nicky Ryden is a part-time tutor on the Social Work Course at the University of Huddersfield. She is a registered social worker with more than 30 years' experience working with children and their families. Nicky successfully completed her PhD in 2009, researching the experiences of very young children in children's centres. Nicky is interested in all aspects of family support work and has participated in the evaluation of parenting support programmes.

Introduction

Social work practice with children and families is one of the most challenging, skilled and rewarding areas of social work practice. Social workers work with a diverse group of children and their families, from babies to teenagers, single parents to two-parent families to multi-carer families. Social workers also work with a diverse group of professionals, such as the police, schools, hospitals, health centres and various community organisations. We believe that safeguarding children and preventing them from suffering significant harm is a rewarding and challenging way to make a difference to the life of a child, which involves the co-operation, consultation and collaboration of many people working effectively together. This book is itself a collaboration between experienced social work practitioners and educators.

Social workers engaged in this work must believe that the work they do makes a difference and that they can make a difference. In order to do so they must have the necessary knowledge, skills and values to achieve this objective. The introduction of the three-year social work degree has brought changes to the knowledge, values and skills of student social workers. They now need to have knowledge of:

- the Professional Capabilities Framework;

- the law and legislation in relation to children;

- the social and political context;

- a number of different assessment processes in the context of working with children and families;

- interdisciplinary working in an ethnically diverse society;

- different types of family support and substitute care for children;

- working with disabled children.

This book relies on this knowledge to inform the protection of children.

Working with children and families requires many skills: communication, preparation and planning, intervention skills, recognition, identification and assessment of significant harm, recording and report writing, managing oneself and the work, problem solving, research and analysis and decision-making skills. This book attempts to review how these skills can enhance working with children and families.

Working with children and families requires that social workers work in a non-judgemental anti-oppressive way. The Professional Capabilities Framework provides guidance to assist workers in this context. The book explores how social workers' values and attitudes can affect the work they do and the safety of children.

Social work practice with children and families is changing as a result of the many public cases of child abuse. These changes will affect the way services for children are managed, as the role of social service departments changes with the introduction of children's trusts and the more extensive involvement of education departments. Social workers engaged in safeguarding work must be able to work within and between various systems and also manage the work they do effectively. In addition, the registration of social workers has made social workers more personally accountable and responsible for their actions, decisions and conduct. The importance of having a good grounding in working with children and families becomes even more important than ever.

This book is intended to be used by social work degree students and social work educators as well as professional practitioners.

Chapter 1 explores the values and ethics of working with children and families. This chapter addresses the social work benchmarks 3.1.1 and 3.1.3, which require social workers to have an understanding of social work processes in a diverse society as well as of the ethical issues and value dilemmas which face those working with children and families. It makes explicit links to the Professional Capabilities Framework. The chapter seeks to address how values and ethics apply in social work practice with children and families. It examines issues that arise in working with children and families, and students are encouraged to examine their own beliefs and prejudices and the implications for practice that these provoke.

The chapter discusses the impact of social differences that affect the position of families in society, for example poverty, race, culture, disability and gender. The tensions between welfare principles, children's rights and protection and the right to family life are considered. Social work practice with children and families is discussed with reference to interpersonal, institutional and structural discrimination, empowerment and anti-discriminatory practice.

Chapter 2 sets out and explores the changing contexts of social work with children and families over time. It considers the historical context of the work that has informed modern practice. Significant legislation and events are reviewed to try to develop the reader's understanding of how current provision developed. Social work practice is defined in relation to working with children and families and the practical aspects of working with children are highlighted throughout the text. The changes and developments post Climbié are highlighted with brief discussion of Every Child Matters (DfES, 2004), the Children Act 2004 and Care Matters (DfES, 2007) and subsequent developments, including the impact of the death of Peter Connelly.

Chapter 3 focuses on family support, considering current policy and its implications for social work practice. It explores how the provision made to support families in the care of their children varies with the age and circumstances of the child and their family. The impact of poverty will be discussed in the context of supporting families. The aims of family support are also explored and a brief outline is given of the relevant legal knowledge. In addition, the role of the social worker is discussed as an assessor, provider and broker of services. The range of different types of support given to families is also discussed, as is the principle of partnership and the impact 'joined up' thinking can have on the quality of service provided.

Finally, some research findings are reviewed and case studies presented to illustrate some of the knowledge, skills and values that are needed to work with children and their families.

Chapter 4 aims to introduce the student to working effectively with children and families in the safeguarding children arena. It expands upon the legislative issues raised in Chapter 2 as well as giving definitions of abuse. Safeguarding children is discussed in the context of the experience of modern families. This includes the impact of domestic abuse, substance misuse and mental ill-health. The main elements of the framework of assessment for children in need and their families is highlighted in the context of multi-agency working. The chapter also discusses the role of the Local Safeguarding Children Boards.

Social work skills and methods of intervention will be discussed and demonstrated at each stage of the safeguarding process with the use of activities.

Chapter 5 is a new chapter for this edition, reflecting the importance of consulting children and young people of all ages and abilities about decisions in their lives and recognising the importance of building relationships as an underpinning social work precept. The chapter addresses direct work with children, discusses approaches to direct work and offers a variety of techniques and tools that social workers can use with differing ages as well as specific discussion of working with children with disabilities.

Chapter 6 covers working with children with disabilities. It looks specifically at the skills required by social workers to support disabled children and their families effectively. It is based on a social model of disability and promotes the values of inclusion for children with disabilities. It enables students to see disabled children as children first, and build on their skills in communicating with children and undertaking family assessments. It makes links to legislation in terms of the 1989 Children Act Section 17, for children with disabilities as 'children in need' (The Children Act, 1989 Guidance and Regulations, Volume 6, Children with Disabilities) and the Children Act 2004. It also refers to the National Service Framework Standard 8 for disabled children and young people and those with complex health needs.

This chapter looks sequentially at some of the issues facing disabled children and their families, building on students' knowledge of human growth and development. Diagnosis, communication, short breaks and leisure opportunities, education, child protection, housing needs and adolescent transitions are explored by the use of case studies to enable students to develop skills in working in partnership with disabled children and their families.

Chapter 7 considers the substitute care of children. This chapter discusses children in the looked after system, reviewing the three main areas of substitute care as well as the Looked After Children (LAC) provisions. Principles of adoption and fostering are considered in the current legal and social policy context. The processes of adoption and fostering are outlined using case study material. The chapter also discusses residential provision as the other area of substitute care, again using case material to highlight principles, procedures and processes.

Throughout the book activities are used to help you reflect on your values, beliefs and practice. Some of these will focus on the Cole/Green family whose experiences will introduce you to and inform you about social work with children and families.

This book has been carefully mapped to the new Professional Capabilities Framework for Social Workers in England and will help you to develop the appropriate standards at the right level. These standards are:

- **Professionalism**

  Identify and behave as a professional social worker committed to professional development.

- **Values and ethics**

  Apply social work ethical principles and values to guide professional practice.

- **Diversity**

  Recognise diversity and apply anti-discriminatory and anti-oppressive principles in practice.

- **Justice**

  Advance human rights and promote social justice and economic well-being.

- **Knowledge**

  Apply knowledge of social sciences, law and social work practice theory.

- **Judgement**

  Use judgement and authority to intervene with individuals, families and communities to promote independence, provide support and prevent harm, neglect and abuse.

- **Critical reflection and analysis**

  Apply critical reflection and analysis to inform and provide a rationale for professional decision-making.

- **Contexts and organisations**

  Engage with, inform and adapt to changing contexts that shape practice. Operate effectively within your own organisational frameworks and contribute to the development of services and organisations. Operate effectively within multi-agency and inter-professional settings.

- **Professional leadership**

  Take responsibility for the professional learning and development of others through supervision, mentoring, assessing, research, teaching, leadership and management.

References to these standards are made throughout the text and you will find a diagram of the Professional Capabilities Framework in Appendix 1 (see page 153). Each chapter also relates to specific parts of the social work subject benchmark statements – you will find extracts from the statements in Appendix 2 (see page 154).

Chapter 1

Values and ethics in social work with children and families

Steve O' Loughlin

Introduction

This chapter will discuss issues that arise in working with children and families in a diverse society. Students will be encouraged to examine their own values and beliefs and the implications these have for practice. The chapter will consider the value requirements for social work practice contained within the Professional Capabilities Framework (2012) and the Health and Care Professions Council (HCPC) standards of conduct, performance and ethics (Van der Gaag, 2008), which are currently completing their development and are untried in practice. The chapter will consider the scope of these new values and ethics as well as discussing the impact. In addition, this chapter will also discuss the impact of social differences that affect the position of families in society, for example, poverty, class, race, religion, culture, sexuality and gender. The tensions between welfare principles, children's rights and protection and the right to family life will be considered.

Diversity of families

Social work with children and families rarely involves working with one individual. It involves working with families that are complex, diverse and constantly changing. The family may consist of one or more parents or carers. It may consist of relative carers such as grandparents, who may be paternal, maternal or by marriage. The family may consist of non-relative carers such as friends. Additionally, it may consist of parents or carers who share the same race, class, culture, religion and sexuality, or alternatively it may consist of parents or carers who have different race, class, culture, religion or sexuality. There may be one or more children in the family, some of whom may share the race, religion and sexuality of their parents and some who do not. To add to the complexity, people constantly enter and leave families, by birth, marriage, adoption, divorce and death. Millam (2002, page 31) describes some of this complexity and diversity when she says that:

> Parents are generally the most important and influential people in a child's life and they usually have more information about their child than anyone else. Some children live with both birth parents, some with one parent, some children live with foster carers, some live in residential homes, and a number of children are adopted.

The child and family social worker needs to both understand and value the complex, diverse and different family forms and be able to assess the relative merits of each one they encounter. The child and family social worker also needs to have a clear idea about why she or he is doing what they are doing as well as being aware of some of the complicated ethical dilemmas which they will encounter. Who is the main focus of the work or intervention: the child or the family? Clearly the child's welfare is paramount but, in order to achieve an outcome for the child, work will also need to be done with the family. Before you begin to think about who you are working with you will need to have an understanding about what you believe is important. The value or importance that you place on the work you are doing and the ethical or moral stance you take (that is simply whether you feel that the work you are doing is right and proper) are the two areas that we are going to explore. As Beckett and Maynard (2005, page 1) have stated: *Values and ethics do not simply exist at the fringes of social work, but are at the heart of social work practice.*

I would go further and state that values and ethics are not only at the heart of social work practice but they constitute the life force that permeates every part of social work practice. Having an understanding of what factors might influence your decisions will help to guide your practice. These factors will include personal values and ethics, professional values and ethics, agency values and ethics, and societal values and ethics. In order to do this you will need to have an understanding of your personal values and ethics.

Developing an understanding of your own starting point

Think about your personal views and assumptions about how children should be cared for while they are growing up. Make a list of those you feel are most important. How do you think you came to choose these?

COMMENT

Your list will be personal to you and many factors will influence your views, for example the experiences you have had as a child or parent, as well as your family's or carers' attitudes, beliefs, religion and cultural backgrounds. This list will almost become an internalised standard by which you judge and will be judged by others, except that you also have to consider that your standards might be challenged as being too high, too low, too narrow or too accepting. They are, after all, exclusive to you. Your standards might even be considered to be appropriate for a certain era, and inappropriate or even wrong for the present. A situation that you might like to consider is whether you should let young children cry or comfort them. Your personal views might be that it is OK to let children cry for a while, but your professional view will be that it depends on how long the child is crying for and whether it is a cry of pain, hunger, discomfort or a cry for attention. Your personal values and beliefs could well mean that you are personally discriminating. It is therefore essential that you also use, understand and adopt some external standard to guide you. You can do this by considering your professional code of practice. This code or standard list will usually contain things that you should and must do if you are to become a more effective, empowering and thoughtful practitioner.

Professional values and ethics

As a professional you will be committed to certain standards of behaviour and conduct towards service users or the children and families you are working with. These are outlined in the Professional Capabilities Framework (2012), which describes the values and ethics for workers at various stages or levels of their careers: Principal Social Worker (PSW), Advanced Practitioner, Experienced Social Worker, Social Worker, Assessed and Supported Year in Employment (ASYE), End of last placement, End of first placement and Readiness for practice and Entry to the profession. In addition, from July 2012 the standards for the social work professional body which regulates and registers practitioners, the Health and Care Professions Council (HCPC), should also be followed. The latter currently includes some fourteen points, three of which (relating in the main to clinical interventions) will need some revision for social workers. For example, removing a child from their family is a serious form of intervention, whereas offering advice about childcare is a less serious intervention. Child and family social workers are concerned about risks and safety to both themselves and others but they are not directly concerned about 'infection' as this is a health matter rather than a social care issue. Finally, health will need to be clarified to include a wider definition, which also covers emotional and psychological health (see Van der Gaag, 2008).

Values and ethics in the Professional Capabilities Framework are much more detailed than before and prospective practitioners should be more aware of the impact that their own values and attitudes can have on relationships with others from when they enter the profession. This is sometimes difficult to ascertain as people vary in their level of insight and self-understanding. For example, you might expect a woman to have more insight and understanding about the oppression that women experience than men, but if a man has been brought up in a family that has more female members he may have more insight than a man who has not had the same experiences. The child and family worker should value and be committed to working with children and their families and this should be reflected throughout their careers.

Having obtained a place on a social work course a prospective practitioner's awareness of their personal values is to be further tested before they are allowed to practice. This can be usefully done by engaging prospective practitioners in activities in which their learning is reviewed and where they are given the opportunity to challenge and be challenged in their views and assumptions.

Your first practice placement offers you, as a prospective practitioner, further opportunities to develop, review, understand and learn about your values and ethics and this knowledge should be further consolidated during the last or final placement. The emphasis will be on understanding and managing the impact of your own values on professional practice and on the ability to identify and (with guidance) manage potentially conflicting values and ethical dilemmas, as well as becoming more knowledgeable, accountable and increasingly autonomous.

Having qualified as a social worker the next stage is to undertake a year being assessed and supported in employment (ASYE) where your ethical reasoning and values are again being tested.

As a qualified social worker the focus on self-understanding continues as you are required to be able to critically reflect on and manage the influence and impact of your own and others' values on professional practice; but equally as a practitioner you are also required to work in partnership with others.

The values and ethics strand of the Professional Capabilities Framework (PCF) for the experienced social worker suggests that the worker should be able to demonstrate, model and promote their skills at this stage whereas the advanced practitioner's knowledge and skills should be such that he or she is able to provide advice, guidance and challenge to others.

To date the values and ethics for the principal social worker have not been formulated. These are vital for those below PSW to follow and aspire to since they should inspire faith and confidence in the leader's knowledge and commitment to working with children and their families. This level of understanding should improve the standard of workers. But how are the current qualified workers to be assessed and supported in having an understanding of the importance of values and ethics as some of the workers undergoing training?

Although the GSCC Codes of Practice (2002) were not described as values or ethics they did form the basis of the professional values and ethics for social care workers. They informed professional beliefs about what is important and right.

The six main points of the Codes of Practice listed below were divided into sub-sections of between four and eight sub-points. The six main points all began with the statement: *As a social care worker you must…* The HCPC standards also begin with the words *you must*. I have attempted to compare and contrast these so that you can see which are currently applicable and which are not.

1. Protect the rights and promote the interests of service users and carers. *This is similar to Standard 1: 'You must act in the best interests of service users', and it uses language which social workers will recognise.*

2. Strive to establish and maintain the trust and confidence of service users and carers. *Trust is not mentioned explicity, though high standards of personal conduct are, in Standard 3.*

3. Promote the independence of service users while protecting them as far as possible from danger or harm. *The independence of service users is not mentioned, though Standard 1 would apply.*

4. Respect the rights of service users seeking to ensure that their behaviour does not harm themselves or other people. *Standard 1 would apply.*

5. Uphold public trust and confidence in social care services. *This is similar to Standard 13: 'You must behave with honesty and integrity and make sure that your behaviour does not damage the public's confidence in your profession'.*

6. Be accountable for the quality of your work and take responsibility for maintaining and improving your knowledge and skills. *This is similar to Standard 5: 'You must keep your professional knowledge and skills up to date'.*

(GSCC, 2002, page 4 and Van der Gaag, 2008, page 3)

As a children and families social worker you will be still be protecting the rights and promoting the interests of children and their families. You will be striving to establish and maintain the trust and confidence of children and their families. You will be promoting the independence of children and their families while protecting them as far as possible from danger or harm, always being aware that the child's interests come first. You will also be respecting their rights while seeking to ensure that their behaviour does not harm themselves or other people. You will also be upholding the public trust and confidence in you and your employer as well as being accountable for your work and taking responsibility for improving your knowledge and skills.

The PCF includes both professional value statements and professional ethical statements, that is, it seeks to outline what social workers should and must do, as well as how they should be and how they should act. You will also be using code of conduct, performance and ethics from the new regulatory body, the HCPC.

The GSCC Code of Practice also sets out what you must not do. The HCPC code currently does not set out what you must not do. Both codes are clear that workers should be accountable for their work and that they should take some responsibility for maintaining and improving their knowledge and skills as well as acting in a professional manner. Rather than the national occupational standards (key roles) you will now be concerned with the Professional Capabilities Framework's nine domains: professionalism; values and ethics (as discussed above); diversity, which we have begun to explore in the introduction to this chapter; justice; knowledge; judgement; critical reflection and analysis; contexts and organisations; and professional leadership.

ACTIVITY *1.2*

Consider the following situation: you have been asked to go to the house of a family following a referral from a family member who wishes to remain anonymous. The family member states that three children, aged 12, 3 and 1, are living in unsatisfactory conditions. List some of the things you might do to meet the PCF and the HCPC code

COMMENT

In order to maintain the trust and confidence of the family (PCF: demonstrate your professionalism, values and judgement [pvj]) you would need to clearly identify yourself by showing your identity card. You would also respect the family (pvj) by confirming that you have the right family. You would be as honest as you can by explaining the purpose of your visit (pvj) and would protect the rights of children (which includes their welfare and well-being) while respecting the confidentiality of the source of the referral. You would respect the family (pvj) by asking if you could enter their house to discuss the situation. This would also give the family some degree of choice. If they refused you might need to use your authority and explain your legal duty under the Children Act 1989. By acting in a consistent way with all families you would be meeting (using your judgement [j] and critical reflection and analysis skills [cra]) and attempting to uphold the public trust in children and family social workers. You would do this by not being abusive or confrontational but by being polite yet firm.

You are invited to enter the house and are greeted with a living room that looks tidy, clean and well decorated. What goes through your mind? Was the referrer malicious? Do you leave and apologise for wasting the family's time or do you invade their privacy and dignity further by asking to see the children's bedroom? You reach the top of the stairs and are greeted by the smell of urine. You enter the children's bedroom, which has excrement on the floor and holes in the floorboards and in the walls. There are dirty clothes everywhere you look. What decision do you make? Who would you consult with?

As a social worker concerned with protecting children from harm and promoting their welfare, you will not only be making individual professional decisions that will be influenced by a code of conduct but you will also need to follow your agency's policies and procedures. These written policies and procedures, together with the unwritten rules of your agency, will together form your agency's values and ethics to which we shall now turn.

Agency's values and ethics

As a professional you will be expected to both act on your own and work as part of a team and consult with others. Your will consult with senior colleagues within your agency about the right course of action. Some agencies will have clearly written guidelines about what you should do and others will leave some things to your discretion.

ACTIVITY **1.3**

Can you think of some of the ways your agency might value and support your intervention in the life of this family?

COMMENT

How about having a policy that you went out to referrals with another colleague? How about giving you a mobile phone so that you could consult with your colleagues at base and seek some advice if necessary? How about having a culture within your team that is flexible and supportive rather than individualistic?

The first thing you would have to decide is whether the children are at risk of significant harm or are likely to be at risk of significant harm. You may have already come to an initial decision that the children may be at risk if the situation continues and may want to seek your agency's view about precisely what should be done about the situation. The consultations with your agency colleagues might lead to the suggestion that steps should be taken to improve the living conditions of the children immediately. In making this decision you will have to monitor the situation to see if there is any improvement and, if not, decide whether further action should be taken as well as consider many dilemmas. What are the family's reasons for the current situation? Are there financial issues or class issues (this is how we care for children in our family)? Are there mental ill-health issues? Is a parent or carer immobilised by illness? Do any of the parents have some kind of disability? Are there issues concerning how to appropriately control and discipline the children?

ACTIVITY **1.4**

Consider your own beliefs/values about how children should be controlled and disciplined. List what you think are appropriate methods.

COMMENT

Social workers need to have an awareness of their own beliefs and how these may impact on their work with service users while promoting core values of respect and empowerment. However, as you are aware that your overriding duty is the welfare of the child you may well be challenging people about behaviours that at one time you accepted without questioning.

Clark (2000) suggests that the core values in social work are concerned with conflict and dilemmas that arise from the dual role of care and control. He identifies eight rules for good social work practice. As well as being personal values these might be some of the core values that your agency expects of you. They are:

- respectfulness;

- honesty and truthfulness;

- being knowledgeable and skilful;

- being careful and diligent;

- being effective and helpful;

and ensuring that work is:

- legitimate and authorised;

- collaborative and accountable;

- reputable and creditable.

(Clark, 2000, page 49)

Have you taken these into consideration in your intervention with the family? Do your agency colleagues share your evaluation of what is dirty and unacceptable? Some may not share your views, and some will have rigid and inflexible beliefs and attitudes, which may be based on religious, political or ideological opinions. Collectively, the rigidity and inflexibility of your agency's beliefs and attitudes when transformed into certain behavioural practices may well result in institutional discrimination. You will need to think about how your agency operates as an institution. Do the attitudes and values of certain members of the agency unwittingly discriminate against certain people? Finally, is there anything that this family could not do, due to the differences and socially constructed disadvantages that exist in society? It is to the societal values and ethics that we will now turn.

Societal values and ethics

Society places a great deal of importance or value on the care, welfare and well-being of children as can be seen in the government's *Every Child Matters* (DfES, 2004) agenda. Families are generally supported providing they are considered to be deserving and conform to society's norms. This is evident from the benefits that are available to a family, for example, the availability of Child Benefit. However, a significant number of children live below the poverty line and that number has increased over recent years – and now even Child Benefit (as a universal benefit) is under review. But society is changing and evolving; some things, 'which were acceptable in the past' are no longer acceptable today. Beckett and Maynard (2005, page 18) describe one of the changes that have occurred in how children are supervised. They state:

> *Forty years ago it was normal for children to be allowed to spend long periods away from their homes without parental supervision, playing with friends. Perhaps due to increasing media coverage of incidents where children have*

been killed or abducted, children are far more restricted now. Parental behaviour
that once was regarded as normal, and even healthy, would now be regarded as
neglectful and irresponsible.

This illustrates how society's values have changed from being quite liberal to being restrictive or even repressive. It illustrates how what was considered to be an acceptable way of caring for children has been modified by current circumstances, and the climate of fear that we live in today, thus becoming a questionable way to ensure children's safety.

Beckett and Maynard (2005, page 18) also describe some changes in sexual behaviour. They state:

In Britain, there has been a huge shift in the last fifty years in what is regarded
as acceptable sexual behaviour. Premarital sex is accepted as the norm.
Homosexuality has shifted from being a criminal offence to something which
MPs and cabinet ministers openly declare. This shift has not occurred in all
societies, however.

This also illustrates how society's attitudes and values have changed. As a child and family social worker consider the following activity.

ACTIVITY **1.5**

Jane is 14. She confides in you that she is having a sexual relationship with Luke, who is
18. You are both Jane's and Luke's social worker. What do you do?

COMMENT

From the minimal details given above there are several points you would need to think
about: first, there is your working relationship with Jane and Luke; second, there is your
knowledge that a criminal offence is being committed; third, there are the consequences
for both parties of any action you might take. Consider what influences you in coming
to a decision about what action to take. What factors might make a difference to you,
for example, if Jane were ten? Or if Luke were 28? Or if Jane or Luke had a learning
disability, or they both had?

The children and family social worker also needs to be able to take account of the different structural perspectives or social differences that influence society's values and ethics if they are to avoid making errors of judgement. The perspectives of age, disability and sexuality have been explored above, but others, such as those of black, white, gender, class and religion, also need to be considered. Thinking about how these perspectives impact on your practice and your life is probably the hardest thing that you will have to do both as a professional worker and as a person. It will mean that you will have to first accept that you are part of a society, which has created the problem in the first place, and that its collective attitudes and beliefs can influence you. Is one stronger or more powerful than another for you or do they all exert an equally powerful influence? Can you imagine how they might all be an issue for you? In addition, have you realised that you can become both the oppressor and the oppressed? You will need to accept that your learning in this area will always need to be revised and updated.

In Activity 1.2 you went to see a family with three children. No information was given about the parents. What assumptions or pre-judgements did you make about the parents? Were they both white/UK? Was one of them black/UK? Were they two male parents/carers or were they two female parent/carers? How old did you think they were? Create a picture of the parents in your head and imagine going to see them. Now imagine that the female parent is African Caribbean and her name is Donna Green. Her partner is Ahmed Khan and he is the father of the two youngest children, Tariq aged three and Nadia Khan aged one. The eldest child, Kylie Cole, aged 12, is African Caribbean/white and has learning disabilities. Kylie is from Donna Green's previous relationship with Alan Cole who is aged 28. Kylie has contact with her father.

In order to make a fair assessment of the above family there are many factors that you will have to think and learn more about. By being aware of the different perspectives or structural differences that exist, you will be more aware of the structural oppression which can be inflicted on children and families, and you will have started to adopt an anti-oppressive and anti-discriminatory empowering approach to social work with children and their families. An empowering approach is one that is aware of factors that can negatively impact on families. An empowering approach is one that seeks to promote and enable choice and user self-determination.

ACTIVITY **1.6**

Look at the Professional Capabilities Framework (2012). Can you identify links between Clark's eight rules (see page 8) and the PCF?

COMMENT

There are clear links between the two, which reflect anti-oppressive and anti-discriminatory practice. Respect is a factor in both, so is honesty, as is being accountable for the quality of your work and taking responsibility for maintaining and improving your knowledge and skills (PCF: knowledge; diversity; values and ethics; judgement; and critical reflection and analysis).

For the children and family social worker there are no easy solutions. You will have to juggle your personal, professional, agency and societal values and ethics when working with children and their families. Although I have attempted to separate them I think that they are inextricably linked. There will be many conflicts and dilemmas. Throughout the rest of this book you will encounter the Cole/Green family who will present you with further dilemmas. If you think about how the different perspectives might influence the work you are doing with the family, you will have begun the process of becoming a reflective, anti-oppressive and empowering practitioner.

In Chapter 2 you will be introduced to a historical account of the legal basis of social work with children and families. When you are reading this account you will need to think about the value of the legislation and how it has changed the way people now work with children and their families. You will also need to think about how difficult it is to change a person's value base or the way a person views the world of children and families. Consider what you can do as a child and family social worker to make a difference to the lives of children who suffer abuse. Can strong values and an ethical empowering approach make a difference? This is something that only you can decide.

In Chapter 3 you will encounter the concept of family support. Supporting families makes good economic sense as they will be able to contribute to the economy rather than exist on state benefits; however, this does not take into account either the cost of childcare or people preferring to care for their children themselves. This can pose a dilemma for children and family social workers who may become aware that some families who are experiencing poverty are also committing benefit fraud. Which values are the most important: personal, professional, agency or societal? What is the ethical or right thing to do in this situation? There are no easy answers to this dilemma. Personally, you might have some sympathy with the family. Professionally, and as a member of an agency which has responsibilities of care and control, you have a duty to warn the family that they are committing an offence. Also as a citizen of society you have a duty and responsibility to other citizens, as you do to yourself, as you are also a citizen.

In Chapter 4 you will encounter issues of child protection. Think about how society's values and ethics have changed towards the care and control of children. Corporal punishment was acceptable in schools, but is no longer. However, parents can reasonably chastise their child – it is still lawful to slap a child. It may be acceptable to the parent but is it acceptable to the child? This is a dilemma for children and family social workers, as physical punishment of children has not yet been made illegal.

In Chapter 5 you will be introduced to direct work with children. This should enable you to think about how your personal and professional values might impact on the work you do with children from birth to ten years, children aged 11 to 15 years and young people aged 16 to 20 years. How do the challenges and dilemmas differ in the different age groups? If you have a preference for working with a particular age group, why do you think this is so and what will you need to do to ensure that it does not have a detrimental impact on your practice?

In Chapter 6 you will encounter the issues around children with disabilities. Think about how society has changed its attitudes towards children/people with disabilities. The provision for children is more inclusive and mainstream than it was in the past, but is it meeting the needs and responding to the wishes of children with disabilities and their carers? The value or importance that society places on children with disabilities has begun to change. Community care has replaced institutional care and marginalisation has begun to be replaced by inclusivity and openness.

In Chapter 7 you will be presented with the dilemma of which type of provision is best for children who cannot live with their parents or carers: foster care, residential or institutional care, or adoption. You will also be presented with the dilemma of who can attend reviews. When considering some of these dilemmas you will need to think about how the structure of society, particularly the way society is divided, can lead to oppressive and discriminatory treatment.

This chapter began with an account of the diversity of families and it is appropriate that it should end by asking you to be aware of the influence that ethnicity/race, class, gender, disability, age, religion and sexual orientation may exert on the work you do with children and families. We have looked at some simple definitions of values and ethics and have considered how personal, professional, agency and societal values and ethics may also influence practice.

We also hope that you will continue learning from the high-profile child abuse cases that have occurred in the past, such as Colwell (DHSS, 1974), Beckford (London Borough of Brent, 1985), and Climbié, (DHHO, 2003), where social workers have been criticised for their lack of action, and the Cleveland Inquiry (DHSS, 1988). This was appointed because of a perceived overreaction from health and social work professionals. More recently there have been the cases of Baby P (DfE, 2010) and Khyra Ishaq (Birmingham Safeguarding Children Board, 2010). We hope that you will consider these issues not only while reading the book, but also during your professional social work career.

FURTHER READING

Beckett, C and Maynard, A (2005) *Values and Ethics in Social Work: An Introduction.* London: Sage.

A very readable introduction to values and ethics in social work with many thoughtful exercises to enable the reader to reflect on practice.

Millam, R (2002) *Anti-Discriminatory Practice*, 2nd edition. London: Continuum.

Provides the reader with much valuable information as well many practical exercises about anti-discriminatory work with children.

Parrot, L (2007) *Values and Ethics in Social Work Practice.* Exeter: Learning Matters.

An easy to understand and thoughtful exploration of values and ethics in social work practice, which will further your understanding.

Chapter 2

The legal and political context of social work with children and families

Maureen O' Loughlin and Julie Bywater

Introduction

In this chapter we will review the historical context of social work with children and families as well as considering current policy and legislation. The chapter will give an outline of the Children Act 1989 before going on to consider subsequent policy developments and further legislation, which underpin this area of work. The chapter should enable you to have an understanding of the legal and policy context of social work with children and families and some of the implications for practice.

Children and young people have been seen by society in different ways throughout history. It is only comparatively recently that they have been acknowledged as people in their own right whose views should be sought and listened to, as shown in the Children Act 1989 sections 3(a), 22(4)(a), 22(5)(a) for example. Frost and Stein (1989) suggest that children have always had diverse experiences of childhood across culture and class, which illustrates the capacity for affection and cruelty across generations within different societies. However, other historians argue that childhood did not exist until the seventeenth century, but agree that the more remote the period of history being considered, the crueller the treatment children experienced (Badinter, 1981). De Mause (1976, page 1) suggests that:

> The history of childhood is a nightmare from which we have only recently begun to awaken. The further back in history one goes, the lower the level of child care, and the more likely children are to be killed, abandoned, beaten, terrorised and sexually abused.

ACTIVITY **2.1**

What do you think were the main areas of concern in society about children and young people in the nineteenth and twentieth centuries?

COMMENT

Until around 1870 four categories of children were identified in relation to childcare concerns by the state. These categories can be summarised as follows:

1. *Children of the street (e.g. beggars, prostitutes, etc.).*

2. *Young offenders.*

3. *Children at work.*

4. *Children looked after by the Poor Law authorities (e.g. orphans, children with disabilities, abandoned children, etc.).*

None of these childcare issues involved direct intervention in the internal aspects of the family until the 1870s (Corby, 2006). We can see from this list that very little has changed; we are still identifying concerns and targeting resources to the same categories of children in 2012. In order to understand the complexities involved in working with children and families, it is important that we have an understanding of how social work practice with children, young people and their families has evolved and been informed by past events and state interventions.

It is therefore useful to review highlights of the preceding two centuries to consider if attitudes and concerns have changed over time.

The nineteenth century

Two of the first pieces of legislation involving the care and protection of children were introduced early in the nineteenth century. The Health and Morals of Apprentices Act

1802, followed by the Factory Act 1833, both focused on children in the workplace rather than in society generally. Other legislation, including the introduction of reform schools and the detention of children separately from adults, highlighted young offenders as another area of concern in society. Children who were not cared for by their families, or who were ill-treated or neglected, were cared for by the Poor Law guardians in institutions with adults, where they received harsh treatment.

There were concerns being raised by individuals and groups about the welfare of children who were looked after in their own families as well as those children who were forced to live on the streets.

* Ambroise Tardieu (1868) a medical professor in Paris described the deaths of children from burning/battering.

* Athol Johnson (1868) noted that children were frequently attending the Hospital for Sick Children in London, having sustained repeated bone fractures. There followed strong resistance from society to his (and the state's) assertion that parents could and were deliberately and frequently injuring and harming their own children. More apparently plausible explanations were offered by others to account for his findings, for example, the devastating childhood disease at the time, rickets.

(Any punishment of the perpetrators of child ill-treatment was only carried out by family members and neighbours on a personal basis.)

The Infant Life Protection Act 1872 was introduced to address the problem of baby farming, followed by the Registration of Births and Deaths Act in 1874 so that births and deaths could be recorded.

* The London Society for the Prevention of Cruelty to Children was founded in 1884, changing its name to the National Society for the Prevention of Cruelty to Children (NSPCC) in 1889. The NSPCC began to develop a national network of centres and inspectors who became involved in 'rescuing' children from their homes. It is interesting and perhaps ironic to note that the *Royal* Society for the Prevention of Cruelty to Animals (RSPCA) came into existence 60 years before the NSPCC, though concern for the welfare of animals did raise awareness about the plight of children. Ferguson (1990) depicts an NSPCC inspector in 1898 grappling with the same contradictions and complexities as present-day social workers.

* Barnardo's, the Church of England Children's Society and National Children's Homes (all with a Christian religious basis), among other philanthropic organisations, had begun their work and were 'rescuing' children who had fled from, or been abandoned by, their families.

In 1889 the English Prevention of Cruelty to Children Act was passed, and this created the option to prosecute perpetrators of cruelty to children. Police were empowered by the Act to search for children thought to be at risk, and the Act legalised their removal to a place of safety. 'Fit orders' (now referred to as care orders) were imposed on children whose parents had been convicted of offences against them.

Other legislation ensured that children's welfare was considered in custody disputes and began to introduce education for various groups of children, including those with sensory impairments (the Elementary Education Act 1870 and the Elementary Education (Blind and Deaf Children) Act 1893).

There was however a further dimension to concerns about children, which the reports of Charles Booth (1889) and Seebohm Rowntree (1901) highlighted, that is the impact of poverty.

ACTIVITY **2.2**

Can you think of how poverty might have impacted on children in the nineteenth and twentieth centuries, and currently?

COMMENT

You have probably identified that although there have been many improvements in the quality of people's lives the impact of poverty remains much the same historically as in the present day. Poverty still impacts on the quality of housing, health and education as well as the opportunities that are available to people.

The 1900s

The concerns the reports into poverty highlighted were substantiated by many recruits being rejected on medical grounds when they tried to enlist for the Boer War. The 1904 report of the Interdepartmental Committee on the Physical Deterioration of the Young provided the stimulus for the Education (Provision of Meals) Act 1906, which gave local authorities the discretion to provide food for children who were undernourished. Further provision was made for school medical inspections along with antenatal and child welfare clinics. The 1908 Children Act was one of the first pieces of legislation that addressed a number of issues relating to children rather than focusing on a particular area of concern. The Act established juvenile courts, abolished imprisonment for under 14s and introduced the registration of foster carers. Following pressure from the NSPCC, the Incest Act 1908 was passed. Interfamilial sexual abuse or incest had, up to that point, received little public attention or recognition. Where it was acknowledged, it was linked to low intelligence and overcrowded sleeping arrangements of the poorer classes; another more popular explanation was attributed to the detrimental effects of alcohol (Gordon, 1989).

You can see from the summary above of the provisions made for children that there has been a move from little intervention by the state in family life to an increasing level of intervention, which continues today.

There were some further developments between the two world wars with the introduction of the first Adoption Act in 1926 (see Chapter 6) and the Children and Young Persons Act 1933, which gave local authorities child protection duties and the power to remove children in an emergency. After the Second World War, according to Douglas and Philpot (1998, page 11), the welfare of children was the motor that drove reform. Evacuation had highlighted the poverty in which children lived and through its process left thousands of children separated from their families. The case of Dennis O'Neill (see Chapter 6) also raised public awareness about the plight of children in foster care. The 1948 Children Act sought to address these issues by the introduction of Children's Departments which appointed Child Care Officers and began the process of replacing large institutions with smaller family group homes. The departments began to expand fostering and adoption as alternatives to residential care. This Act emphasised another shift in policy, acknowledging that children who could not live with their families would be better cared for in smaller residential provision or substitute families, policies which continue today.

After the introduction of this Act another gradual shift in focus occurred. Although there had been some provision through legislation to safeguard children from harm, there was still a lack of awareness of the extent of child maltreatment and the need for children to be protected.

In 1946 John Caffey published a paper which became a landmark in the identification of child abuse (Johnson, 1990). There had been developments in radiology in the 1940s, which made it possible to date fractures fairly accurately. As a result of this Caffey described unexplained injuries to children; however, there was no suggestion at this stage that this was child abuse (Johnson, 1990). Wooley and Evans (1955) were among the first to suggest that adults were causing these injuries to children. Their work was built on by Henry Kempe, an American paediatrician, in 1961. In the UK these developments began to impact with the Children and Young Persons Act 1963 giving local authorities the duty to undertake preventative work with children and families. This reflected an optimistic view that families and local authorities could work together to ensure that appropriate care and conditions necessary for children to develop were maintained. The Children and Young Persons Act 1969 which followed was more focused on child welfare and safeguarding, but also contained elements of control, with one criterion for care order applications being non-school attendance and another beyond parental control. The Act also enabled courts to make place of safety orders, which parents could not challenge for 28 days, sometimes resulting in no parental contact during that time.

In 1971 there was a move from specialist Children's Departments to the creation of a *generic* social work service – available to all and with wide community support, following the Seebohm Report (1968), which made recommendations that social work services should be offered in a holistic way within one department.

In 1973 seven-year-old Maria Colwell died from physical abuse and neglect. In the months before her death professionals from social services, the police, health, education, the NSPCC and housing agencies had all been involved with Maria and her family. In 1974 the inquiry into Maria's death criticised the lack of communication between the various agencies involved with the family. This case was crucial in identifying the issues of major social problems and how agencies were to work together. One of the central themes in the Colwell Inquiry was that failures in interagency communication and co-operation were to blame for 'at risk' children not being identified, and provided with protection (DHSS, 1974). (These themes are still relevant today, and were considered in some detail in the Laming Inquiry (2003 and 2009); see below for further discussions.) In 1975 the child protection register, known until then as the 'At Risk Register', was established as a national requirement for all local authorities to improve contact in such cases between social workers, the police and the medical profession.

During the 1980s it became socially unacceptable to support physical punishment in schools and residential establishments/institutions. (However, in 2012, despite many parliamentary debates, the law still permits parents to hit their children – see section 58 of the Children Act 2004 for details.) Examples from practice, as in the illustration below, indicate that opinions differ on what is appropriate chastisement.

A father explained that he had 'only tapped' his two-year-old son, and had not realised his own strength, which had resulted in the boy being hurled against the wall of their home and sustaining a fracture to his arm.

ACTIVITY 2.3

What are your views on physical punishment and the case illustration above? Do your personal views conflict with your duty to safeguard children? Do you think that not realising your own strength is an acceptable explanation?

COMMENT

Social workers may well have to challenge parents and carers on the appropriateness of the way they control children. You will need to be clear that your primary duty is to safeguard the welfare of the child. This means thinking about the impact on the child, not only of physical controls through hitting, restraining, locking in rooms, etc. but also on psychological controls and exposure to inappropriate activities.

During the 1980s there were developments that impacted on social work with children and families. In 1984 Kidscape highlighted the problem of sexual abuse and was the first organisation to develop a helpline and introduce awareness programmes in schools.

In 1985 the report of the Jasmine Beckford Inquiry (London Borough of Brent, 1985) was published. Jasmine died aged four years in 1984 in an emaciated condition and having been horrifically beaten over an extended period of time by her stepfather, Morris Beckford. Jasmine and her younger sister had been injured in 1981 by Morris, and were taken into local authority foster care with a care order being made in 1981. Morris was prosecuted and given a suspended prison sentence. Both Jasmine and her sister were returned home to the care of their mother and Morris Beckford after a six-month period. Over the following two years social services only saw Jasmine spasmodically and she was only seen by her social worker once during the last ten months of her life. The inquiry made 68 recommendations and stressed concerns that social workers were too optimistic with regard to the families with whom they worked. The report was unequivocal in its view that social work's essential and primary task was to protect children first and consider the rights of parents second, if necessary employing the force of the law to ensure this. Society had begun to realise that children need to be heard. 1985 saw the establishment of Childline, the first phone-in service specifically for listening to children.

In 1986 *Child Abuse – Working Together* was published as a consultation document (DHSS, 1986). As intervention by the state became more overt, it aimed to make the different responsibilities within the system clear. During 1986 and 1987 statistics regarding child protection registration showed a huge increase in the numbers of children registered following the Beckford Inquiry Report. The numbers prior to this had been at the same level for the previous nine years. There was also an increase in the number of children removed from their homes and taken into the care of local authorities as a result of child abuse and neglect.

In 1987 a MORI poll survey suggested that one in ten children had experienced some form of sexual abuse by the age of 15 years; in half of these cases the abuse had been committed either by a family member, or somebody the child knew and previously trusted (Baker and Duncan, 1985). However, in Cleveland in 1987, over a period of six months, 121 children were taken into local authority care and long-stay hospital care on place of safety orders, which parents and carers could not challenge.

There was a general outcry about this with some suggesting that things had gone too far and that parents' rights were being totally disregarded. A public inquiry was set up in 1988 chaired by Lord Justice Elizabeth Butler-Sloss. The Cleveland Inquiry Report (DHSS, 1988) confirmed that child sexual abuse was a more widespread phenomenon than had previously been thought but also criticised individuals from every agency and professional background for not working together more co-operatively. Social workers were criticised for their too hasty interventions and removal of children and for failing to keep parents informed. This resulted in a change to the Working Together guidelines (DHSS, 1986), which stated that it was inappropriate for parents to attend case conferences. The amendment to the guidelines highlighted that parents should be invited to attend and placed greater emphasis on inter-disciplinary consultation before intervention in sexual abuse cases. It was also recommended that police and social services jointly investigate as a norm.

During this time the legislation relating to children was being re-evaluated as it was fragmented, with different laws applying in custody and welfare with no transfer being possible between courts. Wardship proceedings were used for the most complex cases with subsequent delay in decision-making. The resulting Children Act 1989, implemented in October 1991, was a response to the need for a comprehensive piece of legislation, which brought together in one statute many disparate laws relating to children. It introduced new concepts and balances which previous legislation did not have. The Act was also a response both to a number of enquiries into child deaths, which highlighted the need for agencies to work together to protect children, and the need to work in partnership with families using good practice, which the conclusions of the Cleveland Inquiry (1988) highlighted as not happening. Section 44(7) of the Act enabled children of sufficient age and understanding to refuse to undergo medical assessments as some of the children involved in the Cleveland investigations had been examined on four separate occasions.

The Children Act 1989 marked a shift in policy from the previous preoccupation with prevention of the reception of children into local authority care, to a broader concept of children 'in need' and the provision of family support. The Act brought together public and private law to ensure that the welfare of the child is paramount. It was described as: *the most radical legislative reforms to children's services of the (last) century* (Lord Mackay, cited in Franklin and Parton, 1991). The Children Act 1989 sought to balance the protection of children with supporting families while introducing and emphasising the concept of parental responsibility, rather than rights. The Act, unlike previous legislation, did not remove parental responsibility from those parents who had it (mothers by right, married fathers and fathers with parental responsibility orders) even though their children might be subject to court orders. The only way of removal was by adoption. Parental responsibility could be limited to some extent if a child was made the subject of a care order but local authorities were no longer able to terminate contact without a court order.

The Act addressed a wide range of issues concerning children: the provision of services for children in need, including those with disabilities; the regulation of children's homes; childminding; day care and private fostering. The Act contains specific references to the need to ascertain and listen to the wishes and feelings of children and young people and to take into account their racial, cultural, linguistic and religious background. Additionally, the Act acknowledged that young people leaving the care system needed ongoing support beyond the age of 18.

However, the Act was introduced in a hostile political and economic climate. It quickly became apparent that local authorities were failing to fulfil their new responsibilities and were concentrating almost exclusively on their narrow child protection responsibilities and were operating very high thresholds for providing services (Aldgate and Tunstill, 1995; Department of Health, 1995, 2001; Frost, 1992; Jones, 2001; Parton, 1997: all cited by Parton, 2009).

In 1991 the Department of Health published the Working Together guidance (DoH, 1991) to support the Children Act 1989 and stressed the importance of working collaboratively across agencies as specifically outlined in section 27 of the Act. Further developments in policy and procedure have led to this being rewritten in 2006, and the latest version was published in October 2010. Its title (*Working Together to Safeguard Children: A guide to interagency working to safeguard and promote the welfare of children*) reflects the emphasis on 'safeguarding' rather than 'protection' and is indicative of the greater emphasis on consultation and corporate and multiprofessional involvement in this area (DCFS, 2010).

As a consequence of social work practice with children and families being dominated by child protection section 47 enquiries, concerns arose about the lack of support for families before they reached crisis point. Also the lack of services, choice and outcomes for children with disabilities, for care leavers and for children in the looked after system were highlighted within a number of inquiries into abuse in children's homes (see Chapter 6). Rose (1994) suggested that family support and child protection seemed mutually exclusive. She advocated less emphasis on the incident and more on enquiring and assessing whether family support was needed.

The public and political image of social work by the late 1990s was dominated by failures in relation to children, particularly in terms of child abuse. An analysis of press reporting of social work in England in national daily and Sunday newspapers between 1 July 1997 and 1 July 1998 is particularly instructive in this respect (Franklin and Parton, 2001, cited in Parton, 2009). The 15 most common messages, accounting for 80 per cent of the total, were negative with regard to social work and included 'incompetent', 'negligent', 'failed', 'ineffective', 'misguided' and 'bungling'. Over 75 per cent of the stories were also related to children, where the dominant concerns were about child abuse, paedophiles, adoption and fostering. Media stories about the nature, purposes and efficacy of social work were, almost without exception, negative and critical and have since regained momentum following the deaths of Victoria Climbié and Peter Connelly, resulting in low morale in the profession (Parton, 2009).

Research review

Child Protection: Messages from Research (DoH, 1995a) provides a summary of the main findings of 20 research studies commissioned by the Department of Health into child protection practice. A number of issues were highlighted, including a lack of emphasis on planning and intervention to meet children's needs and the over-representation of African Caribbean children on child protection registers, whereas Asian children and children with disabilities were under-represented.

The research indicated the need for departments to refocus resources from the almost exclusive emphasis on child protection towards family support.

> *If policy and practice changes are to follow from this round of research, it should reconsider the balance of services and alter the way in which professionals are perceived by parents accused of abusing or neglecting their offspring.*
>
> (DoH, 1995a, page 55)

This, together with the other concerns highlighted above, informed the government's thinking and resulted in a number of initiatives, regulations and pieces of legislation, all with the aim of improving services for children, including those who are looked after, and their families. Those listed below give an idea of the extent of the provisions that have been made between the Children Act 1989 and the White Paper, *Care Matters: Transforming the Lives of Children and Young People in Care*, June 2007.

- **Children's Service Planning Order 1996**

  A legal requirement for local authorities to identify and assess need and then produce plans for children's services in consultation with those requiring and providing services.

- **Quality Protects 1998 (Children First in Wales)**

  Policy initiatives to ensure the safeguarding and improve the quality of care and outcomes for children in the looked after systems, through establishing specific objectives and the promotion of partnerships between local authorities and other agencies. Eight national objectives were identified to provide a consistent framework with an overall aim of giving children a better deal:

  1. To ensure children are securely attached to carers capable of providing safe and effective care for the duration of childhood.

  2. To ensure children are protected from emotional, physical and sexual abuse and neglect (significant harm).

  3. To ensure children in need gain maximum life chance benefits from educational opportunities, health care and social care.

  4. To ensure **looked-after** children gain maximum life chance benefits from educational opportunities, health care and social care.

5. To ensure that young people leaving care, as they enter adulthood, are not isolated and participate socially and economically as citizens.

6. To ensure that children with specific social needs arising out of disability or a health condition are living in families or other appropriate settings in the community where their assessed needs are adequately met and reviewed.

7. To ensure that referral and assessment processes discriminate effectively between different types and levels of need and produce a timely response.

8. To ensure that resources are planned and provided at levels that represent best value for money, allow for choice and different responses for different needs and circumstances.

- **Sure Start**

  A further government initiative targeted on areas of deprivation, bringing together early education, health and family support in a way that is accessible to and involves the community.

- **Human Rights Act 1998**

  Requires public bodies such as local authorities to act in accordance with the Convention on Human Rights and offers a way of challenge if they do not (for further discussion, see Johns, 2011).

- **Framework for the Assessment for Children in Need and their Families 2000**

  Guidance for assessment in the 1990s had primarily been through that issued by the Department of Health in 1988 known as the Orange Book (DoH, 1988). Research findings, practice and experience led government to recognise that guidance on assessment needed to be developed to focus on the needs of children and their families (Horwath, 2001). The Framework offers detailed guidance that maintains a child focus through providing a systematic way of recording, understanding and analysing a child's developmental needs, the parent's or carer's response to those needs and the wider family and environmental factors which affect the child's situation (see Chapters 3 and 4 for further discussion).

- **Children (Leaving Care) Act 2000**

  This Act focuses on the needs of young people of 16 to 17 years of age who were looked after by local authorities. It gives local authorities the duty to provide a personal advisor and prepare a pathway plan for them. Support and material assistance can be offered until the age of 21.

- **Race Relations (Amendment) Act 2000**

  This Act requires public bodies, including local authorities, to work towards the elimination of unlawful discrimination and promote equality of opportunity and good relations between different racial groups.

- **Carers and Disabled Children Act 2000**

  Gives children with disabilities the opportunity of having services commissioned by their parents through direct payments, with increasing responsibility for this themselves as they become adults.

- **Children's Fund**

  The Children's Fund focuses on 5 to 13 year olds, building on the work of Sure Start. It aims to identify children where there are signs of potential difficulty and to provide support to them and their families through multidisciplinary teams.

- **Children's National Service Framework**

  This initiative sets out standards for the NHS and social services and is intended to break down professional boundaries and achieve partnership working. Following New Labour's re-election in June 2001 a framework for the 'transformation' of children's services was outlined in the 2002 Spending Review in a chapter entitled 'Children at Risk' (HM Treasury, 2002). While presented by the government as a response to the Laming Report (2003) into the death of Victoria Climbié in 2002, the Green Paper *Every Child Matters* was also primarily concerned with bringing forward the government's proposals for changing the organisation and rationale for the delivery of children's services (Parton, 2009). Rather than only be concerned with 'children at risk', as suggested by the Spending Review, the emphasis was instead on integrating services so that universal services were conceptualised as offering early (primary) intervention to prevent the emergence of specific risk factors. The vision was of *a shift to prevention while strengthening protection*, ensuring that all children received early help so that they could fulfil their potential (DfES, 2004b, page 3, Parton; 2009).

- **Care Matters: Transforming the Lives of Children and Young People in Care (2006)**

  This Green Paper highlighted the need for children in the looked-after system to have access to a higher standard of corporate parenting, which would enable them to be supported to achieve more in their lives.

- **The Children and Adoption Act 2006**

  This provided the courts with new powers to promote contact and enforce contact orders. These include taking part in activities to promote contact (for example, programmes or counselling designed to improve contact or to address violent behaviour). The Act gives the courts power to make orders requiring participation in unpaid work if someone fails to comply with a contact order or contact activity condition. The Act also strengthens the protection for children who are adopted from abroad.

- **Staying Safe (Department for Children, Schools and Families, 2007)**

  This sought to build on work already ongoing to improve the safety of all children and young people, through: being involved in play and taking part in positive activities in safe environments; understanding and managing risk to help parents and children and young people themselves understand how to keep safe; promoting safer recruitment practices; addressing 'new' threats to children's safety (for example, from the internet or mobile phones) and supporting the work of the Local Safeguarding Children Boards.

These examples of government policies and legislation show the range of provisions which are impacting on children and their families in different ways. Following the inquiry into the death of Victoria Climbié (2003), further initiatives through the Children Act 2004 and *Every Child Matters: Change for Children* (2004) introduced new and exciting changes to social work practice with children and their families. Victoria Climbié was failed by many of the safeguarding professional agencies involved in working with her and her family, as other children have been in the past. The inquiry into her death and the Joint Chief Inspectors' Report *Safeguarding Children* (DoH, 2003b) were two of the key governmental drivers for change behind the 2004 Act and the *Every Child Matters* (2004) programmes. These publications have a number of key messages which are underlined in the Act. They include:

- the safeguarding and promoting of the welfare of each child;
- the child being the centre of endeavours;
- that all agencies and their staff must work together.

The messages were brought into effect in a number of different ways, both through policy development and legislation. For example, the Children's Commissioner ensures that a voice for children and young people will monitor the effectiveness of services to improve the well-being of children and young people across the country.

In relation to child protection social work, the Children Act 2004 placed a duty on local authorities to make arrangements with key agencies to improve the well-being and support of children and young people by widening the power of services to pool budgets. The 2004 Act established statutory Local Safeguarding Children Boards to replace the existing non-statutory Area Child Protection Committees. In addition, since April 2006, children's services authorities are required by regulations to publish a Children and Young People's Plan (CYPP), setting out their strategy for services for children and relevant young people (see Sections 10, 11, 13–16 and 17). Databases holding information on all children were established to support professionals working together and sharing information, enabling them to identify difficulties and provide appropriate support (see Section 12 of the 2004 Act), along with an integrated inspection mechanism and measures to ensure accountability.

The Children Act 1989 functions of social services have remained unchanged, but how they are delivered at local level has been revised. The Children Act 2004 requires local authorities to lead on integrated delivery through multi-agency Children's Trusts to include health, education, voluntary and independent partnerships. The **Common Assessment Framework** (CAF) for Children and Young People was implemented by all local authorities in April 2006. The CAF is part of the wider *Every Child Matters: Change for Children* programme. Along with other elements, including the role of the lead professional, multi-agency working and the introduction of information-sharing databases as outlined earlier, it should enable agencies to provide a more integrated service to children, young people and families, and help practitioners assess children's additional needs earlier and more effectively (DfES, 2004b).

The introduction of the CAF was seen as an important part of the strategy to shift the focus from dealing with the consequences of difficulties in children's lives, to preventing things from going wrong in the first place (risk minimisation). It should help children and young people, supported by their parents or carers, to achieve the priority outcomes to:

- be healthy;
- stay safe;
- enjoy and achieve;

- make a positive contribution;

- achieve economic well-being.

If a CAF suggests that a child has needs that require input from more than one service, one practitioner will act in the role of lead professional to:

- *provide a single point of contact whom children, young people and families can trust, and who is able to support them in making choices and in navigating their way through the system;*

- *ensure that children and families get appropriate interventions when needed, which are well planned, regularly reviewed and effectively delivered;*

- *reduce overlap and inconsistency from other practitioners.*

(DfES, 2004, pages 2–4)

It will not be necessary to do a common assessment for every child; a checklist will be used to decide whether a CAF is needed or not. The CAF has been designed so that with appropriate training practitioners from any discipline will be able to complete it. This is to help address the tensions in cases where several professionals are involved in the completion of assessments within the current Assessment Framework. Currently social workers have predominantly been left to compile the information in the assessment with health visitors, teachers, community psychiatric nurses, etc. providing verbal summaries in core group meetings. The CAF is part of a wider programme to provide more integrated services. It seeks to improve multi-agency working by being an accessible tool using a common language and maintaining a single overview record of the needs and progress of a child in contact with several agencies, so as to address the problems, highlighted in so many inquiries, of poor communication sharing between agencies, which effectively prevented them working together. The role of children's social work was, however, explicitly restricted to work with the most vulnerable children, particularly 'children in need', including those in need of protection, looked-after children and disabled children. This was made explicit in *ECM: Change for Children in Social Care* (DfES, 2004a), published at the same time as *ECM: Change for Children* (DfES, 2004b). The more preventive and early intervention developments were located primarily in the new children's centres and extended schools. Children's centres were to play a key strategic role in the new developments (Parton, 2009).

The changes introduced by the Children Act 2004 have been expanded on through the Care Matters agenda to focus particularly on looked-after children. These include more social work time for children and young people, better support for carers and improved educational opportunities for looked-after children. It was envisaged that there would be more opportunities for training and apprenticeships, with stronger emphasis on health and support for care leavers for longer. This led to the issuing of guidance including *Promoting the Health and Well-being of Looked After Children* (statutory guidance 2009) and *Personal Educational Allowances for Looked After Children* (2008).

On 10 January 2006, the government launched the *Respect Action Plan* (Respect Task Force, 2006), which aimed to tackle the underlying causes of antisocial behaviour, to intervene earlier where problems occurred and to broaden the efforts to address new areas of poor behaviour. It aspired to build *stable families and strong, cohesive communities* and argued that while it was important to address the causes of problems, it was also important to challenge poor behaviour where it existed. Poor parenting and 'problem families' were seen to lie at the root of the problems.

In February 2007 the United Nations Children's Fund Report (UNICEF, 2007) highlighted that the UK was bottom out of 21 economically advanced nations in terms of the overall well-being of children and young people. The publication of the report coincided with the murder of a 14-year-old boy in South London amidst escalating concerns about young gangs and knife and gun crime. Political and media comment was considerable, asserting that childhood was in crisis and a terrible reflection on the state of British society. In response, the government launched *Reaching Out: Progress on Social Exclusion* (SEU 2007a) in an attempt to address some of the concerns raised. The government also highlighted that a small number of families with multiple problems were proving particularly 'hard to reach' and would need special attention in the future (Parton, 2009).

The Children's Plan: Building Brighter Futures (DCSF, 2009) was launched on 11 December 2007, setting out a 13-year deadline to dramatically reduce illiteracy and antisocial behaviour and eradicate child poverty. Five principles were said to underpin *The Children's Plan*:

1. Government does not bring up children – parents do – so the government needs to do more to back parents and families.

2. All children have the potential to succeed and should go as far as their talents can take them.

3. Children and young people need to enjoy their childhood and grow up prepared for adult life.

4. Services need to be shaped by and responsive to children, young people and families, not designed around professional boundaries.

5. It is always better to prevent failure than tackle a crisis later.

The state was seen as supporting parents rather than supplanting or undermining them, while also recognising that the nature and context of family life was now much more diverse and complex than previously. The Plan aimed to build on ECM, stating that it was important that services worked together *not just to provide a safety net for the vulnerable, but to unlock the potential of every child* (pages 143–4). The government wanted to build a system that provides opportunity and delivers services to meet the needs of children and young people, support parents and carers, and intervene early where additional support is needed to get a child or young person back onto the path to success. (page 144). Whenever possible, it was hoped that services could be co-located and schools, extended schools and children's centres were seen as both central to the plan and, usually, the most accessible places for children and parents.

The Children's Plan envisaged an important role for statutory children's social work, but this was again restricted to work with children in care and child protection (Parton, 2009). This was reinforced further in the White Paper *Care Matters: Time for Change* (DfES, 2007a) and the passage of the Children and Young Persons Act 2008 (which gave the Secretary of State a specific duty to promote the well-being of children in England) together with the publication of *Staying Safe: Action Plan* (DCSF, 2008).

In January 2008 the Social Exclusion Unit Task Force launched *Reaching Out: Think Family* (SEU, 2008). *Think Family* argues that it is crucial that managers and practitioners in the children's and adult services departments *think family*. This was devised following an earlier report from the *Families at Risk Review* (SEU, 2007b). The term 'families at risk' was used as a shorthand term for families with multiple and complex problems, such as worklessness, poor mental health or substance misuse. The focus was upon those who already had complex and ongoing problems as well as those who were at risk of developing them, and as children's services could only ever mitigate the impacts of parental problems such as domestic violence, learning disability or substance misuse, it was important therefore that adults' services not only joined up better with children's services to provide support for the needs of *the whole family*, but that adults' services also needed to consider the parental roles and responsibilities of their clients. In a system that *thinks family*, both adults' and children's services need to join up around the needs of the family (Parton, 2009). Four characteristics were identified as key to the 'think family' approach:

1. Have no 'wrong door', so that contact with any service would offer an open door into a broader system of joined-up support.

2. Look at the whole family.

3. Build on family strengths.

4. Provide support tailored to need.

Baby Peter Connelly died in Haringey, in August 2007 (Laming, 2009). Peter Connelly was being monitored by social services at the time he was being abused. He had numerous injuries, including broken ribs and a broken back, which went undiagnosed by the doctor who had seen him two days before his death. At the time of his death, Peter (then aged 17 months) was the subject of a child protection plan. His name had been on Haringey's child protection register under the category of physical abuse and neglect since 22 December 2006. A total of ten agencies were involved with Peter and/or his family. One of the conclusions/recommendations made by the Panel of the Serious Case Review asserted that:

> *Everybody working as 'safeguarders' in the safeguarding system, especially those working in the universal services provided by health, education, early years provision and local police, needs to become more aware of the authority in their role, and to use it to safeguard the children as well as to support parents. The mode of relationship with parents, especially on first meeting them, needs to be observing and assessing as well as helpful. Those agency roles which are the protectors – doctors, lawyers, police officers and social workers – need to become much more authoritative both in the initial management of every case with child protection concerns, and in the subsequent child protection plan. It is crucial to be sceptical of the accounts which are given for any maltreatment of the children, and they should be tested thoroughly against the facts.*
>
> (*Local Safeguarding Children Board, Haringey, 2009, page 24;*
> *See Lord Laming's Review, 2009 for a fuller appreciation of the case.*)

In 2010 the government commissioned the Munro Review of child protection and children's services, with the final 15 recommendations being published in May 2011. The review emphasised the need to get the right help early to the right children as well as suggesting that the qualities needed in children's and family social work should be explicitly stated in the Professional Capabilities Framework. The review also suggested a revision of the *Working Together to Safeguard Children* guidelines, and the Framework of Assessment, as well as changes to the way services are monitored and inspected. National and local performance data should be published to help benchmark performance, including social work caseloads and social workers' views of caseload manageability.

In addition to the Monro Review the Family Justice Review entitled *Streamlining the System* (January 2011) has made recommendations to speed up the judicial system and try to remove many private law disputes (following partnership breakdown) from the court arena. Child protection cases are to be dealt with in a much speedier way; the government has given six months as the target. These changes will have a significant impact on the welfare of children and, given the increasing legal aid restrictions, will also impact on the access families and other parties have to the justice system.

In 2010 the Care Planning, Placement and Case Review (England) Regulations were issued. These regulations cover all aspects of a looked-after child's life including contact, health and education needs, reviews and planning for the future. Independent Reviewing Officers (IROs) were given additional functions including a role in assisting a child to obtain legal advice or to bring legal proceedings on their behalf. (It is worth noting that there is provision now in law, though this is not as yet in force, to set up an independent reviewing officer organisation.) The IRO handbook was issued as statutory guidance. The regulations also require care plans for children who cease to be looked after and detail the requirements for children's case records.

A whole raft of regulations and guidance came into force in April 2011. These included guidance on securing sufficient placements for children, family and friends placements, minimum standards for fostering and children's homes, and visiting children in long-term care. Regulation also gave local authorities a duty to provide short breaks for children with disabilities.

Following the introduction of National Minimum Standards for Adoption in 2011, further reforms have been announced to try to streamline the adoption system in order to process applications and place more children in a speedier fashion (Action Plan for Adoption, March 2012).

CHAPTER SUMMARY

As this chapter demonstrates, the area of children and family law and policy is complex. This chapter has introduced you to both the historical context and the current provisions. The historical context has shown you how law and policy have developed over time, highlighting the concerns that have been repeated in a number of inquiries as well as showing how the focus of work has changed and is changing. The chapter concludes by briefly considering the Children Act 2004, *Every Child Matters, Care Matters* and the Children and Adoption Act 2006, and the *Staying Safe* provisions, as well as the proposals currently being considered for further reform. These seek to address the underlying problems of multi-agency working,

CHAPTER SUMMARY *continued*

which have so often impacted on children and their families (whether through child protection issues, children in need or with disabilities or for those being looked after). They acknowledge and reaffirm that corporate responsibilities for children must be more appropriately fulfilled and contact promoted following parental separation if the lives of vulnerable children and young people are to be safeguarded and supported to enable them to achieve their potential.

FURTHER READING

Department for Education (2010) *Working Together to Safeguard Children*. London: The Stationery Office.

Useful reading to gain a fuller understanding of the expectations of all those with responsibilities for safeguarding children.

Department for Education and Skills (2004) *Every Child Matters: Change for Children in Social Care*. London: The Stationery Office.

Useful reading to gain a fuller understanding of the new provisions for children post Climbié.

Department of Health and Home Office (2003) *The Victoria Climbié Inquiry: Report of an inquiry by Lord Laming*. London: The Stationery Office.

Reading this report will help you gain an understanding of why things go wrong and why partnership working is so important.

www.dfe.gov.uk provides access documents and continuing developments within the *Every Child Matters* agenda as well as useful statistical information.

The Monro Review of Child Protection (final report) (2011) gives the suggested plans for the revision of the child protection system.

www.education.gov.uk/childrenandyoung people/families/a00205069/action-plan-for-adoption-tackling-delay gives details of the government's plans for addressing the issues of delay in adoption.

Chapter 3

Family support in social work with children and families

Nicky Ryden

Introduction

This chapter will first define family support and then explain how the concept has developed over time so that you will be able to locate your practice in what can be a complex picture. It will explore the characteristics of family support and the related social work practice, how needs are defined, the importance of the assessment process, the need for planning of any intervention and reviewing of that intervention in ways that are sensitive to the individual circumstances of children and their families. It will provide case examples of family support interventions for different problems and outcomes.

Definitions of family support

In 1994 the Audit Commission produced a report on services for children which used the following definition of family support: *Any activity or facility provided either by statutory agencies or by community groups or individuals aimed at providing advice and support to parents to help them bring up their children* (Audit Commission, 1994, page 39). There is an emphasis here on the providers as experts, who can advise and support parents on bringing up their children, rather than a partnership approach, which would see rearing children as the responsibility of all adults in a society, not just of their parents.

A more inclusive definition is one used by Barbara Hearn:

> Family support is about the creation and enhancement with and for families in need, of locally based (or accessible) activities, facilities and networks, the use of which have outcomes such as alleviated stress, increased self esteem, promoted parental/carer/family competence and behaviour and increased parental/carer capacity to nurture and protect children.
>
> (Hearn, 1995, page 6)

The emphasis here is on local provision to overcome the stresses that can make parenting a difficult task. You will notice that this definition refers to families in need, which we will explore later when we consider the families services are provided for and the nature of those services.

ACTIVITY **3.1**

Spend a few moments thinking about family support. What do the words suggest? Make a note of your thoughts. It might help to consider the words separately and then together.

COMMENT

You may have noted that 'family' usually consists of adults and children living in the same place. Those people will have a relationship with each other that might be defined in biological, emotional or legal terms, and there might be dependency and mutual support as well as conflict and violence. You may have considered the different kinds of families: one-parent families, step-families, adoptive families. You might have considered 'family' in terms of responsibility, arguing that the adults are responsible for the care and upbringing of the children so that they reach their potential and, in their turn, contribute to the community by working and by rearing their own family.

Similarly with support, generally we use this to mean a prop or framework which will keep something upright, often a growing thing. We use it in terms of emotional support, friendship and relationships which promote our sense of belonging to a community. Support can be practical as well as emotional. In fact, one could argue that without practical support other forms of support will not be effective.

Continued

When we put the two words together, 'family support', we have a term that might lead us to consider the multiplicity of family groups, the way that families change over time, often splitting and reforming with other individuals or parts of other families. Those families will be expecting and seeking support in the task of raising their children from a whole range of informal and formal support networks: friends, relatives, schools, health services, local authorities and government. Clearly we are dealing with complex relationships, not only between family members, but between families and the state.

The development of family support

There is considerable debate on whether services for children and families should be universal or targeted and on the purpose and intention of the state when it promotes such services. Historically in Britain there has been a reluctance to intervene in the privacy of family life, or to tell parents how they should discipline their children. Until the welfare state was set up after the Second World War, provision for those who could not support themselves and their children was shaped by the Poor Laws. The Poor Law Relief Act 1601 provided relief in the form of a small weekly payment, which allowed the person or family to remain in their home. The Poor Law Amendment Act 1832 decreed that the able-bodied poor could only receive support if they entered the workhouse. For families this often meant being separated, with little hope of being reunited. Generally any provision was designed to discourage people from seeking support. A number of concerned individuals started organisations to support and rescue children who were orphaned or abandoned, to supplement the provision made by the workhouse, for example Barnardo's and the Children's Society. Voluntary organisations continue to have a significant role in providing family support services. Holman (1988) reviews the way that statutory and voluntary agencies developed preventive strategies so that children could be maintained in their own family, rather than in institutions or the homes of strangers.

The role of the social worker in supporting the family

With the launching of the welfare state in 1948, health and education became universal services for children and their families. The financial support of the family in times of unemployment, ill health or disability was ensured, and the introduction of Family Allowance gave every family with more than one child a weekly payment to meet the costs of raising children. When it came to considering support and advice for families it was not considered necessary to have universal services. The Children Act 1948 did not consider prevention, but was concerned with setting out the circumstances in which the local authority would take over the responsibility of parenting children and with the ways in which it would undertake that task. However, the new Children's Officers were soon arguing that in many cases early practical advice and support could avoid the need to receive children into the care of the local authority. Many families living in areas of social deprivation found the new Children's Department a useful source of advice on dealing with children's behaviour or developmental problems. Caring for children at times of intolerable stress or distress helped many families over difficult periods. In 1963 the Children and Young Person Act gave the local authority the power to give practical and financial support to prevent children coming into care.

Lorraine Fox-Harding has given us a useful way of examining the principles that underlie social work practice with families. Fox-Harding's Perspectives in Child Care Policy (1991) outlines the relationship between the state and the family. She calls the first perspective laissez-faire and paternalistic, which characterises the situation where the family is defended from interference by the state unless the child is harmed by its parents or the child is an offender. On those occasions the state, or its representative the social worker, has a right to intervene, but in the interests of maintaining minimal public expenditure most families will be regarded as of no concern to the state.

The next perspective develops from the recognition that children can be the victims of poor parental care and that they deserve to be rescued from such care – this is called state paternalism and child protection. The goal of any intervention is to remove the child from such harmful care and place them in a substitute family, to give the child a fresh start. The Adoption Act 1976 gave local authorities the opportunity to apply for children to be freed for adoption so that children could be established in new families, over-ruling the objections of their birth parents. In reaction to this power of the state the third perspective, defence of the birth family and parent rights, developed. Fox-Harding calls this the modern defence of the family to distinguish it from the original laissez-faire approach and in this she argues the state is providing support for families so that children do not need substitute care: *This may take the form of intensive help directed to those families on the verge of breaking up, or of broader social policies to support all families with children* (Fox-Harding, 1991, page 71).

The Children Act 1989, with its emphasis on parental responsibility and partnership between parents and social workers in resolving concerns about children, reflects this perspective. The maintenance of family links is central to the Act; when a child has to be cared for by the local authority, parents retain their parental responsibility.

Finally, her fourth perspective is that of children's rights and child liberation, in which the child is seen as a subject in his or her own right, with rights and freedoms similar to those of an adult. This perspective has encouraged adults to listen to and to take account of children's own views about their lives and the services provided for them.

Recent developments in family support

Between 1997 and 2010 there was a concerted effort by the government to address the issues of social deprivation and family stress. This involved a shift in thinking about the position of children in our society, from being the sole responsibility of their parents to one of social investment, that is, the state has an interest in promoting the health and development of all children as a means of ensuring the future stability of society (see Frost, 2003, pages 7–9 and Featherstone, 2004, pages 96–100).

In 1998 the Home Office produced a document called *Supporting Families: A Consultation Document*, in which the government outlined a new, supportive and preventive approach to families and children. In particular it recognised that living in deprived circumstances operated to make parenting more challenging and caused children not to reach their potential, with implications for the future prosperity of the country. *Supporting Families* outlined for the first time how the state might actively support parents in parenting, whilst also encouraging as many adults as possible to enter the labour force – to achieve this goal parents need to have reliable and affordable childcare. The high costs to society of family breakdown, particularly if it leads to delinquency and offending, was to be overcome by investing in preventive strategies with young families. The following year the Department of Health issued *Opportunity for All: Tackling Poverty and Social Exclusion*, which launched a number of initiatives, including: increased investment in Early Years education; the launching of Sure Start; the National Child Care Strategy for affordable quality childcare for children aged 0–14 years; and Connexions, an advisory service for young people in education. The report outlined various financial supports to poorer families such as Working Families Tax Credits and Educational Maintenance Allowances.

Following the publication of *Supporting Families*, large sums of money were invested in improving the quality of provision for education and health services for all children. The New Labour government promoted the development of pre-school care for more and younger children. The agencies responsible for providing services were restructured, with children's services being separated from those provided for adults. This new approach was first articulated in *Every Child Matters*, a Green Paper produced by the Treasury in 2003. In the introduction Paul Boateng wrote: *we must be ambitious for all children, whoever they are and wherever they live. Creating a society where children are safe and have access to opportunities requires radical reform* (HM Treasury, 2003, pages 3–4).

The Children Act 2004 formalised this call for radical reform, identifying five outcomes for children: being healthy, staying safe, enjoying and achieving, making a positive contribution and achieving economic well-being (2004, page 4). Alongside these universal aspirations for all children a new framework for safeguarding children, with an emphasis on multi-agency co-operation and working, was published (DoH, 2006). This was further reviewed and revised in 2010.

Since 2010 the coalition government has been grappling with the consequences of a global economic downturn, one aspect of which has been severe cutbacks in public spending and reform of the welfare benefits system. As a consequence, although there is a commitment to maintain family support services, provision has been increasingly focused on those families that are perceived as creating problems within their community.

Provision of family support

There is a wide variety of organisations and services that can be considered to provide family support. Some will be befriending schemes, depending on volunteers who have had similar challenges to face, e.g. Homestart; others may have a long history of supporting families living in areas of social deprivation, e.g. family service units. Other projects may come under the umbrella of large voluntary organisations such as Barnardo's or the Children's Society; others will be run by statutory organisations. Family support is not limited to families with pre-school children. There is a wide range of projects and services which are provided by both statutory and voluntary agencies across the country. Frost has argued that this represents a progressive form of welfare practice (Frost, 2003) at a time when globalisation and rapid social change are impacting on families, creating diverse family structures and challenging traditional role models of parenting. The significance of having a choice of service providers may be particularly important for black and ethnic minority families, who find it difficult to access services that do not reflect their culture (Butt and Box, 1998a, 1998b; Butt, 1998), or who may feel their parenting style is not understood by white workers. In the same way expertise in dealing with particular problems, for example, drug and alcohol dependent parents, may deliver more effective services for those families than a more generic service (see Frost et al., 2003).

The provision of family support by child welfare agencies has often been located in family centres. Such centres have been around for about 40 years; this approach to delivering services invited all of the family to attend, to benefit from advice and support, to access educational opportunities, to give the children play opportunities. Family centres have been categorised according to their function:

- the client focused model;

- the neighbourhood model;

- the community development model (Holman, 1987).

The client-focused model offers specialised activities, only accepts referred clients, often draws its users from a wide area, and the workers will be professionally trained. Often such centres will be concerned with working with families where there are child protection issues and may also undertake core or specialist assessments of family functioning for court proceedings. This model of the family centre will often be wholly funded by the local authority, or have an agreement with the local authority to work with families who have complex needs.

The neighbourhood model is integrated with its local community, has an open door policy and will encourage local volunteers to contribute to the activities and programmes. Any paid staff are likely to be flexible in the roles they undertake, responding to individual need and day to day demands. This model of the family centre will often be funded by a local trust or voluntary organisation, and will be well used by local families.

The community development model is similar to the neighbourhood model in many respects but has a philosophy that is focused on developing the community, encouraging local residents in taking control of local resources and making management decisions. Both neighbourhood and community centres can make a significant difference for children in need by improving play opportunities, developing social activities for families with children and offering advice and support to stressed parents.

There is another model of family centre, the integrated model, which incorporates all of these aspects; some are nationally known. For example, Pen Green in Corby (Koris, 1987: Makins, 1997; Whalley, 1994) is based on an old secondary school site and is well known for its creative and varied approach to supporting families by providing specialist programmes, as well as education access programmes, day care and out-of-school resources for children of all ages and a full programme of activities for both men and women.

Another such centre is the Fulford Family Centre in Bristol (Stones, 1994). The integrated model of the family centre (Warren, 1998) can be identified in government thinking about children's centres, where the intention is to co-locate all local services for children so that they work effectively together and are accessible to all children.

Family centres continue to provide support to families, although many are now developing new partnerships and roles as the government has launched a series of new initiatives to improve provision for young children and to address the implications of childhood poverty (see Tunstill et al., 2007).

RESEARCH SUMMARY

Improving Children's Services Networks

This study by Tunstill et al. (2007) was commissioned by the Department of Health, and aimed to identify learning from family centres that could help to develop practice in children's centres and extended schools. Using both quantitative and qualitative methods, the research explored:

- *the management of partnership;*
- *meeting the needs of a diverse community;*
- *workforce issues;*
- *strategies for engaging service users.*

The authors suggest that family centres, and potentially children's centres, can be conceptualised as 'gateways' to family support services.

Among the findings from the research, professional commitment to partnership with families is more significant than the co-location of services. The relationship between a centre and children's social care can be characterised by frequent change with consequent tensions as established patterns of practice may have to be re-evaluated. Maintaining communication in the face of such tensions can be demanding. It was also established that successful centres worked hard to maintain a broad range of services that would meet the needs of a range of families, permitting early intervention and the capacity to respond to more complex needs.

Sure Start

In the late 1990s the New Labour government established a review of policy for pre-school children, which cut across a number of government departments and was chaired by the Treasury (www.surestart.gov.uk). The process of consultation between government departments and with recognised authorities on Early Years provision, visiting sites of Early Excellence, gave rise to the Sure Start programme. Each programme has its own partnership arrangements for management and governance, including voluntary and statutory agencies, parent representatives, community members and private sector representatives. The programme was launched in 2000, targeted on the poorest communities, and was consistently expanded year by year until 2010.

Sure Start programmes provide support to all families with children under five, in the areas where they are located, by providing a range of resources relevant to families with young children, home visiting to support stressed parents, running parenting programmes and drop-in centres, offering health advice and support, promoting educational opportunities to help adults acquire new skills, and providing ante-natal services, postnatal screening for depression, advice on breastfeeding, home safety advice and equipment loan. Many programmes also provided new childcare places or play and learning opportunities for children (Tunstill et al., 2002). The 2006 National Evaluation of Sure Start (NESS) found that the centres were having difficulty in reaching the most socially excluded families, including those from black and ethnic minority communities. Also there was little evidence that the provision was having much impact on children's attainment, although it recognised that indicators of children's increased resilience would not be demonstrable until they reached their teens (www.bbk.ac.uk/ness, Lloyd and Rafferty, 2006; National Audit Office, 2006). The most recent report from NESS indicates that children's health is better and mothers are providing a more stimulating home environment. Children from the most disadvantaged families, who have accessed Sure Start Children's Centres, are making progress that is comparable with that of children who are not disadvantaged. In addition, 95 per cent of eligible children are making use of the 15 hours' free childcare, exposing them to Early Years education in the pre-school years (NESS, 2010).

Children's Centres

Following the publication of the Green Paper *Every Child Matters* (2003), the government announced in December 2004 that it was extending the Sure Start programme by opening Sure Start Children's Centres in every community. These centres would extend the existing Sure Start provision by providing affordable day care. The target was to have 3,500 centres by 2010. Although this appears to be a universal service, it is in fact targeted, with centres in the 30 per cent most deprived communities being required to provide core services which include integrated childcare and early learning (in other words a structured learning environment for young children), while in less deprived areas the core service must include drop-in activities for children and families. All Children's Centres are expected to promote parental employment, to offer integrated child and family health services, outreach and family support, support for childminders and for children and parents with special needs.

Extended schools

Besides services for pre-school children the Education Act 2002 allows school governing bodies to provide, through partnerships with providers, a range of services to support children and families. Based on *Every Child Matters*, the goal for 2010 was for every school to offer high quality wraparound care for children from 8 a.m. to 6 p.m. The core services are after-school activities, including study support, parent support, effective referral to specialist support services and community access to ICT, sports and arts facilities. Children will therefore be spending more hours at the school site, which will become more accessible to the community. *Aiming High for Children* (DfES, 2007b) outlined the government's strategies for building resilience among families caught in a cycle of low achievement. These interventions are targeted at children who are in receipt of free school meals and include two hours of free activities per week, with two weeks of holiday activities. The Department for Children, Schools and Families was driving this agenda forward, encouraging parents to raise their expectations for their children with a Parent's Charter. Professionals were urged to be proactive in engaging with such families, providing integrated services tailored to their needs. To assist schools, health professionals and other children's services the Common Assessment Framework (CAF) was simplified and promoted as a tool to help identify children's needs and to facilitate multi-agency work (Brandon et al., 2006).

As part of the extended school's agenda the Connexions service, which provides an advice, guidance and personal development service in English schools for 13–19 year olds, was reorganised.

Targeted interventions

There has been considerable political interest in family support activities and in particular whether early interventions can prevent later costs to society created by criminal activity, drug and alcohol misuse and long-term unemployment (see, for example, Allen, 2011). There is an increasing emphasis on targeted interventions, such as the Family Nurse Partnership, which aims to provide a structured programme for young first-time mothers during the first two years of their child's life (DoH, 2011). Families with older children who are engaging in antisocial behaviour may be referred to a Family Intervention Project (FIP). FIPs were launched in 2006, and there were 250 in place by 2010. The projects typically use family support workers, who usually work with six families at any one time, providing advice and guidance on managing children's behaviour, developing parenting skills, and supporting and encouraging parents and carers to deal with family issues: *an assertive and persistent yet supportive approach to addressing and challenging the issues facing the whole family* (Dixon et al., 2010, page 11).

The evidence suggests that 75 per cent of the families referred to such projects show significant improvement, with reduced criminal activity, improved school attendance and less likelihood of being evicted from their home because of antisocial behaviour (Dixon et al., 2010). Social workers need to be knowledgeable about the projects in their local area (and in times of financial stringency there may be sudden changes in provision), and skilled in working with workers from a variety of agencies.

Children and families in need

The Children Act 1989 introduced the concept of a child in need and outlined the duties and responsibilities of the local authority in respect of such a child. Section 17 states that:

> It shall be the general duty of every local authority . . .
>
> a) to safeguard and promote the welfare of children within their area who are in need;

and

b) *so far as is consistent with that duty, to promote the upbringing of such children by their families, by providing a range and level of services appropriate to those children's needs.*

(HMSO, 1989, page 12)

The Act goes on to say that the local authority can ask voluntary agencies or other individuals to provide such service on its behalf, that assistance can be in kind or in exceptional circumstances cash, that any assistance can be subject to a means test, but if the family is dependent on benefits then they will not be liable to repayment of assistance. It then defines a child in need:

. . . a child shall be taken to be in need if –

a) *he is unlikely to achieve or maintain, or to have the opportunity of achieving or maintaining, a reasonable standard of health or development without the provision for him of services by a local authority under this Part;*

b) *his health or development is likely to be significantly impaired, or further impaired, without the provision for him of such services; or,*

c) *he is disabled,*

and family in relation to such a child includes any person who has parental responsibility for the child and any other person with whom he has been living.

(HMSO, 1989, page 13; see also Johns, 2011, pages 46–49)

The Act defines disability in terms of sensory deficit, mental disorder and substantial or permanent handicap by illness, injury or congenital deformity, then goes on to define development as meaning physical, intellectual, emotional, social or behavioural development and health as physical or mental health.

As you can see, the definitions given in the legislation seem to have little relationship to any real child and their family. It also suggests that there are universally understood and accepted standards of health and development. Clearly having a disability means a child is in need, but what is a disability? Being without hearing, sight or speech are disabilities according to the Act, but does suffering chronic inner ear infections also qualify a child as in need? If it could be argued that the infections meant time off from school and that when able to attend the child was unable to learn effectively because of hearing loss, then perhaps they would be regarded as in need, but what kind of service might they or their family require? If the child has parents who are responsive to the need for treatment then the child will be attending the audiology clinic and getting the help necessary to minimise the impact of the hearing loss. If the child has parents who are careless about keeping appointments, or who are not concerned about the child missing school, then there might be a case for intervention, because without help this child is not going to achieve a reasonable standard of health or development. The intervention might take the form of encouraging the parents to take the child to see the appropriate professionals, perhaps providing practical support to attend if the family live in an isolated place or have difficulty with transport.

39

CASE STUDY

Let us consider Kylie, who is a 12-year-old, of mixed parentage, AfricanCarribbean/White. She lives with her mother Donna and sees her father Alan Cole regularly. Donna was in care as a child, and she did not get much education. She says Kylie is like her, not much good at school. Kylie does not like school, where she says she is bullied by other girls, who call her names. Kylie is small for her age; she is not well dressed. Kylie has attended school 60 per cent of the time in the last term.

ACTIVITY **3.2**

Spend some time thinking about Kylie. Do you think she is a child in need? Who is her family? What kind of provision might the family welcome?

COMMENT

It appears that Kylie is a child who finds school a difficult place to be and whose mother may not place much value on education. In this respect she may be like many other children who attend that school. Living with a single parent who is on benefit will mean that money for clothes is in short supply. The local authority may assist with the provision of school clothing. Would there be any need to do more than ensure that the family is receiving all the benefits to which they are entitled?

The Children Act Report 2002 highlighted the high thresholds social services departments were operating for children in need if there was no evidence of risk of significant harm (DfES, 2002, pages 33). The Children in Need Census, which collects information on all children referred over seven consecutive days, showed that 15,400 cases were dealt with, within the first 24 hours (DfES, 2002). In many instances the decision would be that no service will/can be offered.

The government funded a series of research studies evaluating the way services for children in need were being implemented (Colton et al., 1995; Aldgate and Tunstill, 1995; DoH,1995a). Earlier research had suggested that local authorities had misinterpreted the Act and not appreciated that they had as much responsibility for children in need as they had for children who were at risk and in need of protection. Contrary to the Act's intention, services for children and families in need had been service led rather than needs led – in other words, provision had been determined on the basis of reducing demand for more expensive services such as providing accommodation for children, rather than responding to social deprivation. It had also established that families who did receive family support were generally eager for advice and support, particularly when concerned about adolescent behaviour problems and involvement in offending (Tunstill and Aldgate, 2000).

RESEARCH SUMMARY

The Every Child Matters agenda, and the Children Act 2004, has meant that 'children in need' are no longer the sole responsibility of the local authority social worker. All agencies who deliver services for children are obliged to act to support children who are not meeting the goals of Every Child Matters (see Barker, 2009) The introduction of the CAF as a tool to promote multi-agency working and to standardise assessment has already been mentioned. The aim was to improve assessment of need, to ensure that those needs were addressed as early as possible and to facilitate information sharing between profes-sionals. It was also intended that the completion of a CAF would be noted on the national children's database, Contactpoint. This centralised record of all the nation's children has now been ended following much debate about its usefulness and fears about loss of privacy in family life.

CASE STUDY

Kylie is in her first year at high school and struggling. In her primary school Kylie had a lot of support from the ancillary staff; she attended a small nurture group and was close to one of the classroom assistants. At high school Kylie is in a small class for children who need additional support with learning. She has not made friends with the other children in the class and at break times is reluctant to leave the classroom. Kylie's form teacher is concerned that Kylie seems tired and that her attendance is not regular. She seems unhappy and withdrawn. Kylie often goes to see the school nurse complaining of stomach pains or a headache.

The school routinely invites the parents of children new to the school to a meeting to discuss how the children are settling in. The form teacher decides to invite Kylie's parents to school. Kylie's mother Donna comes at the time arranged. Donna is anxious, as she did not enjoy school herself, but the teacher is friendly and encourages Donna to talk about how she thinks Kylie is settling in. Donna tells the teacher that Kylie misses her old school and the adults who supported her, that she often talks about the classroom assistant. Donna explains that Kylie has been complaining a lot about feeling poorly, so she has kept her at home a few times. The teacher asks Donna what she would like Kylie to get out of school. Donna, after some thought, says that she would like Kylie to enjoy school, after all she has to come for another four years! She would like Kylie to have some qualifications that would help her get a job when she leaves school; Donna says she doesn't want Kylie to end up like she did, having a baby before she had time to grow up. After listening to Donna the teacher explains that Kylie seems to be rather unhappy at the moment, that she is very quiet and hasn't made friends. She then asks Donna if she would be prepared to work with school to try and change this for Kylie. Although a bit doubtful about what she can do to help, Donna agrees that she would like things to be better for Kylie. The teacher introduces Donna to another member of the staff team, who is responsible for pastoral care. In discussion with Donna, it is agreed that she and

Continued

the staff member for pastoral care will meet again to complete a CAF, which will identify Kylie's needs and help to create a plan to address those needs.

Donna is still unsure of the school's intentions, but she feels they do care about Kylie and want her to be happy and be able to learn. She tells Kylie about the meeting and that she will be coming to school again.

Once the CAF is complete it is usual to have a meeting with all the people who are involved, including the parents and the child. This is sometimes called a 'Team Around the Child' (TAC) meeting, and one of the team members may be asked to be the lead professional – that is, the person responsible for co-ordinating the plan and reviewing progress.

ACTIVITY *3.3*

Consider the action taken by the staff member. What do you think about the practice? Try to identify the processes that have taken place – can you foresee any problems with the way the staff member decided to respond to the referral?

COMMENT

Once the CAF has been completed by school, a decision needs to made about whether there is a need to involve other professionals, or to support Kylie from the services available within school. At this stage it seems that with some additional support Kylie can be provided for by school; if Kylie receives free school meals there may be no charge for attending activities. Arrangements can be made for her to attend after school club, where she can meet other children and also get help with her homework. She could also be introduced to a mentor, one of the older students who has been trained to support the more vulnerable members of the school. Enquiries can be made to ensure Donna is getting all the benefits she is entitled to, and that she has been given information about the local Children's Centre, where she could get some support and advice about the younger children. A benefit of the CAF is that it attempts to work in partnership with a family, and in many cases will provide a framework that leads to successful outcomes. It is voluntary so people, if they agree to contribute, are more likely to engage in a meaningful way and to contribute to the plans for change. The CAF can also alert professionals to a child's particular vulnerabilities and if there is no improvement can be the basis of a referral to more specialised services.

The assessment process

On receiving a referral Children's Social Care has one working day to decide whether to take any action. The team manager will scrutinise the CAF completed by the school. As the focus of the CAF is Kylie, there may be questions about the well-being of the younger children that are not fully addressed. This and the lack of improvement in Kylie's attendance, her continued unhappiness and general air of being neglected might result in some further exploration. The department's own records show that Donna was herself in care as a child and that there was some contact when Kylie was younger. Although the school was under the impression that Donna was going to the Children's Centre regularly with the younger children, when this is checked it appears she has not been for the last month. Given these concerns the decision is made to make an initial assessment. This must be completed within seven working days. The initial assessment will determine what action may need to be taken. Enquiries will be made of other agencies, e.g. the health visitor and GP, the school and the family. Because Kylie is 12 the social worker will speak to her on her own to discover what Kylie's wishes and feelings are about having help.

The Framework for the Assessment of Children in Need and Their Families (2000) was designed to ensure that children's needs are fully and consistently assessed, using a holistic approach.

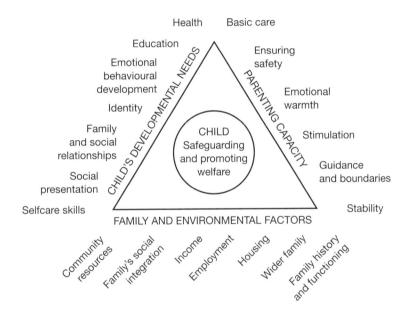

Figure 3.1 *The assessment framework*

Source: Department of Health (2000). *The framework for the assessment of children in need and their families.* The Stationery Office.

The Framework encourages social workers to look at family strengths as well as identifying the difficulties. In Kylie's family there are strengths: Donna has raised Kylie more or less on her own. Although her school attendance is not as good as it should be, there is no suggestion that Kylie is involved in any antisocial activity when she is not in school. Donna attends clinic regularly and has a good relationship with her health visitor. The estate where the family lives has had problems with vandalism. Both Donna and her partner feel that the neighbours avoid them and Kylie has been subjected to racist taunts from other children. On balance the social worker decides that the best way to help the family is to link them up with local resources that will help Donna in her parenting of the younger children, and to encourage Kylie to improve her school attendance. The social worker plans to do this by seeing Kylie regularly and doing some work to improve her self-esteem.

However, this does not satisfactorily address all of the issues – Kylie's small stature and the reasons why her teacher felt concerned enough to refer her. Could it be that the family has not felt able to disclose all of their concerns – are they actively concealing factors which might cause the social worker to consider whether there is a need for further assessment? Let us suppose that the social worker does decide there is a need for a more extended assessment, a core assessment. She might still want the family to make use of local resources while that process is being completed – the family may be invited to attend a local family centre for the purposes of a full assessment. (The core assessment will be discussed further in a later chapter.) The social worker could also liaise with the education department over Kylie's difficulties in school. The school may have referred Kylie for assessment by an educational psychologist. Discussion between the social worker and the educational psychologist may facilitate this in happening rather sooner.

Partnership with the family

Throughout her contact with the family, the social worker will be striving to work in partnership with the family, to listen to their concerns and to consult them about the solutions that they think will work for their family. There is a difficult balance to be held between the rights and needs of the children and the rights and responsibilities of the parents. It is important not to forget Kylie's birth father Alan Cole, who although not living with Kylie does have regular contact with her and should also be consulted about any plans that might be made for Kylie. In the same way, Ahmed Khan should be involved in discussions about Tariq and Nadia.

At this point the children are not considered to be in need of a child protection plan, and the relationship is one of voluntary support. The family may be ambivalent about having a social worker visit them at home, feeling that it indicates they are under surveillance. Although Donna has not recently attended the Children's Centre she felt much more comfortable talking to the volunteer at the playgroup, someone who has lived locally and brought up her children. This may prompt Donna to go back to the centre, as she could recognise that going somewhere that provides play and learning opportunities for the children is preferable to having the social worker calling at the house. There may be the opportunity for Donna and Ahmed to attend a parenting programme, where again some of those leading the group could be parents who have faced similar challenges in the past. Parenting programmes are provided for all ages; some are for parents of young offenders, who may be obliged to attend by a Parenting Order (Crime and Disorder Act 1998) for a period of three months for training and guidance.

There is a variety of parenting programmes used by centres providing support to families. Some are very structured and delivered by professionals, others are more informal and may be delivered by volunteers, or by professionals and volunteers working together. Some examples of parenting programmes that you may have heard of are the Webster-Stratton Parenting Programme, which was developed by Caroline Webster-Stratton, and the Mellow Parenting Programme developed by Christine Puckering, both of which have been extensively evaluated and use a variety of strategies to engage with parents and to help them learn new ways of interacting with their children. The Mellow Parenting Programme has been successful with very vulnerable families, nurturing the parents (usually single mothers) as well as promoting the development of the children. Some programmes such as Supporting Parents on Kids' Education (SPOKES) aim to improve relationships between parents and children by learning together. It is important to ask questions about the purpose of the programme before suggesting it to a family. While all aim to improve relationships and promote children's development, the intensity or method may not be suitable for everyone. Some parents find attending groups daunting – in particular, single parents with drug or alcohol problems and people with low self-esteem or who lack social skills may find a group unsatisfactory. There may be practical issues to consider. Will there be childcare available? Will the family have to travel? When is the session timed – can working parents get there? Will there be men present? What provision is made for the older child?

The social work role in relation to family support requires knowledge of local provision and effective relationships with practitioners from a range of settings and with different knowledge and understanding. It requires considerable skill in communicating effectively with other professionals as well as the family. Supporting families with complex needs to engage with support services in their own community can produce significant change and improvement for children.

CHAPTER SUMMARY

The chapter has looked at what we mean when we use the term 'family support' and explored some of the ways that our approach to family support has changed over time. We have looked at the role of the social worker in family support, considering the way legislation and policy have promoted preventive work, although there are often constraints on how this can be delivered. There has been an emphasis on supporting parents in the care of their children, with the New Labour interest in social investment, which meant a significant shift in how services were structured and delivered to families with children. The concept of 'the child in need' has been considered and the response of social services departments to children in need has been reviewed. We have looked at some of the ways that family support might be delivered, through family centres, Sure Start Children's Centres, and voluntary agencies such as Homestart, together with some of the programmes which are used in those centres.

The impact of the economic downturn and the consequences for service providers will be seen over time. There are already indicators that it is affecting family support, which is being reviewed by many local authorities and may well become much more targeted in the future.

FURTHER READING

Butt, J and Box, L (1998a) *Family Centred: A Study of the Use of Family Centres by Asian families*. London: Race Equality Unit.

This book looks at the reasons why Asian families are under-represented in many family support settings.

Featherstone, B (2004) *Family Life and Family Support*. Basingstoke: Palgrave Macmillan.

This book takes a feminist perspective and considers how recent policy developments are impacting on family life.

45

Frost, N, Lloyd, A and Jeffrey, L (2003) *The RHP Companion to Family Support*. Lyme Regis: Russell House Publishing.

This book, besides exploring theory and policy on family support has, in Part Two, accounts by practitioners of family support in action, and in Part Three a helpful guide to information sharing and networking to find out what services are available to support families.

Quinton, D (2004). *Supporting Parents. Messages from Research*. London: Jessica Kingsley.

This book presents in a readable form the recent government-funded research that is guiding the development of current policy on family support.

Chapter 4

Working effectively with children and families in the safeguarding children arena

Julie Bywater

A C H I E V I N G   A   S O C I A L   W O R K   D E G R E E

This chapter will help you to develop the following capabilities from the **Professional Capabilities Framework:**

- **Professionalism**

Identify and behave as a professional social worker committed to professional development.

- **Diversity**

Recognise diversity and apply anti-discriminatory and anti-oppressive principles in practice.

- **Justice**

Advance human rights and promote social justice and economic well-being.

- **Knowledge**

Apply knowledge of social sciences, law and social work practice theory.

- **Judgement**

Use judgement and authority to intervene with individuals, families and communities to promote independence, provide support and prevent harm, neglect and abuse.

- **Critical reflection and analysis**

Apply critical reflection and analysis to inform and provide a rationale for professional decision-making.

- **Contexts and organisations**

Engage with, inform, and adapt to changing contexts that shape practice. Operate effectively within your own organisational frameworks and contribute to the development of services and organisations. Operate effectively within multi-agency and inter-professional settings.

It will also introduce you to the following academic standards as set out in the 2008 social work subject benchmark statement:

4 Defining principles

      4.3 Contemporary definitions of social work

      4.6 Social work as a moral activity

5.1.1 Social work services and service users

5.1.2 The service delivery context

5.1.3 Values and ethics

5.1.4 Social work theory

7.3 Knowledge and understanding

Introduction

This chapter will focus on the skills and knowledge needed by social workers to work effectively with children and families within the child protection/safeguarding children arena. The categories and definitions of child abuse will be briefly outlined with reference to the current guidance and suggested further reading. Particular reference will be given to the predominant factors currently being addressed by child protection practitioners throughout the country, specifically the impact of parental domestic violence; learning disability; substance misuse and mental illness/distress in relation to children's development, welfare and safety. Current legislation, policies, guidance and the framework for assessing children and families will be briefly outlined, while also highlighting some of the proposed changes recommended in the Munro Review of Child Protection (Munro, 2011, as noted in Chapter 2).

Keeping a child safe from harm is a high profile area of social work practice. Decisions about the protection of children are among the most challenging that any professional has to take, and often involve social workers making difficult judgement calls, such as whether a child should be removed from the family based on whether there is evidence or suspicion of maltreatment, or how best to work with a family unit in an attempt to improve relationships between different family members (Munro, 2011). Following the tragic deaths in Haringey of eight-year-old Victoria Climbié in 2000 from abuse and neglect, and of baby Peter Connelly, aged 17 months in August 2007, Laming (2009) found that a range of professional networks had failed to act on concerns about Victoria's and Peter's safety and welfare. At the time of Peter's death, for example, he was the subject of a child protection plan and 11 different services were involved at the time he was being abused (Laming, 2007). On 11 November 2008, two men were convicted of causing or allowing the death of Peter, including his stepfather. Peter's mother had already pleaded guilty to the charge. During the trial, the court heard that Peter was used as a 'punch bag' and that his mother had deceived and manipulated professionals with lies, and on one occasion had smeared him with chocolate to hide his bruises. There had been over 60 contacts with the family from a variety of health and social care professionals, and he died only 48 hours after a hospital doctor failed to identify that he had a broken spine (Parton, 2011). Laming (2009), as a consequence, highlighted the sheer enormity of working with highly resistant and hostile parents and carers in cases ending in the deaths of children.

The Peter Connelly case provides a striking picture of how it is possible to deceive and manipulate professionals, by covering up the causes of injuries and also by concealing who is actually forming a family unit. There are considerable practice implications when social workers are confronted by resistant or manipulative parents/carers/family members, some of whom have emerged in recent high profile cases, such as Victoria's aunt and Peter's mother, along with Karen Matthews, who claimed that her daughter Shannon had been kidnapped. Highly resistant families is a term which refers to families where interventions are not providing timely, improved outcomes for children, where they may suffer, or are likely to suffer, significant harm because of ill-treatment or the impairment of health or development due to abuse or neglect. A recent study highlights that many of the parents and carers (regarded as highly resistant) had multiple problems including domestic violence, substance misuse, mental health problems and prior history of being abused themselves (Centre for Excellence and Outcomes in Children and Young People's Services, 2010).

Current legislation and practice guidance has been informed by a number of important publications, including relevant research findings and government guidance as highlighted in Chapter 2. It is important that we are aware of these in order to understand how current practice in this area has evolved. The most significant piece of guidance, for this chapter, has been the Munro Review of Child Protection (Munro, 2011), which sets out proposals for reform which have been accepted by the government and which, taken together, are intended to create the conditions that will enable professionals to make the best judgements about the help to give to children, young people and families. Some of the proposed changes will be highlighted throughout the chapter.

The current legislative and practice context of child protection/safeguarding children

In England, the responsibility to care for and protect children and young people rests primarily with their parents, but there is also a recognised need for state involvement to protect children and young people from all forms of abuse or neglect and to support them where necessary (Munro, 2011).

The current legal framework for intervention in the area of child protection continues to be largely contained in the Children Act (1989), but practice must also now be considered within the context of Every Child Matters and the legislative changes introduced by the Children Act 2004. The Children Act 2004 does not introduce a range of new child protection powers, but does set the foundations for good practice in the use of existing powers contained in the Children Act 1989, and covers all aspects of safeguarding the well-being of children through the development of more effective and accessible services focused around the needs of children, young people and their families (see earlier chapters).

Duty to investigate concerns regarding children at risk of significant harm

The Children Act 1989, section 47(1) places a duty on local authorities to investigate where a local authority:

(a) *is informed that a child who lives, or is found, in their area –*

   (i) *is the subject of an emergency protection order; or*

   (ii) *is in police protection, section 46; or*

(b) *have reasonable cause to suspect that a child who lives, or is found, in their area is suffering, or is likely to suffer, significant harm,*

the authority shall make, or cause to be made, such inquiries as they consider necessary to enable them to decide whether they should take any action to safeguard or promote the child's welfare.

Definitions and concepts

The Children Act 1989 introduced the concept of significant harm as the threshold that justifies compulsory intervention in family life in the best interests of children, and a court may make a care order or supervision order in respect of a child if it is satisfied that:

- the child is suffering, or is likely to suffer, significant harm; and

- the harm, or likelihood of harm, is attributable to a lack of adequate parental care or control (section 31).

A 'child' refers to anyone who has not reached their eighteenth birthday (Children Act(s) 1989 and 2004), so although 'child' is used throughout, it applies to both children and young people.

> The fact that a child has reached 16 years of age, is living independently or is in further education, is a member of the armed forces, is in hospital or in custody in the secure estate for children and young people, does not change his or her status or entitlement to services or protection under the Children Act 1989.

> (DCSF, 2010, page 34)

The Children Act 2004 extended the five outcomes in Every Child Matters for children's services, as areas for improving the well-being of children in section 10(2), relating to:

- physical and mental health and emotional well-being;

- protection from harm and neglect;

- education, training and recreation;

- the contribution made by them to society; and

- social and economic well-being.

Section 11 of the Act further imposes the duty to make arrangements to safeguard and promote welfare on a wide range of bodies, including for example, a children's service authority, district council, Primary Care Trust, NHS Trust, police authority, probation board, youth offending team, etc. (see section 11(1) for others listed). Inter-agency working is the focus of this section and the duty to safeguard and promote the welfare of children is broader than preventing child abuse or responding to children in need, in that it is defined as:

> protecting children from maltreatment, preventing impairment of children's health or development; ensuring that children are growing up in circumstances consistent with the provision of safe and effective care; and undertaking that role so as to enable those children to have optimum life chances and to enter adulthood successfully.

> (Section 11, para. 2.8, Children Act 2004)

Alongside the Children Act 2004, several volumes of guidance were issued, including for example:

- interagency co-operation to improve the well-being of children;

- duty to make arrangements to safeguard and promote the welfare of children;

- *Working Together to Safeguard Children* (DfES, 2006) – which incorporates an important additional chapter on Local Safeguarding Children Boards.

Working Together to Safeguard Children (DfES, 2006) was updated in October 2010 fol- lowing the government's acceptance of all 58 of Lord Laming's (2009) recommendations; 23 of those recommendations are addressed in the 2010 revised guidance.

Following a recommendation in the Munro Review, the government is working with part- ners to revise and shorten the 2010 guidance, and to remove the distinction between initial and core assessments, and the associated timescales in respect of these assess- ments in the Framework for the Assessment of Children in Need and Their Families (DoH, 2000b). Any proposed changes to the assessment framework will be consulted upon as part of the *Working Together* consultation. Until the revised version of *Working Together to Safeguard Children* is published and implemented, the current guidance (DCSF, 2010) remains operational. It contains detailed procedural guidance and research studies to pro- vide an integrated approach to safeguarding and promoting the welfare of children and families, within which agencies and professionals – individually and jointly – have a shared responsibility:

> *In order to achieve this joint working and safeguard and promote the child's welfare, all agencies should:*
>
> - *be alert to potential indicators of abuse or neglect;*
>
> - *be alert to the risks of harm that individual abusers, or potential abusers, may pose to children;*
>
> - *prioritise direct communication and positive and respectful relationships with children, ensuring the child's wishes and feelings underpin assessments and any safeguarding activities;*
>
> - *share and help to analyse information so that an assessment can be made of whether the child is suffering or is likely to suffer harm, their needs and circumstances;*
>
> - *contribute to whatever actions are needed to safeguard and promote the child's welfare;*
>
> - *take part in regularly reviewing the outcomes for the child against specific plans; and*
>
> - *work co-operatively with parents, unless this is inconsistent with ensuring the child's safety.*
>
> (*DCSF, 2010, page 32*)

To meet these requirements professionals involved will need to follow and adhere to the guidance provided in *Working Together to Safeguard Children* (DCFS, 2010) and the *Framework for Assessment of Children in Need and their Families* (DoH, 2000b), which incorporates the theoretical frameworks and underpinning knowledge base of child development, parenting capacity and the environmental factors that impact upon children's needs and safety. This ecological approach has been central in informing policy and provides an analysis to be made of the key risk factors that are likely to have an adverse effect on children's development and the corresponding protective factors that may help children to develop the resilience they will require if they are to thrive in relation to the outcomes listed in *Every Child Matters* (DfES, 2004a; Scott and Ward, 2005). By ensuring that practice is evidence based and in accordance with statute/government guidance and agency policy, practitioners will have a safe framework within which to practise (Walker and Beckett, 2011).

The categories and definitions of abuse

ACTIVITY *4.1*

Make a list of the following:

- *What do you think constitutes child abuse?*

- *Can you think of some of the types/categories and definitions of child abuse?*

- *Who do you think are the main abusers of children?*

COMMENT

Somebody may abuse or neglect a child by inflicting harm, or by failing to act to prevent harm. Children may be abused in a family or in an institutional community setting, by those known to them or, more rarely, by a stranger, for example, via the internet (DCSF, 2010, (1.32) page 37).

The most commonly agreed types of abuse are: emotional, physical and sexual abuse and neglect. These categories are used to define abuse in child protection registers. Other forms of abuse, however, are also recognised, which the guidance details.

Working Together (DCSF, 2010) provides the following descriptions of the four major types of abuse:

Physical abuse may involve hitting, shaking, throwing, poisoning, burning or scalding, drowning, suffocating, or otherwise causing physical harm to a child. Physical harm may also be caused when a parent or carer fabricates the symptoms of, or deliberately induces, illness in a child.

Emotional abuse is the persistent emotional maltreatment of a child such as to cause severe and persistent adverse effects on the child's emotional development. It may involve conveying to children that they are worthless or unloved, inadequate, or valued only insofar as they meet the needs of another person. It may include not giving the child opportunities to express their views, deliberately silencing them or 'making fun' of what they say or how they communicate. It may feature age or developmentally inappropriate expectations being imposed on children. These may include interactions that are beyond the child's developmental capability, as well as overprotection and limitation of exploration and learning, or preventing the child participating in normal social interaction. It may involve seeing or hearing the ill-treatment of another. It may involve serious bullying (including cyber bullying), causing children frequently to feel frightened or in danger, or the exploitation or corruption of children. Some level of emotional abuse is involved in all types of maltreatment of a child, though it may occur alone.

Sexual abuse involves forcing or enticing a child or young person to take part in sexual activities, not necessarily involving a high level of violence, whether or not the child is aware of what is happening. The activities may involve physical contact, including assault by penetration (for example, rape or oral sex) or non-penetrative acts such as masturbation, kissing, rubbing and touching outside of clothing. They may also include non-contact activities, such as involving children in looking at, or in the production of, sexual images, watching sexual activities, encouraging children to behave in sexually inappropriate ways, or grooming a child in preparation for abuse (including via the internet). Sexual abuse is not solely perpetrated by adult males. Women can also commit acts of sexual abuse, as can other children.

Neglect is the persistent failure to meet a child's basic physical and/or psychological needs, likely to result in the serious impairment of the child's health or development. Neglect may occur during pregnancy as a result of maternal substance abuse. Once a child is born, neglect may involve a parent or carer failing to:

- provide adequate food, clothing and shelter (including exclusion from home or abandonment);

- protect a child from physical and emotional harm or danger;

- ensure adequate supervision (including the use of inadequate caregivers); or

- ensure access to appropriate medical care or treatment.

It may also include neglect of, or unresponsiveness to, a child's basic emotional needs (DCSF, 2010, pages 38–39).

The concept of significant harm

The Children Act 1989 introduced the concept of significant harm as the threshold to justify compulsory intervention in family life, to uphold the best interests of the child.

ACTIVITY **4.2**

Make a list of what you understand by the following terms:

- *'harm'*

- *'significant harm'*

Can you think of any examples that would equate to the term 'significant harm'?

COMMENT

Unfortunately, there is no absolute definition to rely upon when trying to judge/assess what constitutes significant harm. Working Together to Safeguard Children (2010, page 36) states that:

> *consideration of the severity of ill-treatment may include the degree and the extent of physical harm, the duration and frequency of abuse and neglect, the extent of premeditation, and the presence or degree of threat, coercion, sadism and bizarre or unusual elements. Sometimes, a singly traumatic event may constitute significant harm, e.g. a violent assault, suffocation or poisoning. More often,* **significant harm** *is a compilation of significant events, both acute and long-standing, which interrupt, change or damage the child's physical and psychological development. Some children live in family and social circumstances where their health and development are neglected. For them, it is the long-term emotional, physical or sexual abuse that causes impairment to the extent of constituting significant harm. In each case, it is necessary to consider any maltreatment alongside the family's strengths and supports.*

Under section 31(9) of the Children Act 1989 (as amended by the Adoption and Children Act 2002):

- *'harm' means ill-treatment or the impairment of health or development, including, for example, impairment suffered from seeing or hearing the ill-treatment of another;*
- *'development' means physical, intellectual, emotional, social or behavioural development;*
- *'health' means physical or mental health; and*
- *'ill-treatment' includes sexual abuse and forms of ill-treatment which are not physical.*

Under section 31(10) of the Act:

> *Where the question of whether harm suffered by a child is significant turns on the child's health and development, his health or development shall be compared with that which could reasonably be expected of a similar child.*

An excellent diagram is provided by Johns (2011, page 66) to demonstrate the threshold criteria for significant harm.

Working openly and in partnership with parents in order to gain their involvement and participation is one of the underlying principles of the Children Act 1989. Parents have a central role in their children's welfare and protection from harm, and should therefore be included in all decisions and actions taken by professionals, wherever possible, when they have concerns about a child. In order to prevent and protect children from abuse, professionals need to help the child's parents provide good enough care of their children. In addition, *Working Together to Safeguard Children* (DCSF, 2010) requires local authorities to refer parents to independent advice and advocacy as soon as inquiries commence under a section 47 (Children Act 1989). If a parent or child is disabled, they may also require additional support with communication in order for them to fully participate. Interpreters should also be provided for those whose first language is not English.

> *Helping children, families and adults who are in crisis or in difficult or dangerous situations to be safe, to cope and take control of their lives again requires exceptional professional judgement. Social workers have to be highly skilled in their interactions and must draw on a sound professional understanding of social work. They have to be able to do all of this while sustaining strong partnerships with the children or adults they are working with and their families: sometimes they will be the only people offering the stability and consistency that is badly needed.*
>
> (Social Work Taskforce, 2009, quoted in
> Munro Review of Child Protection, 2010, page 30)

However, as highlighted earlier, social workers may experience a range of difficulties when working with some parents and families to achieve effective partnerships, particularly with those who are highly resistant or deceitful. Adults perpetrating abuse are often skilful at hiding abuse from social workers and other professionals (Munro, 2011). Moreover, some parents go to extreme lengths to conceal the truth. Whatever the resistances from adult parents and carers that social workers have to confront, their primary professional responsibility is to the child. It is this that must drive the decision-making. Whatever the attitudes and reactions of adults, it is the needs of the child that have to be uppermost in driving all judgements and decisions about whether parents can carry on being parents to their children (Ferguson, 2011). Managing 'risk to self' is also a priority of professional practice, and having the ability to handle stress and crisis situations or managing 'decision calls' is something that cannot be taught, it is learned through practice experiences, critical reflection and skilled supervision. Supervision is a critical priority and in some cases could mean the difference between life and death (Walker and Beckett, 2011).

When inquiries are being made within the context of section 47, the local authority must take steps to obtain access to the child (section 47(4), Children Act 1989), and if access is denied or the local authority is denied information as to the child's whereabouts, the local authority may need to apply for an emergency protection order, a child assessment order or a supervision order (section 37, Children Act 1989), unless the local authority are satisfied that the child's welfare can be satisfactorily safeguarded without doing so (section 47(6), Children Act 1989).

Emergency protection powers

As highlighted above, there is a range of powers available to local authorities and others, such as the NSPCC and the police, if required to take emergency action to safeguard children.

The court may make an emergency protection order under section 44 of the Children Act 1989, if it is satisfied that there is reasonable cause to believe that a child is likely to suffer significant harm if:

(a) s/he is not removed to different accommodation; or
(b) s/he does not remain in the place in which s/he is then being accommodated.

Continued

An emergency protection order may also be made if enquiries (e.g. made under section 47) are being frustrated by access to the child being unreasonably refused to a person authorised to seek access, and the applicant has reasonable cause to believe that access is needed as a matter of urgency. An emergency protection order gives authority to remove a child, and places the child under the protection of the applicant, who then also acquires parental responsibility (section 44(4) c) which is limited to what is necessary to safeguard the welfare of the child. During the order, the child must be able to have reasonable contact with his/her parents or those with whom the child was living immediately before the order, subject to any specific directions given by the court. If it appears safe during the order the local authority may return the child home, however, if circumstances change the child can be removed again (section 44 (12)). An emergency protection order lasts for eight days but it is possible to be extended, once only, for a further seven days.

The court may also include an exclusion requirement in an interim care order or emergency protection order (sections 38A and 44A of the Children Act 1989).This allows a perpetrator to be removed from the home instead of having to remove the child. The court, however, must be satisfied that:

(a) there is reasonable cause to believe that if the person is excluded from the home in which the child lives, the child will cease to suffer, or cease to be likely to suffer, significant harm, or that enquires will cease to be frustrated; and

(b) another person living in the home is able and willing to give the child the care that it would be reasonable to expect a parent to give, and consents to the exclusion requirement.

Under section 46 of the Children Act 1989, where a police officer has reasonable cause to believe that a child would otherwise be likely to suffer significant harm, s/he may:

(a) remove the child to suitable accommodation and keep him or her there; or

(b) take reasonable steps to ensure that the child's removal from any hospital, or other place in which the child is then being accommodated, is prevented.

A child may only be kept in police protection, however, for 72 hours (Brammer, 2010).

The assessment framework and legislation (specifically relating to safeguarding children/ child protection)

The current framework for assessment will be revised (as recommended in the Munro Review) but, until the changes are implemented, practitioners will continue to use the current *Framework for the Assessment of Children in Need and their Families* (DoH, 2000b), which provides for a systematic assessment of children and their families. The Framework embraces three key areas/dimensions: the child's developmental needs; parenting capacity; and the wider family and environmental factors. The aim of the assessment is to identify and clarify the needs of the child in relation to their overall development and safety and the parents' ability to empathically understand and give priority to meeting the child's needs. An important component in addressing parenting capacity in the context of child abuse is to gain the parents' understanding and acceptance of their behaviours/ actions that have resulted in harm to the child. Jones (1997) points out that if parents do not acknowledge that their caring has been seriously compromised, it may not be possible to begin the process of rectification, and the continuation of that particular parent-child relationship is likely to be untenable.

Assessment of the child's/family's race and culture should also be addressed integrally, and consideration given to whether any racial/cultural stereotyping of black or minority ethnic families have led to the intervention, or if there has been a failure to protect black or minority ethnic children from abuse. Cohen (2003, page 2) highlights that issues of race can have a powerful impact on the choices that practitioners make:

> Sometimes race and culture may lead to more intrusive interventions, but at other times, they seem to normalise unacceptable behaviour. The cultural and racial background of families influences the specific factors that workers consider in assessing the severity of risk and level of intervention. Decisions are more likely to be made on the basis of deficits in available resources, accepted agency practice, personal values and biases, and notions of an ideal family than by application of consistent case rules.

It is important, therefore, for practitioners to differentiate between parenting practices that enhance a child's well-being and safety, and those that are potentially harmful, and it is essential that all practitioners involved in child protection investigations develop an understanding and level of proficiency in working with a range of diverse cultures, and develop an understanding of their own cultural identity and attitudes. An understanding of the impact of oppression, prejudice and discrimination and the influences these have on cultural biases and stereotypes is very important to demonstrate culturally responsive practice (Connolly et al., 2006). Practitioners must also be aware that child abuse and neglect exist within all cultures and communities, and if cultural and religious factors are accepted as offering an explanation for abuse, it could increase the risk of greater harm for some children. Practitioners must therefore avoid colluding with abuse and challenge sensitively any behaviour that is being perceived as harmful (Barker and Hodes, 2007).

The Framework for Assessment currently has specific timescales for the completion of assessments following a request/referral to the local authority children's care services. An initial assessment should be undertaken within ten days, and if a decision to initiate section 47 enquiries is made, then a social worker will lead a core assessment to be completed within 35 working days. (See the flow charts in *Working Together to Safeguard Children* (DCSF, 2010, pages 186–190).)

The rest of the chapter gives a brief overview of the procedures and requirements involved at each stage.

1. Referral to social services

Referrals raising concerns about children's welfare are received by local authorities from a variety of sources, for example:

- other professionals (e.g. GPs, health visitors, teachers, etc.) who have a legal duty (section 47 of the Children Act 1989) to report concerns and help the local authority with its enquiries;

- members of the public (e.g. the child/young person themselves, family members, neighbours, etc.). There is no legal obligation for this group to report concerns.

Almost all referrals will require some level of investigation but a relatively small number of these will go on to court proceedings. Sometimes while working with service users in other settings, for example, working with adults or young people in drug and alcohol services, mental health services and youth offending teams, social workers will encounter new information that raises their concern about the welfare of a child. In these situations the worker should discuss these concerns with the service user, and where possible, seek their agreement to make a referral to the children and family team. However, in certain situations caution may be needed when discussing the concerns, and seeking agreement with the service user may result in the child being placed at increased risk of significant harm. The welfare of the child is paramount. Information should therefore be conveyed to the child protection team that the service user has not been informed of the referral (DCSF, 2010). Practitioners should never delay emergency action to protect a child from harm; they should always record in writing concerns about a child's welfare and of the decisions about the child's welfare, including whether or not further action was taken, and if action is to be taken, a record should be made of who will be taking that action (DCSF, 2010).

If a referral constitutes, or may constitute, a criminal offence against a child the police should be informed automatically. This will enable both agencies to consider jointly how to proceed, while maintaining the best interests of the child. Where there are offences against a child, social services and the police will work in partnership during the initial enquiries. It is the responsibility of the police to instigate criminal proceedings but in less serious cases it is usually agreed that the best interests of the child are served by interventions led by social services rather than a full police investigation (DCSF, 2010).

a) **Receiving a referral:** as the social worker on duty responding to incoming referrals, it is important that you check and correctly record concerns about a child with the person making the referral: for example, what is the nature of the concerns?; how have they arisen?; what appear to be the needs of the child and family?; what involvement they are having or have had with the child and/or family members? The referrer should have the opportunity to discuss their concerns with a qualified social worker. When processing the referral you should always identify clearly whether there are concerns about maltreatment and of any associated risk factors (e.g. domestic violence, mental illness, substance/alcohol misuse, learning disability, past criminal activities, etc.) – these will then be considered with respect to informing any urgent actions required to safeguard the child from harm. If the referral is made by another professional by phone then they should follow up their referral in writing using the CAF within 48 hours.

b) **Within the first working day:** clarity about any action to be taken, by whom and all decisions made will be recorded in writing by the relevant team manager. A referral at this stage can lead to no further action, or to the provision of support (see section 17 of the Children Act 1989) and/or to further investigations, with the possibility of seeking to obtain an emergency order to safeguard the child. The current timescales for an

Initial Assessment are a maximum of ten working days following the referral to determine whether:

- the child is in need;

- there is reasonable cause to suspect the child is suffering, or is likely to suffer, significant harm;

- any services are required and of what types;

- whether a further, more detailed core assessment should be undertaken (paragraph 3.9 of the Framework for the Assessment of Children in Need and their Families (DoH, 2000a, see also pages 145–148 of *Working Together*, DCSF, 2010)).

The government statistics for year ending March 2011 indicate that child abuse and neglect accounted for 44 per cent of initial assessments being undertaken (www.education.gov.uk/rsgateway/DB/STR/db001041/index.shtml).

An initial assessment should be led by a qualified and experienced social worker who is supervised by a highly experienced and qualified social work manager. It should be carefully planned in collaboration with all those involved with the family, and with clarity about what information will be shared with the parents and what processes the initial assessment should include, for example:

- seeing and speaking to the child, including alone when appropriate;

- seeing and meeting with parents, the family and wider family members as appropriate;

- involving and obtaining relevant information from professionals and others in contact with the child and family;

- drawing together and analysing available information (focusing on the strengths and positive factors as well as vulnerabilities and risk factors) from a range of sources (including existing agency records).

The above information should then be recorded in writing. The assessment will then be viewed and authorised by the team manager and discussed with the child and family/caregivers, the referrer, and other agencies involved while respecting confidentialities and not jeopardising further action in respect of concerns about harm (which may include police investigations), and confirm in writing any further actions to be taken. The initial assessment is a brief assessment used to determine whether a child is a child in need and if so what services are required to address the need identified. It may be very brief. However, if the initial assessment determines that there are reasonable grounds to suspect a child is suffering or likely to suffer significant harm and that initiation of section 47 enquiries is required (DCSF, 2010), a fuller, core assessment will be undertaken. If during the course of an initial assessment it emerges that a criminal offence may have been committed the process may develop into a joint enquiry with the police. Social workers therefore need to be aware of the need to:

- keep accurate notes of any interview;

- be alert to the potential for medical and forensic evidence.

Section 47 enquiries should be opened immediately where any agency receives information, which already amounts to an allegation or suspicion that a child has suffered or is likely to suffer significant harm. Such a referral must always be discussed between the police and the local authority at the earliest opportunity but in any event before the end of that working day. A decision to undertake section 47 enquiries and a core assessment (DoH, 2000a) will then be made to establish if any short-term emergency actions are required.

c)   **A strategy discussion** with social services, the police, health or other agencies as appropriate will be held following concerns about a child who is perceived to be at risk of significant harm. Any section 17 (child in need) referral that involves the suspicion of a criminal offence will also be the subject of an early strategy discussion between the police and children's social care. The outcome in any strategy discussion/meeting will be a decision as to either take no further action, to proceed with a single agency enquiry, or to proceed with a joint working agency enquiry. If a joint investigation takes place, the strategy meeting will also determine the role the social worker will play in the Achieving Best Evidence interview. Children's social care completes a record of the strategy discussion/meeting and agreed actions, and circulates copies to the police and any other agencies involved in the discussion.

Where there is a risk to the life of a child or a likelihood of serious or immediate harm, an agency with statutory powers should act quickly to secure the immediate safety of the child. The need for emergency action may, however, only become apparent over time as more is learnt, and neglect as well as abuse can result in a child suffering significant harm to the extent that urgent protective action is necessary. It is also important to consider whether action is required to safeguard other children in the same household, or in the household of an alleged perpetrator or elsewhere. Decisions will be agreed between the referrer and the relevant manager in line with *Working Together to Safeguard Children* (DCSF, 2010) and Local Safeguarding Children Board procedures about what the referrer, other agencies and the child's parent/s will be told, by whom and when.

The child protection practitioner and any other professionals already involved with the child will begin to work together at this point, for example, health visitor, midwife, GP, teachers, school nurse, community mental health, drug/alcohol specialists, etc., to establish the core group. Lead responsibility for action to safeguard and promote the child's welfare will lie with local authority children's social care. However, in all cases where the police are involved, the decision about when to inform the parents (about referrals from third parties) will have a bearing on the conduct of police investigations.

As part of the initial section 47 investigations, records held by social services, NSPCC, health, education, police and probation services will be checked to establish if any of the family members/adults involved with the child have had any previous involvement with any of the agencies, and if any criminal convictions or allegations of offences against a child have been recorded.

A child protection medical assessment may also be required to inform decisions by the lead agencies about how best to safeguard the child. In all cases of alleged sexual abuse and serious physical harm, a paediatrician should be invited to attend the strategy meeting. Where this is not possible, their views should be established prior to the strategy meeting and then used to inform the discussion and agreed actions. The medical examiner and assessment must:

- assess the child's general presentation at examination including any injuries;

- establish if any medical treatment is required and action as appropriate;

- establish if the physical evidence supports or negates any explanations given by the child or parent/carer;

- ensure that any forensic evidence that may inform an investigation is recovered and injuries photographed where appropriate (if the age-appropriate child consents);

- provide a verbal opinion and written report/statement in relation to the allegations made and any explanation offered as to the likely cause and to make this available for any subsequent conference or court hearing;

- provide advice regarding any specialist assessment needed.

Those conducting child protection enquiries must always secure consent for the child to be medically examined, treated, photographed and/or interviewed, unless to do so would place a child at further risk of harm. In the majority of cases, this consent will be given by parents/carers. In some instances involving complex cases, where a parent is believed to have harmed a child and there are grounds to suspect that obtaining consent may put that child or other children at risk of harm or seriously undermine an investigation, a joint decision between the police and children's social care must be made as to the most appropriate course of action to be taken regarding the obtaining of consent. Occasionally it will be necessary to gain consent by court order.

Young people aged 16 years and over are able to give their own consent to be medically examined, treated, photographed and/or interviewed. However, it is good practice to involve parents unless to do so would jeopardise the child's welfare or is against their wishes. Account should always be taken of the age and ability of the child to give consent. Some children under 16 years may be assessed by the medical practitioner to be *Fraser* (previously Gillick) Competent to give informed consent (Brammer, 2010). Legal advice should nevertheless be sought if this is against the parent's wishes. Children must not be medically examined against their wishes unless the medical practitioner believes that there is a need for emergency medical treatment. Whenever a child protection medical assessment is sought for a particular child, consideration must also be given as to whether the siblings/other children in the same household should also be medically assessed.

The outcome of any medical assessment is only one part of the child protection enquiry. Medical examinations should not be relied upon to prove or disprove that a child has suffered significant harm. The outcome of a medical examination and the information obtained within the core assessment and subsequent police investigation should provide a holistic picture of the child and family. Best practice is when all the information gathered is taken into account and analysed to inform the level of need and risk.

Medical assessments within child protection enquiries, however, can be pivotal in assisting children's social care services or the police to make informed decisions on whether it is both appropriate and legally possible to take immediate steps to protect a child and/or their siblings.

Thresholds for medical assessments are based on the following:

- Where non-accidental injury or neglect concerns exist. Even where the injury appears minor, medical assessment is required to ensure that there are no concealed injuries found on the child.

- Where allegations concerning sexual abuse of a child have been made. In cases of suspected sexual abuse, the child should be 'Achieving Best Evidence (ABE) Interviews with Children' video interviewed prior to any medical assessment, unless there are concerns regarding physical injury that may require emergency treatment. The purpose of interviewing the child prior to medical assessment is to establish the exact nature of the alleged abuse. A joint judgement to decide the necessity and nature of any medical assessment needs to be made based on the outcomes of the enquiries conducted in the investigation and the ABE interview with the child.

If emergency protection orders are authorised, the local authority Looked-After Children and Substitute Care social work teams (see Chapter 6) will be notified of the possible emergency accommodation of the child(ren), and appropriate placement with wider family members will also be pursued. Placements will need to take account of the child(ren)'s ethnicity and cultural background.

CASE STUDY

A referral is made to social services by the school nurse involved with Kylie Cole. Kylie is 12 years old, she is of African Caribbean/White heritage, and has learning disabilities. The nurse states that she has had growing concerns about Kylie over the past few weeks. She is not mixing well with other children, and her teachers have commented that her behaviour in class over the past couple of months has become more disruptive and difficult to manage. Kylie went to the nurse this morning complaining of stomach pains. When the nurse examined Kylie, she was concerned about how thin and emaciated she appeared. She was dirty and smelly, her skin was very dry, cracked and sore, she had severe and extensive new and old bruising and bite marks to her chest, inner thighs and buttocks. Upon weighing her, the nurse notes that Kylie has lost two stone in weight since starting at the school nine months ago. The nurse adds that Kylie appeared frightened and would not comment on how the bruising might have happened.

The nurse has not informed Kylie's mother, Donna Green, of the referral. Kylie's father, Alan Cole (who no longer lives with Kylie and her mother), usually collects Kylie from school, but is currently on holiday abroad and not expected back until next week. Kylie lives with her mother, her mother's partner Ahmed Khan who is Asian, and their children Tariq aged three, and Nadia aged one who both have African Caribbean and Asian dual heritage. The nurse also reports that the school have tried to discuss their concerns in the past many times, and again last week about Kylie's behaviour – with her father in person, and her mother by letter – but were met with little or no response/concern.

ACTIVITY **4.3**

From the information in the case study and your reading so far, consider the following questions.

- *What do you think the categories of abuse may be?*

- *How would you categorise the concerns in relation to the criteria for initiating a section 47 enquiry?*

- *What do you think has been happening to Kylie?*

- *How does this information make you feel? How do you think you would respond to Kylie's mother, her mother's partner, and her father?*

COMMENT

From the information available at this time, the social worker will need to be aware of the agency procedures, the legal duties and requirements, and therefore be aware that there is a statutory duty to investigate as from the information available at the time of referral, Kylie is presenting with the appearance of being emaciated and with extensive bruising and bite marks, it would appear that Kylie is possibly suffering from neglect and possibly also emotional, physical and/or sexual abuse.

The history of the school's and nurse's concerns would indicate that these issues have been long-standing, and therefore there is reasonable cause to suspect that she is suffering, or likely to be suffering significant harm (Children Act 1989, section 47(1) (b)). The nature of the referral and its context will require the social worker and team manager to make a cautious response – they will need more information before deciding whether a full investigation is warranted. The team manager will ultimately decide the current status of Kylie's case and this will involve communications with the police, a medical examiner, education and health professionals.

How did you think you would feel? Were you surprised by any of the feelings that the case study raised for you?

Working with children in situations like this raises emotive feelings and reactions. You will need to know what kinds of situations you find most difficult and which you find easier to deal with. Understanding feelings that may arouse a desire to 'rescue' children and what kinds of parental actions make you feel punitive is crucial in child protection work. You need to be aware of how your feelings and reactions could influence your judgement of the situation and the needs of others. Feelings of anger may motivate social workers involved in child protection to work hard for the child, but anger can also cloud their judgement and increase the likelihood of mistakes being made. Sometimes the reactions to abuse can result in some professionals being intimidating, cold and rejecting towards parents and other professionals. Being respectful of parents is not, however, incompatible with making the child's needs paramount and failing to recognise and respect the importance of parents and family for a child would be to ignore one of the child's most basic needs. Even abusive and neglectful parents love their child and see themselves as the protector of the child. It is also important to remember that in the majority of cases, children will not be removed from their families. Social workers will therefore need to build an alliance with the child's parents and family to promote and maintain the safety and welfare of the child.

Social workers may also try to avoid painful or frightening responses. Witnessing the distress of a seriously abused child may be very difficult to bear and can result in avoiding interventions that need to be made; this can also be very dangerous in child protection work. Fear is another major feature of child protection work, for example, fear of making a mistake, of being blamed, of anger and hostility of others, and fear for your own safety when dealing with violent, threatening individuals. A result of the responses highlighted can end up with professionals being as preoccupied with protecting themselves as with protecting the child. Being aware of your own needs and addressing them openly and honestly in supervision is essential if you are to offer the best service to a child and their families (Beckett, 2007).

As soon as the assessment process begins, practitioners start hypothesising about what they know and observe in order to try to understand the child and family's situation – some of these hypotheses will be confirmed, others aborted or replaced with new ones as more information is gathered and analysed. What is important, however, is that practitioners keep an open mind and do not ignore information that doesn't fit with their original hypothesis (Munro, 2002). All of the tasks involving social work interventions involve decision-making, for example: at the referral stage; when undertaking assessments; what and when to enquire/question; planning; when signposting/allocating support/resources, and reviewing etc., all of which can involve very complex issues, be problematic and require a careful balancing act. However, many decisions social workers make will be informed by and/or involve joint collaboration and consultation with other professionals. In some situations it will involve making decisions when there is uncertainty about what is happening and when there are no clear-cut answers to questions/concerns. Subsequently, it is not always possible to ascertain which options will be effective in achieving identifiable outcomes, and achieving good/safe outcomes can never be guaranteed (O'Sullivan, 2011). However, social workers need to be mindful of a reluctance to make decisions, both in avoiding decisions altogether, or in having a tendency to procrastinate so that decisions are made in reaction to crisis rather than as part of a long-term plan (Munro, 2002).

2. The core assessment

The core assessment provides a systematic basis for collecting and analysing information to support professional judgements about how to help children and families in the best interests of the child. A risk assessment in relation to the child's developmental needs, the capacity of the parents to respond appropriately to those needs – including the capacity to keep the child safe from harm, and the impact the wider family and environmental factors have on the parents and the child, are incorporated and analysed. Government statistics for the year ending 31 March 2011 indicate that 185,400 core assessments were completed with 111,700 subject to section 47 enquiries and of these, 53,000 were subject to initial child protection conferences with 42,700 children being made subject to child protection plans. Neglect accounted for 42.5 per cent; emotional abuse for 27.3 per cent; physical abuse for

13 per cent, multiple abuse for 11.7 per cent and sexual abuse for 5.4 per cent. Of those 42,700 children, 6,500 were made subject to a child protection plan for a second or subsequent time. For the child protection plans that came to an end in that year, 2,700 had lasted for two years or more (www.education.gov.uk/rsgateway/DB/STR/db001041/index.shtml).

ACTIVITY 4.4

Make a list of what you consider to be the developmental needs of children in relation to the following age groups:

- *0–2yrs   3–4 yrs   5–9yrs   0–14yrs.*

Check your list as you read through the dimensions of the child's developmental needs. (You will refer back to this list in the next activity.)

Dimensions of the child's developmental needs

Child development theories are essential underpinning knowledge for social work practice within children's services, but in the area of child protection, they are crucial. Understanding developmental milestones will provide generalised guidelines for undertaking assessments (refer to Chapters 2, 3, 4 and 5 in Crawford and Walker (2010) *Social Work and Human Development*, and Horwath (2010) *The Child's World* for guidance). The comprehensive checklists developed by Mary Sheridan in the *Framework for Assessment* guidance (DoH, 2000b) will also provide a helpful tool for practitioners.

The *Framework for Assessment* (DoH, 2000b) identifies five dimensions of undertaking direct work with the child during assessments in order to obtain knowledge and an understanding of the child:

- seeing the child;
- observing them;
- engaging with them;
- talking with them;
- doing activities with them.

(Bell and Wilson, 2003)

Spending time with the child(ren) is crucial as evidenced in Munro's final report (2011), where she argued that the child protection system had lost its focus on the one thing that matters most – the views and experiences of the children themselves. The *Working Together to Safeguard Children* (DCSF, 2010) guidelines for all professionals also require that children are seen by social workers on their own.

Working together, the allocated social worker with health and education professionals involved with the child (for example, health visitor, GP, school nurse, paediatrician, designated teacher, child protection, educational psychologist) would undertake an assessment of the following areas.

The child's health

This would include their growth and development, as well as their physical and mental health well-being; the impact of disability and any genetic factors; if the child has received appropriate health care if needed in the past, an adequate and nutritious diet, immunisations, optical and dental care; whether the child or a family member may be likely to suffer sickle cell disorder; and whether past life experiences or trauma have had any detrimental effects on the physical health of the child. The extent to which the family have direct access to appropriate services and advice in relation to health care should also be considered. If the child is disabled or has an impairment, consideration of whether this has a direct effect on the child's growth, development and physical or mental well-being is required. It is also important to ascertain if there are any disabling barriers that limit the child or hinder their development (Horwath, 2010 ; DCSF, 2010). Assessments of children with a disability should also include the question: Would I consider that option if the child were not disabled? Clear reasons are necessary if the answer is no (Middleton, 1996).

The child's education

This would cover all areas of the child's cognitive development, which begins from birth – focusing upon the opportunities provided for the child to play and interact with other children; have access to books and stimulating toys, etc. However, children's learning can also be encouraged in a range of different ways and the provision of toys is not a guarantee of a stimulating environment. Assessments of educational and cognitive development should also take account of racism, and address whether the child has the opportunity to realise their potential – without the limitations of negative stereotyping.

The child's emotional and behavioural development

This would address the appropriateness of responses demonstrated in feelings and actions by the child, initially to parents and, as the child is growing older, to others beyond the family. Assessments would address if the child is loved and/or valued for who they are; if they are listened to, and if their personal care is being undertaken respectfully. You will need to consider if there any concerns in relation to the child's emotional development. For example, is the child being treated in ways that are appropriate for their age and development, and what messages is the child receiving about their disability? If a child is seen to be unable to give or withhold their consent and is resisting any treatment/interventions, this will need to be acknowledged and addressed. It is important to assess if the child is supported in taking reasonable risks in every situation; if the acquisition of a positive racial identity has been considered, and whether the cultural and linguistic backgrounds of the child and family have been fully taken into account. An observation and understanding of the pattern of attachment for this family in particular is essential – this may include attachment figures who are not necessarily birth relatives. The impact that migration, separation and trauma may have on the child and family as well as the nature and quality of the child's early attachments should also be acknowledged. The child's temperament, resilience and vulnerability factors, adaptation to change, and their response to stress and appropriate degree of self-control should also be assessed.

The child's identity

This would focus upon the child's growing sense of self as a separate and valued person. An assessment is required of the extent to which the child has the opportunity to learn/ maintain their family language(s) and whether any action is needed to support the child's identity development with regard to family and community life. This will include the child's view of themselves and their capabilities, self-esteem and self-image. Issues about their ethnicity, culture, religious beliefs, gender, sexuality and disability may all contribute to this. It is very important to ascertain if the child has feelings of belonging and of being accepted by their family, peer group and the wider society.

The child's family and social relationships

This would focus upon the child's development of empathy, and the capacity to place themselves in someone else's shoes. This would ascertain if the child's relationships with their parents or care providers, siblings and friends were stable and affectionate for the child. Who are the important people in the child's life? What supports are available to help the family with their disabled child? Are any of the key adults aware of the increased vulnerability of disabled children to being abused? Are any family members/adults discriminating against the child due to their parentage? These are all important questions within this context.

The child's social presentation

This would focus upon the child's growing understanding of the way in which appearance, behaviour and any impairment are perceived by the outside world and the impression being created. This would include the child's appropriateness of dress for age, weather conditions, gender, culture and religion, cleanliness and hygiene and the availability of advice from parents or caregivers about presentation in different settings.

The child's self-care skills

This would focus upon the child's practical, emotional and communication competencies that are required for increasing their independence. This would include their early skills in dressing and feeding themselves, participating in activities away from the family environment as older children and using problem-solving approaches.

Note that when undertaking core assessments within the above domains, it is important to recognise that the intention of the assessment is not just to enquire into a particular or single event or incident, but to reach as deep as possible an understanding of the child's world (Horwath, 2010). Practitioners may be overwhelmed by the amount of information gathered, as well as the accuracy, detail, value and significance of it. A study by Cleaver and Walker (2004) found social workers expressed anxiety about analysing all of the information collated as part of the assessment.

Prevalence of parental disorders in the UK (Cleaver et al., 2007)

- 30 per cent of adults with a mental illness/disorder have dependent children;

- 7 per cent of adults with a learning disability are parents;

- 200,000 to 300,000 children living in England and Wales have a parent who misuses drugs – only one-third of fathers and two-thirds of mothers still live with their children;

- 1.3 million children in England are affected by parental alcohol problems;

- 200,000 children in England live in households where there is a risk of domestic violence.

But there are also high levels of complex cases involving more than one parental disorder, for example:

- 25 to 40 per cent of adults with a learning disability have mental health problems;

- 86 per cent of adults attending alcohol services and 75 per cent attending drug services have mental health problems;

- 48 per cent of women exposed to domestic violence experience depression and 64 per cent experience post-traumatic stress disorder.

A combination of parental issues leads to a *toxic combination for children*, as highlighted in a Review of Serious Case Reviews, which found that nearly 75 per cent of children lived in families where two or more of these issues were present (Brandon et al., 2010).

A brief review of the impact that parental mental illness, learning disability, substance misuse and domestic violence have on children's development

Infants aged 0–2 years

They may be damaged before birth (for example, foetal alcohol syndrome, and substance dependency). Infants may be harmed if their parent's concentration is impaired because of drug or alcohol misuse or mental illness (for example, depression), as the needs of the child for nourishment, nappy changes etc. are not met, they may be dressed inappropriately and their personal hygiene grossly neglected, or be in an unsafe environment (for example, with used hypodermic needles, or in situations of domestic violence). An infant's cognitive development may be delayed through inconsistent, neglectful or under-stimulating behaviour and by parents with a learning disability. Babies may also be suffering with withdrawal symptoms from foetal addiction and be difficult to manage. A lack of commitment and increased unhappiness, tension and irritability in drug/alcohol using parents may result in inappropriate responses, which can lead to faulty attachments. Depressed mothers may also be more irritable, tense, unhappy and disorganised and therefore interact with the infant less, or convey anger which may result in insecurely attached children. Some mothers experiencing violence from the child's father may also emotionally distance themselves from their children. The child's cues may be also be missed, for example their cries for warmth or comfort, and they may be met with anger and criticism.

Children aged 3–4 years

They may be physically at risk from drugs and needles when they are left at home alone while their parents go out to buy alcohol/drugs, or left with unsuitable carers. Children may not be fed or provided with sufficient clothing due to lack of money, as priority is focused upon buying drugs/alcohol. Children are at increased risk from parental mental illness if they are subjected to hostile and aggressive behaviour, neglected and/or experience rejection. Children's cognitive development may be delayed through parents' disorganisation, limited parental interaction and engagement, and failing to attend pre-school facilities. Attachments may be damaged due to inconsistent parenting and children may learn inappropriate behavioural responses from witnessing domestic violence and display emotional symptoms similar to those of post-traumatic stress disorder. The impact of adverse parenting for this age group is more damaging – as the children may blame themselves for their parent's problems and being neglected. Children can also be affected if they have been the subject of their parent's delusions or hallucinations. They may also attempt to correct their parent's behaviour and try to put it right, believing themselves to be responsible, for example trying to protect their mother from domestic violence and sustaining injuries. Children may be left for periods of time with inappropriate adults and exposed to abuse. In peer settings children may have learnt to resolve conflict through violence and have problems establishing friendships with other children as a result. Children may be reluctant to form other attachments and relationships through believing they are in constant danger and by being unnaturally fearful and vigilant. Basic hygiene may be neglected and children may be left in a filthy condition; they may take on responsibilities beyond their years and abilities because of parental incapacity and be increasingly at risk as a result.

Children aged 5–9 years

They may have an increased risk of physical injuries and medical problems. Many children develop psychosomatic problems relating to anxiety, for example, headaches, stomach pain and discomfort, difficulty sleeping, and bedwetting, and show symptoms of extreme anxiety and fear as a result of domestic violence. Academic attainment is usually poor due to lack of concentration and the child's behaviour in school is often problematic, with low attendance etc. Children may be suffering with depression and poor self-esteem, blame themselves for their parents' problems, and may show their distress by uncontrolled behaviour, emotional distress and fear. Children also have a higher rate of conduct disorder if their parents are suffering from depression. Children witnessing domestic violence have also shown problems in controlling their temper, emotions and behaviour. For some children, being the same gender as a parent who has problems appears to be more traumatising and psychologically distressing, resulting in a negative self-image and low self-esteem. They may have already developed anxiety and faulty attachments and therefore fear hostility and unplanned separations. Children may also feel embarrassed and ashamed of their parent's behaviour and curtail friendships and social interaction with their peer group. Children may experience shame and embarrassment if their clothing is inappropriate. They may be expected to take on too much responsibility for themselves or their younger siblings, or a caring role for their parent(s).

Young people aged 10–14 years

They risk having to cope with puberty without support; are at increased risk of psychologi-cal problems, neglect and physical abuse; and when living with parents with depression, young people can develop suicidal behaviour and depression. They may suffer increased anxiety due to their fear of being hurt when there is domestic violence or of being injured while trying to protect one parent from the other. Education is hampered by the young person's inability to concentrate and by missing school because of caring for siblings and/or parent(s). They may be at increased risk of emotional disturbance and conduct disor-ders, including bullying and school exclusion. There is an increased risk of sexual abuse in adolescent boys, while being in denial of their own needs and feelings. They may have a poor self-image and low self-esteem and blame themselves for their parent's prob-lems and actions. The problems of being a young carer may also feel stigmatising and they may not receive any respect or praise for their efforts from their parent(s) or others. Relationships with parents are usually poor and they may fear exposing their family life to peers – and so restrict friendships. Many young people may resort to wandering the streets to avoid parental violence, go missing and sleep rough, and are more likely to become involved in crime and avoid school. Stigma may be acutely felt at this age because young people are self-conscious about their appearance and sensitive to how others per-ceive them. If they have learnt that violence is an accepted way of dealing with problems, they may use violent or aggressive means towards their peers and other adults, resulting in them becoming rejected and feeling alienated. They may be forced to assume too much responsibility for themselves and other family members, which may result in them failing to look after themselves and their own development needs.

Teenagers aged 15 years and over

They are at greater risk of accidents; may have problems related to sexual relationships; may fail to achieve their potential due to lack of parental encouragement and poor concentration; are at increased risk of school exclusion; have poor life chances due to exclusion and poor school attainment; have low self-esteem as a consequence of incon-sistent parenting; experience increased isolation from both friends and adults outside the family; may use aggression inappropriately to solve problems; develop emotional problems that may lead to suicidal behaviour; have increased vulnerability to becoming involved in crime; sacrifice their own needs to meet those of their parents and siblings; are more likely to become teenage parents, and more likely to be involved in early drinking, smoking and drug use (Cleaver et al., 2007).

Children and young people affected by domestic violence, parental substance misuse and mental health problems may find disclosure difficult or may go to great lengths to hide it.

It is also important not to generalise or make assumptions about the parenting capacity of parents with learning disabilities, mental health problems or alcohol/substance misuse issues. It is more likely to be a combination of these additional stressors that result in high risk contexts. (See Chapter 9, 'Lessons from research' in *Working Together to Safeguard Children* (DCSF, 2010) for a fuller discussion.)

ACTIVITY **4.5**

Make a list of what you consider to be the skills and qualities of a 'good' parent/caregiver.

Now try and match these lists up with your list of children's needs at their various stages of development (see Activity 4.4).

Check your new list with your reading of the section below regarding the dimensions of parenting capacity.

Dimensions of parenting capacity

For the assessment of parenting capacity good observation and analytical skills are crucial in order to gather the information required. A comparison can then be made in relation to the standards of good enough parenting.

Basic care

This involves assessing the parent's capacity to access and provide for the child's physical needs, their need for appropriate dental and medical care, including the provision of food, drink, warmth, shelter, clean and appropriate clothing and adequate personal hygiene.

Ensuring safety

This involves assessing the parent's capacity to ensure that the child is adequately protected from harm or danger; including their capacity to protect the child from significant harm or danger; preventing the child having contact with unsafe adults or other children and from self-harm. Parents should be able to demonstrate a recognition of the hazards and dangers both in the home and other places where the child spends time.

Emotional warmth

This involves assessing the parent's capacity to ensure that the child's emotional needs are met and give the child a sense of them being specially valued and a positive sense of their own racial and cultural identity. This will include the parent's capacity to ensure the child's requirements for secure, stable and affectionate relationships with significant adults are promoted with appropriate sensitivity and responsiveness to the child's needs, and that parents provide appropriate physical contact, comfort and cuddling sufficient to demonstrate warm regard, praise and encouragement.

Stimulation

This involves assessing the parent's capacity to promote a child's learning and intellectual development through encouragement and cognitive stimulation, by promoting social opportunities. This will include the parents or caregivers facilitating the child's cognitive development and potential through interaction, communication, talking and responding to the child's language and questions, encouraging and joining in the child's play and promoting educational opportunities. Parents should be enabling the child to experience success and ensuring school attendance or equivalent opportunities, while also facilitating the child to meet the challenges of life.

Guidance and boundaries

This involves assessing the parent's capacity to enable the child to regulate his or her own emotions and behaviour. The key parental tasks are demonstrating and modelling behaviour; control of emotions and interactions with others; guidance that involves setting boundaries, so that the child is able to develop an internal model of moral norms and conscience, and social behaviour appropriate for the society within which s/he will grow up. The aim for the parent is to enable the child to grow into an autonomous adult, holding their own values and able to demonstrate appropriate behaviour with others, rather than having to be dependent on rules outside themselves. This involves parents not being over-protective and enabling the child to explore and learn from their own experiences, thereby developing social problem-solving, anger management, consideration for others and effective self-discipline.

Stability

This involves assessing the parent's capacity to provide a sufficiently stable family environment to enable the child to develop and maintain a secure attachment to them in order to ensure the child's optimal development. This will include the parent's capacity to ensure secure attachments are not disrupted, provide consistency of emotional warmth over time and respond in a similar manner to the same behaviour of the child. It is also important that parents' and caregivers' responses change and develop according to the child's developmental progress, and in addition, that they ensure children keep contact with important family members and significant others.

Daniel et al. (2010) also provide brief summaries of some of the basic parenting tasks required for children of different age groups and a guide to the assessment of parenting responses to children's needs at different stages.

When working with families it is important to 'think fathers' as well, including when the father is himself a young person. A child's father can have a significant, positive impact on the child's outcomes but only where he is causing no harm to the child – for example, research shows that children with highly involved fathers do better at school and are more empathic in the way that they behave. More and more fathers want to be involved within their family and in their children's upbringing, even if they are no longer living with the children and their mother. However, many fathers find this difficult and feel they are not recognised or encouraged to get involved, by schools or health services. For example, children's services as a whole can still be very mother-focused and fathers can, often inadvertently, be made to feel unwelcome or uncomfortable when they try to use them. *The Dad Test* (2009) available at www.education.gov.uk/publications/standard/publicationDetail/Page1/DCSF-00287-2010) sets out practical steps organisations can take to remove these barriers to fathers' participation.

In addition, Family Intervention Projects (FIPs) funded through the local authority 'Think Family' grant may also be appropriate when undertaking parenting assessments/intervention where the needs of a family are complex and require a high level of face-to-face contact and family-focused interventions. Where a FIP team is involved with a family they should continue to be involved, as appropriate, in any assessments, section 47 enquiries and subsequent work led by children's social care.

Summary of parenting/caregiving and child development

Children's needs can be met by several people, but there are aspects of parenting that are more helpful than others in enabling a child to reach their developmental milestones and potential. Daniel et al. (2010) and Cleaver et al. (2007) present some basic positive parenting tasks and protective factors for children in different age groups that can assist social workers in their interventions with parent/s to promote/improve their parenting capacity:

- **Babies and children under five years:** developing a secure attachment between the parent and the child is of central importance. Infants need parent(s) who can offer: overt control; attentiveness; warmth; stimulation; responsiveness; and non-restrictive care. Babies and children under five years need the presence of a caring adult who: has sufficient income and good standards within the home; has access to wider family support and good community facilities; maintains the child's attendance at clinics for immunisations and developmental reviews; will actively engage in regular, long-term support from primary health care services, children's social care and community-based resources; will ensure that the child attends nursery and pre-school provision; will acknowledge their problems and accept treatment programmes, and who will access a safe residence if subjected to domestic violence.

- **During middle childhood:** children's lives should expand emotionally, intellectually and socially with good peer friendships, as play and companionship can offer children respite from family concerns, therefore the parent will need considerable flexibility and responsiveness. The child needs: nurturing to acquire coping strategies so that they know what to do when a parent's behaviour deteriorates; encouragement of internalised control; increased use of induction and reasoning; encouragement with schooling to maintain regular attendance, consistent discipline and expression of warmth and receipt of regular medical checks. Additional protective factors will also include supportive older siblings and/or relatives/appropriate adults; effective bullying policies within schools; access to young carers' projects and belonging to organised, out-of-school activities.

- **During adolescence:** adolescents require from their parent: empathy; parents who can see things from their point of view and offer constructive discipline not criticism and constraint; good communication; and an active and warm involvement. Additional protective factors for adolescents include having: a close and trusted friend who can provide a source of support; practical and domestic help; sympathetic, empathic and vigilant teachers; regular attendance at school, further education or work-based training; the support of a trusted adult who acts as a champion for the young person; factual information about sexual practices and contraception; and knowing who to contact in the event of a crisis regarding their parent(s).

Appropriate non-stigmatising support from all involved practitioners has the potential to overcome some of the stresses of parenting and reduce the likelihood of abuse and neglect. Social workers need to assess and support the parents' ability to make use of the support that is available. Interventions need to focus upon shifting the parents' perceptions of their own ability to change, assessing what is blocking their ability to use support and what therapeutic help is needed to overcome the block, for example, using a motivational interviewing/solution-focused approach, while helping the parent to step back and reflect on the quality of their relationship with the child. The main message that is helpful for both practitioners and parents is the importance of the combination of warmth and no criticism, with appropriate discipline and expectations (Daniel et al., 2010). Rutter argues that it is possible for children to achieve relatively good outcomes despite living with major developmental risks (Rutter, 2000, cited in Brandon and Thoburn, 2008). To discern what might make a difference, Sroufe et al.'s (2005, cited in Brandon and Thoburn, 2008) longitudinal study of 180 children born into poverty over three decades identified factors that protected maltreated children from repeating cycles of abuse as parents. These were emotional support from an alternative, non-abusive adult.

To promote children's and young people's understanding and involvement during all practitioner interventions, it is crucial to ensure that children and young people are: provided with information about their parent's disorders/difficulties; supported to understand records and reports produced about themselves and their situation; provided with opportunities to discuss their concerns and worries with adults whom they trust; given sufficient time to build a relationship and that the practitioner listens to and respects the child/young person; offered real choices when possible, and that the practitioner will always keep the child/young person 'in view' (as under-recognition of the child's/young person's difficulties occurs when practitioners over-identify with parents or become desensitised to the child's maltreatment) (Cleaver et al., 2007).

Working with parents

All practitioners need to work in partnership with parents, and this involves a high level of interpersonal skills and a high degree of active participation from everyone involved. Practitioners will need to be able to ask difficult questions, for example, asking a parent outright if they have punched/kicked their child. Practitioners will need to: be cautious (check out parental responses and accounts with others etc. as they may be given false accounts/lies by the parent); authoritative, and avoid colluding with the parent; be clear about their role and clarify this in relation to the purpose of the assessment; listen, involve and consult with parents, and when possible, offer choices regarding the services on offer; reassure parents that identifying a need for support is a way of avoiding rather than precipitating child protection measures; gain a shared understanding of the family problems; and challenge parents who are actively or passively unco-operative (Cleaver et al., 2007). This can be very frightening and result in practitioners avoiding questions that could provoke a violent response from the parent. All practitioners working with the child's family must ensure that they have due regard for their personal safety when working with parents whose violent behaviour raises child protection concerns. Team working and involving police officers in these situations can often be appropriate.

The implications for collaborative working should be focused upon ensuring: the early identification, assessment and monitoring of children to ensure that they are not left in dangerous and abusive situations; the involvement of specialists to ensure parenting capacity is accurately assessed; that plans are well-targeted and realistic; that procedures between children's and adult's services (e.g. mental health, learning disability, drug and alcohol, probation and domestic violence units) are robust to ensure wider collaboration during assessments, service provision and reviews, and to provide long-term support/funding to children living in families with complex needs (Cleaver et al., 2007).

Dimensions of the family and environmental factors

Any assessment needs to consider the wider context of the child including:

a) **Family history and functioning:** this includes a chronology of events based on information and from documents; a genogram; genetic and psychosocial factors; details of significant events and relationships; concerns about childcare and other problems that have come to the attention of other professionals, and interventions attempted in the past and whether they were beneficial. An assessment is made of: how the family is functioning and influenced by the people living in the household; how these people relate to the child; if there have been any significant changes in the family/household composition; the parent's childhood experiences; a chronology of the significant life events and their meanings to family members; the nature of family functioning, including sibling relationships and their impact on the child; parental strengths and difficulties, including those of an absent parent; and the relationship between separated parents. Munro (2008) highlighted that practitioners often get caught up in the here and now and fail to give sufficient attention to information from the past, leading to failures in considering the chronology and pattern of previous events. She asserts that *the best guide to future behaviour is past behaviour. The family's way of behaving to date is the strongest evidence of how they are likely to behave in the future* (Munro, 2008, page 77).

b) **Wider family:** it is important to ascertain who the child considers to be their family members. This may include related and non-related people. It is also important to ascertain what their role and importance to the child is.

c) **Housing:** an assessment will include the following: does the accommodation have the basic facilities and amenities appropriate to the age and development of the child and other people living there? Is the housing accessible and suitable to the needs of disabled family members? Do the basic amenities include water, heating, sanitation, cooking facilities, sleeping arrangements and cleanliness, hygiene and safety, including the impact on the child's upbringing?

d) **Employment:** who is working in the household, what patterns of work and any changes would be noted in relation to the impact this may have on the child, as would the family member(s)' views of work or the absence of work and how this affects relationships within the family.

e) **Income:** an assessment would include whether there was sufficient income to meet the family's needs; if there are any financial difficulties which could affect the child; if the family were in receipt of all available benefits and if the income is regular and sustained.

f) **Family's social integration:** an assessment would cover an exploration of the family's wider context in relation to their local neighbourhood and community and the impact that this may have on the child and parents/caregivers; the degree of the family's integration or isolation; their peer groups, friendship and social networks and the importance attached to them.

g) **Community resources:** an assessment would identify all facilities and services in the neighbourhood, including primary healthcare provisions, day care facilities and schools, places of worship, transport, shops and leisure activities, including the availability, accessibility and the standard of, or lack of, resources and the impact these may have on the family, including disabled family members.

Summary of research findings

As you can see from the core assessment dimensions and research studies presented, professionals working with children in the child protection arena need to practise with full commitment to anti-oppressive practice by being aware of the impact of their own values in order to assess the child's needs holistically and by considering the impact that racism, parental mental ill-health, learning disability, gender, class, sexuality, disability, social exclusion and poverty have upon a parent's capacity to meet the child's needs.

The provision of appropriate services should not wait until the end of the assessment process but should be determined according to what is required, and when, to promote the welfare and safety of the child.

The assessment process

As the investigation/assessment proceeds and information is gathered from all required sources as discussed, it is then assessed, analysed, measured and evaluated in relation to risk. All three dimensions of the core assessment are of equal focus and importance, as an over-emphasis on any one may jeopardise the child's welfare. If significant harm is viewed as likely, that information is carried forward to the next stage of the process. If it is decided that there are no risks of significant harm, the child may then be referred as a 'child in need', to identify and implement any services that may still be required by the child and their family.

Specialist assessments involving a range of professionals (for example, adult psychiatrists, community psychiatric nurses, community mental health social workers and drug agency workers) may be needed in a range of situations when there are serious concerns about a child's development being impaired through the impact of parental mental illness, drug or alcohol misuse, domestic violence or learning disability. The family's supportive/protective networks need to be identified, promoted and maintained. In some cases parents find it difficult explaining their inability to cope to their partner or other family members. This could be an important contributory factor in explaining severe and unexpected injuries to the child (Horwath, 2010).

Throughout the assessment the professionals involved and the family should be working in partnership in trying to understand and address why the present concerns have arisen, or why they may arise again in the future. Professionals also need to be constantly mindful of the stages involved in child development and avoid delays in assessment and interventions, as outcomes have the potential to affect the future. For example, lack of cognitive development in infancy due to neglect and lack of stimulation may result in poor academic performances in later childhood and successful outcomes to early interventions are likely to have a positive impact on a child and vice versa as an adult (Widom, 1991, cited in Horwath, 2010). The assessment process also provides an opportunity for the family to reflect with the help of the worker, enabling them to develop and understand the explanations for concerns, and to develop improved coping strategies for possible solutions.

Messages for social workers undertaking a core assessment/section 47 enquiry

- Assessment time needs to be carefully planned.

- Adequate time needs to be allocated to complete the work, with targets set for completion.

- Clear and adequate recording is an essential component of a good assessment.

- Assessment reports require a recognisable structure, should demonstrate the decision-making process which led to a specific plan and always be shared with the relevant parties.

- Involve staff with specialist skills, including direct work with children.

- The views of the children, families and carers should be clearly identified in all reports.

Plans that follow an assessment of need should have clear objectives, timescales, details about the purpose of intervention, and the services to be provided, when and by whom (Seden et al., 2001).

The impact of section 47 enquiries on the family and child

Section 47 enquiries should always be carried out in such a way as to minimise distress to the child and to ensure that families are treated sensitively and with respect. Local authority children's social care should explain the purpose and outcome of section 47 enquiries to the parents and to the child (having regard to their age and understanding), and be prepared to answer questions openly, unless to do so would affect the safety and welfare of the child. It is particularly helpful for families if local authority children's social care provides written information about the purpose, process and potential outcomes of section 47 enquiries.

In the great majority of cases, children remain with their families following section 47 enquiries, even where concerns about abuse or neglect are substantiated. As far as possible therefore, section 47 enquiries should be conducted in a way that allows for future constructive working relationships with families. When handled well and sensitively there can be a positive effect on the eventual outcome for the child.

Local authority children's social care should decide how to proceed following section 47 enquiries, after discussion between all those who have conducted, or been significantly involved in, those enquiries, including relevant professionals and agencies (as well as foster carers where involved) and the child and parents themselves. The local authority children's social care record for the child should set out clearly the dates on which the child was seen by the lead social worker during the course of the enquiries, if they were seen alone, and if not, who was present and for what reasons. Parents and children of sufficient age and appropriate level of understanding (together with professionals and agencies who have been significantly involved) should receive a copy of this record, in particular in advance of any initial child protection conference that is convened. This information should be conveyed in an appropriate format for younger children and those people whose preferred language is not English.

Consideration should be given to whether the core assessment has been completed or what further work is required before it is completed. It may be valuable, following an evaluation of the outcome of enquiries, to make recommendations for action in an interdisciplinary forum if the case is not going forward to a child protection conference. Section 47 enquiries may not substantiate the original concerns that the child was suffering, or was likely to suffer, significant harm but it is important that the core assessment is completed. The provision of services to these children and their family members should not be dependent on the presence of abuse and neglect. Help and support to children in need and their families may prevent problems escalating to a point where a child is abused or neglected.

In some cases, there may remain concerns about the child's safety and welfare despite there being no real evidence. It may be appropriate to put in place arrangements to monitor the child's welfare. There may be substantiated concerns that a child has suffered significant harm but it is agreed between the agencies most involved and the child and family, that a plan for ensuring the child's future safety and welfare can be developed and implemented without having a child protection conference or a child protection plan. Such an approach will be of particular relevance where it is clear to the agencies involved that the child is not continuing to suffer, or is likely to suffer, significant harm. This may be because, for example, the caregiver has taken responsibility for the harm they caused the child, the family's circumstances have changed or the person responsible for the harm is no longer in contact with the child. It may be because significant harm was incurred as the result of an isolated abusive incident (for example, abuse by a stranger). This judgement can only be made in the light of all relevant information obtained during a section 47 enquiry, and a soundly based assessment of the likelihood of successful intervention, based on clear evidence and mindful of the dangers of misplaced professional optimism. Local authority children's social care has a duty to ascertain the child's wishes and feelings and take these into account (having regard to the child's age and understanding) when deciding on the provision of services.

When the agencies most involved judge that a child may continue to, or be likely to, suffer significant harm, local authority children's social care should convene a child protection conference. The initial child protection conference brings together family members, the child who is the subject of the conference (where appropriate) and those professionals most involved with the child and family, following section 47 enquiries. Its purpose is:

- to bring together and analyse, in an inter-agency setting, the information which has been obtained about the child's developmental needs and the parents' or carers' capacity to respond to these needs to ensure the child's safety and promote the child's health and development, within the context of their wider family and environment;

- to consider the evidence presented to the conference and, taking into account the child's present situation and information about his or her family history and present and past family functioning, make judgements about the likelihood of the child suffering significant harm in future and decide whether the child is continuing to, or is likely to, suffer significant harm;

- to decide what future action is required in order to safeguard and promote the welfare of the child, including the child becoming the subject of a child protection plan, what the planned developmental outcomes are for the child and how best to intervene to achieve these.

The timing of an initial child protection conference will depend on the urgency of the case and on the time required to obtain relevant information about the child and family. If the conference is to reach well-informed decisions based on evidence, it should take place following adequate preparation and assessment of the child's needs and circumstances. At the same time, cases where children are continuing to, or are likely to, suffer significant harm should not be allowed to drift. Consequently, all initial child protection conferences should take place within 15 working days of the strategy discussion, or the strategy discussion at which the section 47 enquiries were initiated, if more than one has been held (DCSF, 2010).

Conclusion

Although child death in child protection practice is a rare event considering the number of children involved in child protection cases, the emergence of the 'blame culture' by the media and public for failing to protect children has gained significant momentum over the past decade, and is particularly targeted at social workers. Risk in child protection today is acknowledged in the sense that everyone knows that whatever is done, there can be no guarantees that children will be safe (Ferguson, 2011).

Arguably, social work with children and their families will be viewed more positively when we acknowledge and learn from the routinely 'good' practice that is undertaken through the thousands of interventions made each year by social workers. We should be able to celebrate this effective, demanding, often harrowing area of social work practice and commend those practitioners who continue to deliver this service every day, year in year out (Ferguson, 2005).

> *I believe that every day social workers and other professionals help many children to escape from intolerable abuse and neglect, and many families to steer themselves into happier, less self-destructive paths.*

> (Beckett, 2007, page 212)

FURTHER READING

Cleaver, H, Unell, I, and Aldgate, J (2007) *Children's Needs – Parenting Capacity: The Impact of Parental Mental Illness, Learning Disability, Problem Alcohol and Drug Use and Domestic Violence on Children's Development*, 2nd edition. London: The Stationery Office.

A useful text looking at issues that may impact on parenting.

Corby, B (2006) *Child Abuse: Towards a Knowledge Base*, 3rd edition. Maidenhead: Open University Press.

This book provides a broad knowledge base for practitioners and students in all aspects of child protection.

Daniel, B, Wassell, S and Gilligan, R (2010) *Child Development for Child Care and Protection Workers*, 2nd edition. London: Jessica Kingsley.

A helpful text that relates child development and child protection, particularly for attachment theory.

Department of Health, NSPCC and the University of Sheffield (2010) *The Child's World*, 2nd edition. London: Jessica Kingsley.

This book focuses on assessment practice and achieving better outcomes for children and usefully discusses all aspects from the Framework for Assessment, including children's developmental needs and parenting capacity.

Horwath, J (2007) *Child Neglect: Identification and Assessment*. Basingstoke: Palgrave Macmillan.

This book clarifies the issues and processes involved in identifying and assessing neglect and particularly explores the impact that neglect has upon the child's development and attachment strategies.

O'Hagan, K (2006) *Identifying Emotional and Psychological Abuse*. Maidenhead: Open University Press.

This book is particularly useful in providing case studies and vignettes to highlight normal development and abusive situations.

Chapter 5

Direct work with children and young people

Julie Bywater, Jackie Hughes, Nicky Ryden and Steve O' Loughlin

A C H I E V I N G   A   S O C I A L   W O R K   D E G R E E

This chapter will help you to develop the following capabilities from the **Professional Capabilities Framework**:
- **Professionalism**
Identify and behave as a professional social worker committed to professional development.
- **Diversity**
Recognise diversity and apply anti-discriminatory principles in practice
- **Knowledge**
Apply knowledge of social sciences, law and social work practice theory.
- **Judgement**
Use judgement and authority to intervene with individuals, families and communities to promote independence, provide support and prevent harm, neglect and abuse.
- **Critical reflection and analysis**
Apply critical reflection and analysis to inform and provide a rationale for professional decision making.

It will also introduce you to the following academic standards as set out in the 2008 social work benchmark statement:
5.5 Problem solving skills
    5.5.2 Gathering information
    5.5.3 Analysis and synthesis
    5.5.4 Intervention and evaluation
7.3 Knowledge and understanding

Introduction

This chapter will provide an introduction to direct work with children and young people, setting the context for exploring young people's views and the role of the social worker in that task. The planning and process of direct work will be discussed, together with practical ways to approach and relate to children and young people. This chapter will consider four different groups of children and young people to highlight the differences, as well as the similarities, that need to be considered by practitioners when planning their work. Within the chapter there is a general introduction followed by four sections: working with children with disabilities; working with children from birth to ten years; working with young people 11 to 15 years and finally working with young adults aged 16 plus.

The importance of direct work with children and the skills it needs can often be over-looked when workers are focusing on safeguarding or struggling to provide a service. This should not, though, be at the expense of ensuring that the wishes and views of children and young people are listened to and respected, even though they cannot always be fol-lowed. In the past, the voices of children and young people were little regarded, but over time it has been recognised that children and young people have rights, including the right to be listened to. The fact that children and young people have keenly felt (and feel) that their wishes and views have not been taken into account is best illustrated in their own words by the following quote. This is a message specifically for social workers.

> *Explain to children what's going on. Like give them information about their parents, birth parents, foster parents ... And, oh, really help them understand what's going on.*

> *(Thomas and Beckford, 1999, page 140)*

The legal recognition, which encompassed the moves to 'hear' children (DHSS, 1974) has been further broadened and enhanced in subsequent legislation to arenas outside the court setting.

The Children Act 1989 states that the wishes and views of the child must be ascertained before any decisions are made about him or her, although this is qualified by refer-ences to age and understanding. This commitment to discuss with children their views is extended in the Children Act 2004 to not only ascertaining wishes and feelings but also to giving them 'due consideration'. The UN Convention on the Rights of the Child (UNICEF, 2006) also asserts that children have the right to express their view and to have it taken into consideration when decisions affecting the child's life are being considered. The *Framework for the Assessment of Children in Need and their Families* (DoH, 2000b) guid-ance states that direct work with children is an essential part of any assessment. It goes on to suggest that such direct work will have five components: seeing the child, observa-tion, engaging with the child, talking to children and engaging in activities with children (DoH, 2000, para 3.42). Social workers are expected to engage directly with children and young people, regardless of their age, when conducting an assessment of their needs. Children and young people report that social workers rarely speak with them (Butler and Williamson, 1994); children with communication difficulties are even more excluded from consultation, while young children are often regarded as too young to have a view. Brandon and colleagues suggested that *the ability to work competently and sensitively with children should be a basic skill in child and family social work rather than a specialist activity* (Brandon et al., 1998, page 63).

The inquiry into the death of Victoria Climbié (DoH and the Home Office, 2003) in its re-commendations for social services, contains at least five recommendations that emphasise the need for social workers to speak with children and their carers when there is a con-cern about the child's safety and well-being. The findings of the inquiry, on the practice of social workers, suggests that the observation by Aldgate and Simmonds on the lack of any culture of direct work with children in social work practice and the lack of managerial support for such activity still holds true (Aldgate and Simmonds, 1988, page 20).

Social workers who restrict their communication with children and young people to interview techniques that rely on verbal interchanges may find children and young people unresponsive informants, who are challenging to know and understand. Vulnerable children and young people can raise strong feelings in adults and finding a meaningful way to communicate, to overcome their distrust of adults (based on previous experience of abusive and neglectful adults), represents a formidable hurdle to establishing effective communication (Aldgate and Simmonds, 1988; Brandon et al., 1998). Direct work is a concerted attempt to engage with children and young people in ways which will make it possible to understand their perspective on their experience of the world, with all its unique features (Jones, 2003, page 102). As such it needs as much preparation and planning as any other communication undertaken in a professional capacity. It requires an understanding of child development, of theories which promote an understanding of interactions between family members, and a willingness to consider playful approaches to communication. The younger the child the more significant play as a means of communication will be, while creative approaches to communication may well enable children and young people to both explore and express complex feelings and solutions (Bannister, 2003; Cattanach, 1992; Doyle, 1997).

Children and young people communicate in a variety of ways, and social workers will need to consider each child or young person's development, their experiences of talking to (and with) adults, their language of choice and their culture, in order to promote effective communication. When attempting to explore issues relating to past events which may be painful, social workers would do well to remember that children and young people may find it easier to express themselves through creative media rather than interviews that rely on verbal interchanges. Rinaldi (2001) suggests that children have *a hundred languages,* meaning the many and varied ways that they express their feelings and explore and make sense of their world. If adults restrict themselves to a dialogue in only one 'language' then children's communication will be judged inadequate. The younger the child the more restricted their verbal language is likely to be, but this does not mean they have nothing to contribute. All forms of abuse to children, and neglect in particular, can have an impact on a child's language and communication skills. Neglect appears to have the effect of depressing children's language ability (Buckley, 2003, page 183) while physical abuse can increase children's distractibility, and reduce their persistence, so that they find it difficult to learn new words and ways of expressing themselves. Poor self-esteem undermines children's ability to try new ways of communicating and learning, so that their language skills are depressed in comparison with their peers. In such circumstances children's non-verbal communication and creativity will be important extensions of their verbal communication.

Being child- and young person-centred

Being child- and young person-centred requires adults not only to have the child or young person and their needs central to their thinking, but also to develop a relationship with the child or young person that allows them to lead, that values their spontaneity and creativity, with the adult being prepared to follow the child or young person's lead, rather than assuming that the adult perspective is right (Bannister, 2003, page 48). It means that adults need to be comfortable with children, willing to sit or lie on the floor with them as they play, to get messy, and to tolerate expressions of violence or swearing in the course of play. Adults should be willing to learn from the children who are experts on their own situation (Doyle, 1997, page 41).

Being child-centred should also encompass the practicalities for the work, choosing a time and place that is suitable for the child, materials that are age appropriate and that engage their attention, and the opportunity to have fun, as well as a focus on the work that needs to be done. Negotiating with carers about the work can be critical to its success. The adults in the child's life need to be informed about the purpose of the work and how it will be undertaken. There needs to be a discussion about the child's privacy in respect of the work. Carers need to be alerted to the fact that if the work involves revisiting difficult experiences it may have an impact on the child's behaviour, so they need to be prepared for distress or changes in behaviour. They need to be involved in the arrangements for the sessions, so that there is no confusion about who is transporting a child or about the time at which they will be seen. Carers who are not committed to the work can 'forget' arrangements or if the child enjoys and looks forward to the sessions could refuse to let them attend as a punishment for misbehaviour. It is best to take all such eventualities into account and to negotiate a clear contract with carers.

Once the negotiations with carers have been concluded, the child needs to be informed about the nature and purpose of the work, and why the social worker will be doing it. It helps to share with the child information that is already held, for example that their carer has told you they've been upset by an event, that this has made them sad or caused them to be cross, so they shout at people and then get into trouble. The child can be asked if they would like things to be different, and if they say yes, the suggestion can be made that the social worker might be the person to help with this and an explanation offered of how it will be done, that is by meeting once a week and playing with some special toys. When the focus is preparing a child for a transition, they can be reminded that this is the plan, and the social worker can explain that to get ready for this event it might be good to make a book that can be shared with their new carers that will tell them about their life so far. The explanation should be commensurate with the child's age and understanding, and expressed in terms that make sense to them. Children and young people may not want to engage in the work, and this reluctance should be respected, although they might be encouraged to meet for at least one session to find out a bit more about what it means. Most younger children will agree to this, and will hopefully be reassured; if not, then their wishes should be respected and progress monitored until they are ready to engage.

Social workers should have the ability to maintain sufficient structure and boundaries to promote a feeling of security and stability for the child, by discussing plans and negotiating any rules. This also means being able to plan and control other work which might make conflicting demands. Being late, changing the venue, not having a favoured toy, will all undermine any developing sense of trust that the child may have for the social worker. If plans have to be changed the worker should personally explain to the child or young person why and make an alternative arrangement as soon as possible, while being prepared for some expression of anger from them when next seen.

Direct work with children with disabilities

When we are thinking about direct work with children with disabilities it is important not to lose sight of the fact that disabled children are children first, and we need to recognise that they have the same rights, feelings and hopes as all other children. We need to ensure that we adopt the same rights perspective in our work with disabled children that we strive to achieve with all children.

Young people say they want to: *Be listened to when decisions are made about their lives* (NSF for Children, Standard 8, 2004, page 8). This has to be the basis of our involvement with disabled children, so that their views and wishes are central to decision-making about their lives. Historically, social work with disabled children has focused on working with the parents of disabled children (Middleton, 1996). It is important to recognise that there may be a conflict of interest between children and their parents (Marchant, 2008) and also to acknowledge that despite the importance of involving children, children and their families will need support in making some decisions, so as not be overwhelmed by the decision-making process (Russell, 1995). The terminology of 'respite' for short breaks is an example of how the focus may be on the parents' needs, rather than the experience of the disabled child. However, Platts et al. (1996) found, in their research on the needs of learning disabled children with additional health needs, that for parents to benefit from a child's short break, they needed to know that their child was happy and well cared for.

RESEARCH SUMMARY

Disabled children have the same rights to protection and the safeguards of legislation as non-disabled children, yet research indicates that disabled children in residential education or respite placements may not be treated as looked after children and not be afforded the safeguards of the Children Act (Russell, 1995; Platts et al., 1996; Morris, 2005). The way that support services are provided to disabled children and their families may increase their vulnerability, with more adults caring for them than non-disabled children and periods of time spent in 'respite' or residential settings (Morris, 1995). Disabled children are more vulnerable to abuse than non-disabled children (Westcott and Cross, 1996), and yet they are less likely to be represented in the child protection system (Morris, 1995, 1998a, 1999a; Marchant, 2008). Disabled children are twice as likely as non-disabled children to be living away from home (Marchant, 2008).

CASE STUDY

Joanna is ten, and she has cerebral palsy. She lives with her mum and dad and two brothers in a three-bedroom house in a small town in the north of England. She attends a school with resourced provision for children with mobility impairments as she uses a wheelchair. She uses an electric wheelchair at school, but the family home is not adapted for her to use this at home. You have been asked to do an assessment with Joanna and her family. Her parents are requesting short breaks for Joanna, so that they can spend some time on their own with their sons, and also an assessment for adaptations.

What do you need to know to be able to work effectively with Joanna and her family?

COMMENT

You may have thought about your existing knowledge of attachment and child development, and how this might help you in conducting an assessment. Marchant (2008) reminds us that disabled children are more likely to be separated from their families and have fewer friends than non-disabled children. She suggests that a key social work task with disabled children is thus to value and protect children's positive relationships: with their family, with their friends, and with others involved in their lives (Marchant, 2008, page 163).

Your understanding of the social model of disability may help you work with Joanna and her parents to identify barriers and help her access mainstream facilities (Office of Disability Issues, 2006). Beresford (2002) identifies the variety of ways in which children with disabilities are excluded from mainstream society: transport, leisure, housing and decision-making are all key aspects of disabled children's lives where they may experience social exclusion. Beresford highlights the way that children may participate in local parent and toddler groups, and in pre-school facilities, but with the admission to school many children find themselves increasingly using 'special' facilities, and this increases with transfer to high school. Once children are separated from their communities, it is increasingly difficult to integrate into mainstream opportunities. The way that decisions are often made for children with disabilities may mean that they do not develop the confidence or abilities to be able to undertake these themselves.

You may also have identified the way that access for Joanna in the family home may be limiting her involvement in family and community activities. Beresford (2006) identified that unsuitable housing affected disabled children's opportunities to enjoy everyday activities.

You may have decided that you need to start from the basis of finding out more about Joanna and her family by spending some time getting to know Joanna in both the home and school environment. Remember your 'tool kit' of activities that you could use with Joanna to find out more about the things that she enjoys doing and what she hopes for the future. This will help you identify with Joanna and her parents to secure valued opportunities for her. Remember that individual budgets or direct payments can be used to support Joanna's and her parents' choices to enable them to develop a flexible package of support which is person-centred (DoH, 2000c).

Communication

We need to recognise that children with disabilities may have additional needs that must be taken into account when planning direct work (although it is important not just to focus on the impairment). Too often, review reports will refer to children with disabilities as *unable to communicate* or even *not applicable* because the child may not use verbal communication, rather than to have someone who knows them well communicating directly with the child to ascertain their views (Marchant, 2008).

Just because some children with profound disabilities may not communicate with speech does not mean that they do not have things they want to say. Listening to children is key to identifying what they wish to communicate.

> *Listening to children and young people with special educational needs or disabilities will present constant challenges. But it is also an opportunity for 'open learning' and a reminder that simplistic expectations about low participation rates and the inability to discuss sensitive issues in a positive way are often confounded.*
>
> *(Russell, 1996, page 117)*

Communication with disabled children builds on the skills that social workers will develop in working with all children, as you found in Activity 5.1.

When working with children with complex needs, it is important to think about how we broaden our understanding of communication, as you did when you were observing younger children. Communication is not just about speech, but total communication with a child. Therefore, being alongside a child is important. You have already thought about the importance of observing children in different settings and with different people. This may be particularly useful with children who do not use verbal communication. You can both observe their patterns of interaction, but also find out from people who know the child well how they communicate different emotions, such as expressions of pleasure and happiness, discomfort or dislike of activities.

Not all children with disabilities will have additional communication needs, but there is a range of impairments that may affect children's expressive or receptive communication. For instance, some children may repeat words, or other people may find their articulation difficult to understand. It is important to avoid closed questions to ensure that the child has the opportunity to express choices. You may need to rephrase your question to ensure that the child has understood. Some children may use a range of different communication systems, including symbols and signing (BSL or Makaton). As children with complex needs may have very individual ways of communicating, it may be helpful to involve someone else. This may be someone who is a BSL interpreter, but could be someone who knows the child well, and is trusted by them. You need to offer the child a choice about who they would like to support them in this way, so that they have some control over the exchange and they feel confident and respected by you (Marchant, 2008). Remember that as you spend time with a child, you may begin to understand their communication so that you can communicate directly with them (Marchant, 2001a).

Fitton (2000) describes the needs of her daughter, Kathy, who had profound disabilities, and the ways that she developed to help others communicate with her. Her use of a communication and care book outlined the importance of people taking time to get to know Kathy, her routines, and what was important to her and the things that she enjoyed doing. As Fitton indicates, getting to really know Kathy was the first step in learning to interpret her gestures and actions to enable communication to take place.

> **CASE STUDY**
>
> *Usman is 15, and has autism and learning disabilities. He lives with his parents and three younger siblings, one of whom has ADHD. During the week, he attends a residential school for young people with autism, and in addition he has some 'respite' during school holidays at a residential respite centre. Usman has had his Transition Review, and it was decided that his social worker should work with him to identify future plans, as he will leave school at 19. It has been recommended that you should work with him on a Person-Centred Plan.*

> **ACTIVITY 5.2**
>
> *Think about what you need to know to enable you to work effectively with Usman. How will you work with him to produce a Person-Centred Plan?*
>
> **COMMENT**
>
> *You will have realised that Usman is being supported at two different residential placements, in addition to living with his family. You will need to find out his language of choice, and whether he has additional communication needs. He may use a symbol system, such as PECS, to support him in his routines. You will have recognised that he has a younger sibling with a disability, and this may be important for the support needs of his parents.*

Person-centred planning is a requirement for all young people moving from children's to adult services (*Valuing People*, DoH, 2001d). It involves a number of different ways of developing plans, from Essential Life Style Plans, to PATHS and MAPS. Person-centred planning places the person at the centre, so it is an effective way of working with a young person and the people who know and care about them to plan for the future with them. It encourages a flexible approach to working with the young person to enable plans to reflect their interests and skills in a visual way. You may want to encourage the young person or a facilitator to draw some of the things that they want to include in their plan. You may want to find out some more about this and look at some examples of plans, which you will find on the North West Development Team website (www.nwtdt.com).

Marchant and Gordon (2001) demonstrate how skills in communicating with disabled children will enable social workers to communicate effectively with all children. Listening to the views of disabled young people will help you work alongside them to help them build positive futures. Charlotte explained what this meant for her:

> *If anyone were to ask me what message I might have for others I would tell them that they should listen to, believe and respect young people. In my experience it is very difficult to tell anyone how you feel when they won't listen; if you aren't believed then you stop believing in yourself; if you're not respected then you lose your self-respect and everyone needs self-respect.*
>
> (Morris, 1999b page 4)

Working with children aged from birth to ten years

Children in this wide age grouping will experience considerable developmental changes, and having a good level of knowledge of child development will provide a sound foundation for those undertaking this work. This knowledge will provide a basis for planning the work, including how you will explain what you are doing to the child.

ACTIVITY 5.3

Explaining your role and the purpose of the work to children

Take a few moments to think about three children aged two years, five years and eight years of age. For each child consider how you would explain your role and the work you are going to do with them. Record your thoughts, writing down the phrases and words you might use. You might want to consider having some material that helps you to explain – give a detailed description of what this might be and of how you would use it to engage the child's interest.

COMMENT

You have probably decided that for the youngest child you will use a simple form of words, and that it would be important to engage their carer as well as the child. You could tell them your name and that you have talked to their carer. You might have a puppet or toy to engage the child's interest and it will be sufficient to explain that you will be coming to play and to get to know what they like and don't like. With the five-year-old you would tell them your name and ask for theirs; again, you might want to involve their carer. You can explain that your job is to listen to children and to find out what they think about important things that happen in their lives. You could explain what the issue is – to find out how they got hurt, to find out what they think about living with ... (use the name the child uses for that person). A simple explanation about not telling other people what happens in your meetings with the child, unless they tell you someone is hurting them, when you will have to tell ... (a safe person) so that it can be stopped, will deal with confidentiality. With the older child the same issues need to be discussed; it is important to check what the child would like you to call them and to tell them what they may call you. Again, you need to give an explanation of your job and the nature of the work, with some discussion of privacy and the bounds of confidentiality.

Observation

Undertaking an observation requires negotiation with parents and carers, so that the nature of the activity by the observer is understood. It will need to occur more than once and preferably in settings to which the child has regular access. Such observation will be informed by a sound theoretical understanding of child development in the early years, of the implications of attachment and by a willingness to take seriously the child's communication (see Buckley, 2003). When working with babies from birth to three years, there is a need for careful and systematic observation of the child as they engage with their carers, family members and social context.

> *CASE STUDY*
>
> Thirteen-month-old Jamie had been neglected and was the subject of care proceedings. He was being observed in order to consider the possibility of reunion with his mother. It was noted that he was very passive when his mother undertook any caring tasks, not engaging in any interactive activity with her, and that he did not go to her for comfort. When he felt stressed he preferred to sit in his pushchair. Jamie demonstrated avoidant attachment, and it was decided that it would not be appropriate to attempt reunion with his mother.

With older children, observation will continue to be a central activity, along with the recording of what has been noticed, with a clear distinction made between factual observations and the more subjective ones arising from the social worker's responses to the child, that is, how the child makes the worker feel. In the first category might be information about the child's dress, state of cleanliness and apparent health – for example, are there holes in their shoes? Do they have a runny nose? Do they seem tired or hungry? These observations should be substantiated by the reasons for thinking this, such as the child having eaten two packets of crisps and six biscuits during the period of observation, or having repeatedly yawned and shown a lack of energy. The more subjective observations arise from how the child makes the worker feel and could range from anger and resentment to concern and a desire to protect the child. These feelings need to be explored in supervision, so that the processes that are creating such feelings can be understood and the worker enabled to retain a balanced relationship with the child. Such feelings can be projections from the child, that is, the worker is feeling as the child does, or reactions to the child's behaviour and communication, which may elicit either rejecting or care-giving behaviour.

Observation is also central to understanding the content and meaning of children's play. Direct work implies that the social worker will engage with the child's play, being attentive to the child's actions and verbalisations as they engage in activities, whether it is making a scene with small toys in a sand tray, painting a picture or playing a game of 'Snap' or 'Snakes and Ladders'. As the activities progress there may be opportunities to ask open questions about what is happening, to check out whether the worker has understood.

Developing a relationship

Children respond best to consistency. When possible, meetings should take place at the same time and in the same place, with the same toys and materials available. Children from three upwards can be given simple explanations about the purpose of work, and will usually be willing to engage directly with the social worker, in order to explore issues of concern. Using a range of play materials can help to keep the communication focused and give the child opportunities to express their views, through drawing or role-play. The older the child, the more sophisticated their play will be, and the more complex the ideas that can be explored.

CASE STUDY

Phillipa is eight. She was in hospital for some investigations, as she complained of frequent stomach ache and pain. She told the nurse she did not want to go home. Asked why not she was unable to say but, given some small dolls, she was able to role-play how she experienced living with domestic violence. The little girl doll and her sister are in the park playing on the swings. The daddy comes and says they must go home, the mummy is crying, a glass is smashed and there is blood.

This brief role-play, with some minimal play material, demonstrated the tension of living with violence, and how the violent incident intrudes into the enjoyment of the sisters' play in the park. It allowed Phillipa to circumvent the family rules about not talking about what happened at home. The telegraphic style of the verbal explanation that accompanied her play demonstrates the regression of language to an earlier stage of development when recalling a difficult issue. Adults who exploit children's vulnerability impress upon children that they must not talk about their experiences, and it is often only when children begin to feel safe, having been removed from the abusive situation that they are able to 'talk' about their experiences.

Children usually respond well to new toys or play material, but will be disappointed if a familiar or favoured item is missing. Often as the relationship develops, rituals will arise which facilitate the transition into the session – it might be about removing and hanging up outdoor clothes, having a particular snack and a drink in a 'special' cup before starting, or it might be playing with a particular toy first, so one child will always start a session by drawing a picture, another might use playdough. Such rituals reduce anxiety, and promote a feeling of trust in the relationship for both child and worker; each knows what to expect of the other. Similar rituals may develop to mark the end of sessions.

CASE STUDY

Henry, aged five, on first entering the room to be used for work, began to rearrange the furniture, using a great deal of effort. When it was arranged to his satisfaction he said it should always be like that. He then played happily for the allotted time. Before he left he asked if the furniture would be moved. He was told that it would be put back how it was, because other people used the room and they liked it that way. The worker said that she would make sure it was how he liked it when he came next time. Before the next session, the worker moved the furniture as Henry had before he arrived. When he came into the room he checked the layout, and told the worker one item was in the wrong place. This was moved by them both to his satisfaction. Once Henry knew the room would be as he preferred, he developed another ritual before the session began, about getting a drink of milk in a particular beaker, which he filled himself and which was then carried for him by the worker into the room.

Honesty about what can and cannot happen is important. Being open about uncertainties and only making commitments that can be met will all help to promote a relationship. Children recognise adults' willingness to listen or otherwise, and respond to genuineness, empathy and warmth.

Techniques and tools

Having a dedicated space in which to work is not often available to social workers, so most will have to create their working space wherever the child is located, so it may be a corner of the family living room, the kitchen table, the hallway at the foot of the stairs, or a school hall. Wherever it is there needs to be some agreement with others who live in the same place about privacy, the minimising of interruptions, whether anything will be shared with carers about the work, how many times the child will be seen and what is the purpose of the work. Creating a space can be symbolic, or actual. It can be agreed with the child, 'this is our space for the next hour' or by using a special mat or rug the space can be delineated – 'we will play on the rug' (see Cattanach, 1992). If at all possible, avoid using a child's bedroom, particularly if the content of the session might involve recalling upsetting events. The nature of the space may create limitations to the activities that can be undertaken; paints might not be a good idea if you have to worry about the fitted carpet or wallpaper. A washable table cover which could also be used on the floor, can take care of concerns about spills and mess with sand or water, paints and dough. With very young children, a single hand puppet or cuddly toy might be the only equipment required, used as a focus for interacting with the child, playing simple games such as 'Peek a Boo', determining whether the child can demonstrate warmth or affection by stroking and hugging the toy, or whether it gets hit and thrown about. A basic kit for preschool children could include small people, cars, farm animals, a plastic tea set, a puppet, soft toy, one or two soft-bodied baby dolls with clothes and feeding bottle, a piece of fabric, a soft ball, some A4 paper in a variety of colours, washable felt-tip pens and chalks, playdough in airtight tubs, a plastic place mat and rolling pin and cutters for the dough. The fabric can be a blanket for the dolls, a cloak for a child, a screen to hide behind. Items should be kept together in bags, so that the child can explore the kit without feeling overwhelmed. A small cardboard or plastic box, used to hold the felt-tips and chalks might also be used as a building or a doll's bed.

For children from five to ten years, a basic kit might contain a more extensive range of people, including current heroes and anti-heroes such as Ninja Mutant Turtles, Spiderman, Batman and Robin, Cinderella, Peter Pan, the Simpson family. A selection of cars and trucks, animals (including dinosaurs), buildings and fences for role playing could also be included. Again, items should be kept in separate bags, so the child can control access to and the amount of material in use. Drawing materials, A3 paper in a variety of colours and textures, card, pencils, felt-tips, crayons, collage materials, scissors, glue stick, sticky tape and paper clips are useful resources as are playdough, plasticine and clay for modelling, together with some modelling tools and a plastic placemat to work on. Games that can be played by two people such as, 'Snap' and 'Snakes and Ladders', plus pencil and paper games such as 'Noughts and Crosses' or 'Hangman' can be useful with children who are not ready to play. Books with stories relevant to the child's issues can be included. With older children, worksheets that will help them to identify their strengths, or which promote their sense of identity will provide structure to sessions (Plummer, 2001, 2006) and may be directly relevant to the work – for example, 'My Life and Me' (Camis, 2006) for children preparing to move to an adoptive placement. With older children it might be appropriate to provide a special file or box to contain their work. There needs to be a discussion about who will look after such a file or box while the work is ongoing, and who will see its contents. Some children need support to be able to keep things private and safe; not all adults will respect the child's work, so this needs to be discussed before the work begins.

Finding out about a child's family might be first stage of work. This can be done in a variety of ways such as using dolls to represent family members or inviting the child to draw their family. Observation of where the child places themselves in relation to other family members might give some clues to interactions within the family group. In drawings, the relative size of the figure representing the child and their position on the page might indicate whether they feel central to the family or peripheral. The use of small figures allows people to move and this might help to convey change within the family group. Older children often enjoy creating a 'family tree', which can be done using a genogram or by using other objects such as buttons and shells, placed on a piece of paper, with lines drawn to show relationships. Most school-aged children are able to provide an accurate representation of three generations, although they may be a little unclear about the exact status of relationships (married, cohabiting) in the extended family. They usually have a good understanding of such relationships in their own family, for example, whether brothers and sisters have the same father and mother, whether parents are married or in a stable relationship, compared to more recent partnerships, which are usually described as girl/boyfriend. It is always useful to ask a child who else lives in the house with them. Taking the time to find out about family pets can also convey something about the stability of family life (and whether there are any hazards to be faced when visiting the home!), and of shared interests between family members.

Younger children will spontaneously engage with any play materials. Careful observation of their play may convey considerable information about family life – a baby doll may be lovingly held and rocked before being put to bed, or thrown aside with a threat to get to sleep or else! School-aged children can be equally spontaneous, but may need more explanation and encouragement to engage in activities. They may find it easier to begin with some activity that involves sitting down together and talking while either drawing or modelling. The mutual engagement in the activity and avoidance of eye contact is less confrontational and demonstrates that here is an adult who is willing to engage on a level with the child.

As a trusting relationship is established, the child will become more spontaneous, and be prepared to risk role playing or imaginary play. Older children may find it easier to express feelings through a puppet or soft toy, or by creating stories about another child. The making and recording of such stories gives children an opportunity to both recount their own experiences and to experiment with alternative solutions. This can be particularly helpful with children who find it difficult to express themselves through language.

CASE STUDY

Eight-year-old Peter's adoptive placement was threatened by his challenging behaviour. He found it almost impossible to speak about his feelings, but using a dragon puppet and some models of animals he was able to explore his experience of going to live with an unknown family in a strange part of the country, his difficulties in making friends and his ambivalence about being adopted. The various scenarios were suggested by him, acted out with the toys and the dialogue audio taped. The audio tape was transcribed and later made into a book which Peter kept. This process gave Peter a voice, and enabled him to process his feelings about losing his mother and making relationships with a new family. His placement stabilised and his performance in school improved.

Recording the work

Recording is a central part of the work, and can be done in a variety of ways, some of which will have different purposes. The artefacts that children produce – pictures, models, stories and worksheets – constitute one form of record. The use of a digital camera can help to make a record of scenes created with small toys or other symbols. Photographs of artwork might be easier to store than the original items. This record of the work is the child's and what happens to it should be their decision, although they can be encouraged to find a way of retaining significant material. It might be appropriate for the child to dispose of some material, perhaps with some ceremony to signify the rejection of negative beliefs about self. The social worker will also need to maintain their record of the work.

Working with young people aged 11 to 15 years

Using chronological age to define a 'young person' is problematic due to the influences of social and cultural factors on the process of ageing as well as the diversity of subjective experiences. Although the chronological age span for this group is small, the developmental changes and growth are considerable. It must be remembered also that the term 'young people' has a tendency to assume homogeneity, where in fact the people who are included bring with them a range of differences in terms of gender, ethnicity, class, disability, sexual orientation and age (Bywater and Jones, 2007).

Being able to communicate and engage effectively with young people will involve both verbal and non-verbal communication as well as viewing the young person as a unique individual. This will provide the optimum foundation for understanding and establishing a trusting relationship. To demonstrate person-centred practice the practitioner will need to engage with the young person by taking account of their own and the young person's:

- particular vocabulary;
- communication skills/abilities;
- culture;

- emotional and behavioural needs;

- strengths and difficulties.

They will also need to demonstrate an age- and developmentally-appropriate approach.

Being or becoming aware of the emotional world of the young person is extremely important when undertaking any type of intervention if their needs, wishes and feelings are to be heard, identified and subsequently met. Being aware that most young people/adolescents will, during this period of their development, be experiencing puberty, *adjusting to changes in their bodies* and striving for *their own identity, emotional maturity and independence* (Crawford and Walker, 2007 page 73), will enable the social worker to respond more sensitively to issues of power and autonomy, and ensure that young people are able to express their individuality and autonomy within any interventions. This will, however, raise several pertinent questions for the practitioner to consider before meeting with the young person, for example, how to create and respect autonomy in the context of working with the young person, and how to balance this with the duty to safeguard their welfare. These questions can, if not addressed appropriately, result in tensions between the young person and social worker and could result in a lack of continuity in establishing and maintaining a positive working relationship. For example, at what point will a decision be made if a young person's wishes are unsafe or clearly against their interests, and consequently overridden (Golding et al. 2006), and how will these decisions be conveyed back to the young person?

Preparing for and beginning direct interventions with young people

Interventions with young people could be as a 'one-off' session, a series of sessions planned to address an assessment framework or on a more statutory basis in relation to duties and responsibilities as a 'lead/key worker' for the young person.

You will also need to prepare yourself for undertaking interventions with young people as working with abused, distressed and traumatised young people is distressing. You may experience overwhelming feelings of sadness or anger as you hear the young people recall their abuse. You will therefore need to prepare carefully for direct interventions; consider your critical reflection skills; build a supportive network of colleagues; and ensure that you are able to access skilful supervision to manage your own feelings (Koprowska, 2008).

ACTIVITY **5.4**

Take a few moments to think about the context of your social work practice and the variety of tasks that involve you directly engaging and communicating with a young person. Make a list and a brief summary of these before reading further.

COMMENT

You will have thought of a range of tasks linked to your agency context; the roles and functions on the list below are by no means extensive or exhaustive. You may, for

Continued

COMMENT *continued*

example, have listed the need to undertake some direct work sessions with a young person who is looked after by the local authority, leaving care or subject to a care order; is disabled or experiencing health/mental health issues; is being assessed and you need to ascertain their wishes and feelings or for a pending court report; to ascertain their views/ opinions following allegations of abuse or a referral from their caregiver/school about their behaviour etc.; or even that you may need to respond and engage with a young person unexpectedly while on duty who is homeless and/or a substance user. You need to be clear about the context of your involvement so that you can then share this with the young person.

ACTIVITY 5.5

When undertaking any direct interventions involving young people (children and adults, too), it is important to establish ground rules regarding confidentiality, personal safety and consent issues. Using your list from Activity 5.4 and your own reflections, think about how you would establish some ground rules in your first meeting with the young person.

COMMENT

Issues of confidentiality and consent need to be considered thoroughly in relation to the agency, policy and legal guidelines. Most young people aged between 16 and 18 years are presumed to be competent to give their consent and should be treated as such, unless there is evidence to suggest otherwise. However, there may be instances when a young person aged 12 to 16 years may be able to give consent, for example, to a medical examination. However, in some circumstances welfare provisions may well outweigh their views. With regard to confidentiality, young people are only entitled to limited confidentiality. You will therefore need to establish with the young person right at the beginning of your session that their confidentiality will be maintained as long as it does not put them or others at risk. You will need to clarify that, if you are concerned about any information they share with you regarding safeguarding issues, you must report this to your manager and possibly the police. If criminal investigations and proceedings are already being undertaken you will need to liaise closely with the police/legal department regarding any planned direct interventions to ensure that the case is not jeopardised. You will also need to explain to the young person what sort of information will be passed on to others, how and what will be recorded and where records are stored. Be mindful, however, that you use the proper tone when explaining the limits of confidentiality, so that you present this as an enabling process rather than a restriction on communication. However tempted you may be, promising confidentiality is very unhelpful and a promise that you cannot keep; it could also result in the young person finding it difficult to trust professionals in the future.

CASE STUDY

Imagine you have just joined a looked-after children's team in a statutory social services department. You are to work with Steven who is twelve years old and has been living with his long-term foster carers for the past eleven months. One of your forthcoming roles and responsibilities is to prepare for Steven's 'looked-after' review meeting. Think about what would assist you in engaging with Steven and forming an effective, supportive relationship with him.

COMMENT

The following comments are generalised so that you are able to consider these in any context with a young person, even in situations where you will be responding to the unexpected. If you have time in advance, as you would with Steven, arrange for a suitable venue and for transport if required; inform the young person briefly about what you want to discuss with them, the arrangements and how long you are expecting the meeting to take.

You would begin by introducing yourself and explaining what it is that you want to talk privately with them about and why. It is also worth checking with the young person why they think they have come. Explain what will happen during the session and clarify any expectations you have in terms of wanting them to talk to you. (In the case scenario you will want to focus upon establishing a relationship with Steven so that you can begin to gain information from Steven for his review.) You may then need to address any immediate concerns or anxieties and help the young person to dispel any fears or uncertainties. Some young people may not have been able to trust anyone (see Erikson's theory of developmental stages in Crawford and Walker, 2007), so you will need, over time, to prove that you are trustworthy. Building an effective relationship will also depend upon you conveying genuine interest in the young person and exploring their feelings; respecting their individuality; providing alternative information/messages in relation to any misconceptions they may hold about themselves; acknowledging their diversity; and by being empathic and reliable.

Being able to provide the young person with a structure and focus for the session can help to reduce any anxieties. It is important to ensure that you provide a suitable setting for your direct work session with the young person, for example, a room in their own home if they wish; at school; a family centre; or in the agency setting, which offers privacy and no interruptions from the telephone or other people. The setting should be welcoming, warm and comfortable with age-appropriate materials and furnishings. A wipe board with pens may be useful for young people to share their thoughts and feelings and reassures them that they can wipe the board clean before leaving. Having an opportunity to draw can also be a useful way for young people to express themselves if they are 'stuck for words'.

ACTIVITY 5.6

Now take a few moments to think about how you could empower Steven within the session and how long you consider the session should take.

COMMENT

As previously, the following comments are generalised so that you are able to consider these in relation to any young person.

It is important to sit beside the young person as this is less intimidating and less confrontational than sitting opposite them. It is also worth ensuring that your seat is at the same level as theirs so that you are not towering over them. Involving the young person in having some choice within the agenda of the session (within mutually agreed limits) will convey respect, and promote their autonomy and empowerment. Enable the young person to decide what is most relevant and appropriate for themselves to discuss at this time, and also to have a choice about whether they want to attend or not. Even in situations where there is a mandatory requirement to work with the young person, it is important that they still feel able to make a choice by enabling them to consider the consequences of their decision. You will need to understand that most young people are seeking to gain some control of their lives and you will have a higher chance of maintaining their involvement if they do not feel that decisions are being made for them.

Timing the session is very important, although it is sometimes hard to judge in advance when meeting someone for the first time. However, having some notion in advance will help to put the young person at ease. If you are rushing or appear distracted about time, the young person may assume that you are not interested in them. You will need to respond to the young person's concentration span – half an hour to one hour is usually long enough and further sessions can be arranged if needed. You may have planned the session to take place after school so you will also need to be mindful of the young person feeling tired and hungry.

ACTIVITY **5.7**

Whenever possible all interventions should have a beginning, middle and ending. What would you consider to be the beginning component of your very first session with Steven?

COMMENT

The beginning of the session should allow the young person to relax and feel comfortable. Talking with them generally about their interests, family and friends, music and hobbies may help them to become familiar with you and the setting. For example, you could say, 'I don't really know much about you and I am very interested to learn more'. You could then begin by asking them what they like to do when not in school. It is important to listen out for any potential strengths in their abilities/relationships etc. Offering refreshments is another useful strategy, especially if they are meeting with you after school; it is also a way of conveying care and warmth.

It is then important to focus upon establishing ground rules and acknowledging that some young people may want to add their own, for example, having 'time out' if they are feeling uncomfortable or experiencing difficulties, or even having clarification that

Continued

COMMENT *continued*

they can stop the session. Ground rules should, however, address issues of personal safety and be clear about what types of behaviour are acceptable. For example, you should clarify that neither you or the young person will hurt themselves, each other or any property and will not touch themselves or each other in ways that makes either feel uncomfortable (Doyle, 2006). If a young person is prone to shouting, swearing or being verbally abusive it may be a reflection of their distress or experiences, and may therefore need sensitive handling and an agreement made between you as to what degrees will be acceptable. If you feel unsafe then you, too, can stop the session and, if necessary, arrange a colleague to be present in future sessions.

ACTIVITY **5.8**

Communicating with young people is different to communicating with another adult. Think about what communication and engagement skills you will need during the middle part of the session to ensure that you remain focused upon establishing the young person's views, opinions, wishes and feelings.

COMMENT

You will need to try to be open-minded and curious and approach the session as an explorer. Putting the young person into the position of being the expert about their own lives will enable you to set aside your own frame of reference. Anderson and Goolishian (1992) assert that practitioners never know the significance of the service user's experiences and actions; so instead, you must rely on their perceptions and explanations. The best way to do this therefore, is to take the position of not knowing. You will need to demonstrate genuine curiosity, a need to know more about what the young person is saying, rather than convey any preconceived opinions and expectations. Learning how to take this approach will require your commitment and practice. However, when we listen we are usually not only listening but also reacting to what is being said so it is important to be aware of your own body language. It takes commitment and practice to suspend our own frame of reference because we are more used to filtering other people's conversation through our own experiences, values and beliefs, and social workers particularly are trained to listen as a means of gaining assessment information.

So a useful place to begin will be for you to listen first for who and what are important to the young person using appropriate/attentive non-verbal body language. In their efforts to describe their situation, difficulties and needs, young people will talk about those people, relationships and events that are significant to them. Some young people may prefer to communicate by drawing or writing about their experiences, feelings and opinions. By enabling the young person to express them using their own preference and by listening to what they say, you hear what the young person is presently experiencing and are more able to help them to focus upon solutions to their current difficulties and problems. Young people, like most other service users, are sensitive to whether we

Continued

are listening carefully and respectfully, and may come to a conclusion very quickly about this. To reassure them that we are listening, it is useful to convey non-verbal behaviours/ responses, for example:

- *maintaining eye contact;*

- *nodding our head;*

- *varying our facial expressions in response to what they are saying;*

- *smiling when appropriate to convey warmth and understanding;*

- *occasionally hand gesturing or sitting in closer proximity to them and leaning slightly toward them to indicate interest and concentration.*

Listening, acceptance of, and reflecting the way the young person feels about themselves and others will help to form the basis for a helping professional relationship. Reflecting back and paraphrasing what the young person is saying is another crucial skill in communicating with young people and will provide rich sources of information for any ongoing assessments, reviews/evaluations, reports or decision-making. For example, young people may use language and expressions that are unfamiliar to you, so repeating or echoing key words used by them is a useful way to gain mutual understanding. The key words are those used by the young person to capture their experiences and the meanings they have attributed to those experiences. For example, if a young person said to you, 'my life is a mess' you would want to know more about what that meant to them, so you could echo 'a mess' with a rising intonation, or simply ask them what they mean.

Most young people do not have personal autonomy nor are they free from the influences of their family and social environments. As a result, they may lack certainty about the extent to which they can make choices for themselves because they are not yet adults. However, within their developmental process of identity formation, sexual identity, relationships with peers and individuation, they may believe that they can have more control over their lives than they did when they were younger. We therefore need to consider and respect the young person's developmental dilemma regarding the extent to which they can make their own choices and take responsibility for their own actions/lives. You will need to provide a reflective summary of the session in the last ten minutes. This will ensure that you have a shared understanding with the young person about the issues discussed that are both important to them and your agency. Follow-up meetings can be arranged and you should ensure that the young person has a copy of your contact details in case they want to convey additional information, clarify any issues or make any changes.

ACTIVITY 5.9

Bringing the 'one-off' intervention to a close or ending a series of contacts with a young person may be the last time the social worker sees the young person. It is important therefore that time is taken to end the session sensitively and positively. Take a few moments to think about how you would plan to end the session and schedule any future contact with the young person.

> COMMENT
>
> *If your session is a 'one-off' brief intervention you will need to manage the session in a timely way to allow for you to spend the final ten minutes summarising and clarifying the issues with the young person. If you or the young person feel unclear about the need to meet again, sharing each other's contact details and offering to make a follow-up telephone call provides for a positive ending and closure.*
>
> *If you are expecting to be meeting with the young person on a regular basis for a number of specific purposes, you will need to inform the young person at the outset that they will be seeing you for possibly six meetings. After each meeting you will then remind them and yourself of the remaining number of sessions and jointly agree the agendas for the following sessions. As the final two sessions are drawing near, the young person will need to be prepared for the last session. Social workers need to think about how to structure the final session so that the ending is positive and enables the young person to review their progress and development. You could award them with a certificate for their achievement or bravery, for example. Although the sessions may have been emotionally painful or frustrating for the young person they may have become significant to them as a time and place in which they have felt safe, respected and valued. They may also become attached to the social worker and it is not uncommon for young people to ask for a photograph as a memento. Social workers may also experience a strong connection to the young person and initially find it difficult and emotionally upsetting to draw sessions to a closure. Social workers often give the young person the drawing pad and pens used during sessions to signify the ending. Occasionally, young people (as do adults and younger children) disclose very painful and distressing feelings during their last session. You will need to arrange a follow-up session for the young person to convey that you are concerned about them, are not rejecting them and that you have not been harmed or deterred by anything the young person has disclosed.*

It is also very important to be aware of our own beliefs, values and attitudes and how these influence our practice and decision-making when working with young people. Seedhouse (2005) asserts that as we become aware of our own aims, plans and the means to achieve these, as well as becoming aware of those of other people and our professional body, our understanding and decision-making should become easier. For example, we may be more tolerant of a young person who is currently displaying anger management difficulties if we are aware that they have experienced longstanding physical abuse from their parent, than perhaps we would be if we did not have this insight and an understanding of the psychological effects of abuse.

Direct work with young adults aged 16 to 20 years

We began this chapter with the importance of being child-centred, reviewed direct work with children with disabilities, direct work with children from birth to ten and those from 11 to 15; this section will consider direct work with young adults aged 16 to 20 years. We will now return to exploring an important principle of working with children and young people, but become youth-centred in order to help young adults make a successful transition into the adult world. Before any work can begin with young adults we must explore some of the attitudes that exist towards them. One commentator has described direct work with young adults as being either the most frustrating or the most rewarding experience for a social worker, as young adults are often seen as being either a threat or a victim (Garret et al., 2007). It is as a threat rather than as a victim that many media commentators will portray young adults. In addition, many social workers will work mainly with young adults who are in trouble or who are perceived as a problem. This makes seeing young adults in a positive way difficult but not impossible.

One notable exception is the work of Camilla Batmanghelidjh (2008) of the Kids Company organisation, which strives to work directly with children and young adults to provide practical, emotional and educational support to vulnerable inner-city children and young people. The organisation sees young people positively and states: *We are constantly inspired by the courage and dignity expressed by vulnerable children in the face of overwhelming challenges, and in everything that we do the child is put first*.

The work should consist of helping the young adult to develop a growing sense of awareness of the adult world, find their own pathway, develop a commitment to establishing a secure and solid identity that can resist the worse excesses of peer pressure, as well as the ability to challenge any oppression that they may face.

A good introduction to working with young adults can be found in the work of Roger Smith (2008) who provides an up-to-date account of who young adults are and some of the challenges that they face, particularly the difficult transitions that they face. Also covered is the impact, experiences and expectations of social work on young adults.

This section will reflect on work that has been undertaken with young adults aged 16 to 20. There is no typical 16-, 17-, 18-, 19- or 20-year-old. All are different and all will be at different stages of development and maturity. Some will be easy to engage while others will be difficult to engage and will resist engagement. Working with young people involves being youth-centred, developing a relationship with young people and, observing young people and communicating with young people.

What constitutes a young adult is open to different interpretations. Indeed, there are many differing legal responsibilities that the social worker should be aware of. Carolyn Hamilton (2005) gives a comprehensive review of these, which includes the use of drugs, alcohol, cigarettes and solvents, and sex, including the age of consent, unlawful sexual relationships and gay and lesbian relationships.

Youth-centredness or young adult-centredness

Being positively youth-centred is like being child-centred: putting the needs and interests of young people first should be the principal consideration. Being youth-centred is about giving young people clear messages about what they can and cannot do. It is also about giving them time to explore, learn, grow and develop into adults who can function effectively in a world which presents them with many confusing, complex and contradictory messages. More importantly, it is about valuing them and building and maintaining a trusting relationship with them so that they can be fully engaged in making choices and decisions that will affect their lives. Being youth-centred is also about being aware of the power that adults have in comparison to young people (Wheal, 2004).

Berlins (2008) in a discussion about the age at which a young person should be able to vote in political elections argues that, *there is no particular birthday on which a person becomes mature enough, aware enough, sensible enough or knowledgeable enough to be trusted with the vote,* and makes the case for not reducing the age at which young people can vote from 18 to 16 years. This, however, leaves young people confused about their rights, devalues them as individuals and delays their transition from young person to adult. If we are to truly engage and work meaningfully with young people then they need to be sure about where they stand, where they can sit, where they can run and where and when they should walk slowly, and we need to see the young person's potential. Our attitudes towards them must be positive and we must have their interests and rights as our most important consideration; we must become young adult-centred rather than youth-centred.

Developing a relationship

Gender, race, religion, class, sexual orientation and disability all have an impact on the relationship that you develop with young people. The effects can range from subtle to profound. Young people are different; they can be full of fire and passion, feelings and emotions, hopes and aspirations, which if supported and encouraged can be a tremendous positive force. This fire and passion can warm the hearts and minds of those who work with them for years to come, but more importantly it can help them to stand up for what they believe in and enable them to achieve their full potential. The fire and passion that some young people have can make some of them feel powerful, but often their contact with the adult world has the opposite effect and renders them relatively powerless. Developing relationships involves breaking down the activity into discrete components, practising the individual parts, putting the whole together and then visualising the entire process and the end product.

The first point in developing any kind of relationship with a young adult is making contact. When making contact it is good practice to ask first if it is okay to talk to the young person rather than assume that you have the 'power' to do so. If the young person rejects this attempt at making contact it is good practice to try to focus on that feeling. The timing of this first contact is also important because if the young person is engaged in another activity then their focus is on other things. The other factor to take into consideration is the young person's environmental situation. Is it somewhere they feel safe, is it private or is it somewhere that is new and unfamiliar? Are there other young people who could give them support and reassure them that it is safe to make contact?

The next step is to say hello. This hello should be confident, friendly and assured. How many ways can you greet someone? Think about the different ways that people in your life greet you and indeed you greet them. The extremes are characterised by closeness and warmth at one end and by coldness and distance at the other end. Think about the greeting from a parent, a sister, a brother, an uncle, an aunt, a cousin, a school acquaintance, a work colleague, and an authoritarian boss. What are the subtle differences? Some will encourage communication and others will positively discourage it.

The exchange of first names is part of the start of the relationship as it makes a connection between the young person and the interviewer. This connection will be firmly established if the name is remembered or it will be lost if it is not. We should think some more about this early connection. How is the name said – with confidence, with pride, with passion, or quietly and softly? Is eye contact made or not? If it is made, how long is it held? Think about how long eye contact is held with a stranger, a partner, a work colleague. What assumption would you make about the nature of the relationship if you could accurately measure the visual interaction? Is it an indication of trust or mistrust? What other non-verbal cues would you look for?

You have now made a connection with the young person and hopefully the young person will reciprocate. This is a good opportunity to continue to engage informally with the young person. This involves developing not only your observational skills but also your thinking and feeling skills. It is important to be able to pick up if there is an 'atmosphere' and to be able to identify what it is – friendly, calm, accepting, rejecting or indifferent. Use this to extend the conversation so that you can test the feeling temperature of the interaction, before you can begin to discuss the reason for your involvement.

Again, what you say and how you say it is important if you are to begin to develop a helpful and supportive relationship with a young person. It is important to rehearse what to say, not verbatim but the broad areas that you want to discuss. It is important to begin with a question that gives the young person a choice as this gives them power to choose and helps them to feel valued and appreciated. If contact is positive the next step is to again seek permission to discuss the reason for talking with the young person and to state clearly the reason for your involvement and who will have access to the information that is discussed.

This careful approach to beginning the relationship should be considered whether the contact you have with the young person is fleeting or more sustained as it lays the foundations for a way of working which helps the young adults to engage positively in the process of developing a helpful and supportive relationship.

If the start of the process is important then so is the end. You should be working towards the end when you begin. Planning in social work is important and is one of the National Occupational Standards. What kind of plan will you have? Firm or loose? Written or unwritten? Will you have any alternatives, A or B? Or is the interaction too focused on a single objective? Should there be multiple objectives? Should there be short-, medium- and long-term goals and objectives? Consideration will need to be given to the plan before the start of the work and to reviewing it during the course of the interaction.

Observing young adults

Finding out as much as possible about the young person is important and time should be spent reading records and files, but also on developing your skills and knowledge. How much time should be spent on the former? This will depend on what how much information you need to devise a plan of action to work with the young adult. How much time you need to spend on the latter will also depend on how competent you wish to become. As a general rule your competence will come with practice but time, patience and determination is required to become skilled and proficient. The skills that should be developed include observing the young adult's size, reading the face, recognising and identifying the nature of the young adult's verbal interaction, the visual interaction and body language.

Is the young adult small for their age, large for their age or average for their age? Size might be an indicator of whether a person is likely to be bullied or be a bully. Size might also not be an indicator of whether a person is likely to be in need of protection as the six foot two 16 year old is just as likely to be in need of protection as the 16 year old who is five foot two. The importance that a young person attaches to the clothes they wear can give you an indication of their individuality and their ability to resist and/or conform to peer pressure. Trendy and fashionable might tell you that they are prepared to conform to fashion and want to be accepted. Unkempt might tell you something about their current situation, but this could be misleading as it may not accurately reflect their general demeanour. What else would you look for? What about cleanliness and correct size of clothes?

Their face should be studied. Is it clear and unmarked or is it bruised? Is it a young-looking face or a mature-looking face? This may give you an idea about how others will interact with the young adult, and whether this will be positive or negative interaction.

Verbal interaction includes the tone of the conversation. Is the verbal tone of the conversation warm, friendly and fully engaged, lukewarm and partially engaged, or cold, unconnected and unengaged? A fully engaged person will not be distracted easily and will reciprocate the tone or timbre of the conversation. If it is friendly then this will be reciprocated. A partially engaged person will be easily influenced by and distracted some of the time by objects or things, and the tone or timbre of the conversation will fluctuate between full reciprocation and partial reciprocation. An unengaged person will avoid any form of reciprocation. In this situation, you should focus on what is being done to distract you and ask the young adult if they want the interaction to end.

Similarly, some observations should be made about the nature of the verbal interaction. Is the verbal interaction confident and sure or is it hesitant and unsure? If it is the former this person should be able to make their wishes and feelings known. If it is not then the person may need some support to voice his or her wishes and feelings. Is the person fully engaged, partially engaged or unengaged in the verbal interaction? Again, there will be some degree of reciprocity to a greater or lesser extent, questions will be answered in sentences or monosyllabically respectively. This may give you some clues as to the person's readiness to engage, their ability to focus and their concentration span.

The visual interaction is more difficult to observe unless it is excessive, avoidant or absent. Observing the extent of the visual interaction is important as it informs your impressions about the way the person is feeling. This could be scared, nervous, indifferent, uninterested or confident. One way of focusing on the visual interaction is to take note of the colour of the person's eyes as this focuses the attention on that part of the face.

A strengths and weakness analysis should be done of the activities that young adults like to engage in. Are they more group orientated or are they more inclined towards solitary activities?

Communicating with young people

This is a two-way process. It will be either a verbal interaction or an activity-based interaction that involves some verbal interaction. It is important to communicate clearly the purpose of the interaction and the limits of the interaction. The limits should be established early in the interaction, but may be affected by the person's ability to process the information. The skills and techniques in working with children, young people and young adults are similar as you will need to pay attention to some of the micro-skills that are involved in developing relationships with others. The differences are in the ability to engage and the type of activities that you will use with the various age groups. We have already described ways of communicating with children and young people who have communication difficulties; there are also alternatives to verbal communication that may be used with young adults, which should be considered. For some young adults the alternative could involve drama groups, cooking, drawing and painting, model making and involvement in activities such as motor vehicle studies.

Working with 16 to 20 years olds is challenging and should challenge your attitudes and beliefs about young adults. It can be exciting to work with young adults provided you are prepared and respect their feelings and views.

CHAPTER SUMMARY

This chapter has sought to give you insight into some of the methods and skills you will use when you are working with children, young people and young adults at their different, and differing, stages of development. We have highlighted the areas that are common to all these situations as well as those that are not.

We have raised some of the issues that are involved in direct work, including the safeguarding and rights tensions, which are explored further elsewhere in the book.

We hope this chapter has helped you to further your understanding of direct work and of children and young people's rights to be 'heard' and included, even though this can, at times, be challenging for practitioners.

FURTHER READING

There is a variety of very useful and accessible materials for social workers to utilise in their interventions with young people. For example:

Bellhouse, B, Fuller, A, Johnson, G and Taylor, N (2005) *Managing the Difficult Emotions*. London: Paul Chapman Publishing.

This is a humorous, punchy book with a CD-Rom packed with facilitator notes and worksheets, activities and quizzes, which enable the young person to consider their feelings.

Stallard, P (2002) *Think Good – Feel Good*. Chichester: John Wiley & Sons Ltd.

This book includes free online resources offering a range of flexible and highly appealing exercises and worksheets to address a range of psychological problems.

Chapter 6

Social work with children with disabilities and their families

Jackie Hughes

ACHIEVING A SOCIAL WORK DEGREE

This chapter will help you to develop the following capabilities from the **Professional Capabilities Framework**:
- **Values and ethics**
Apply social work ethical principles to guide professional practice.
- **Diversity**
Recognise diversity and apply anti-discriminatory and anti-oppressive principles in practice.
- **Justice**
Advance human rights and promote social justice and economic well-being.
- **Knowledge**
Apply knowledge of social sciences, law and social work practice theory.

It will also introduce you to the following academic standards as set out in the 2008 social work subject benchmark statement:
5.1.1 Social work services and service users
5.1.4 Social work theory
5.1.5 The nature of social work practice
5.5 Problem solving skills
    5.5.2 Gathering information
    5.5.3 Analysis and synthesis
    5.5.4 Intervention and evaluation
7.3 Knowledge and understanding

Introduction

In this chapter you will consider some of the issues facing disabled children and their families so that you can develop your understanding, knowledge and skills to enable you to work effectively to support disabled children within their communities (Children Act 1989, section 17).

Different models of disability will be explored and an understanding of the social model will be used to help you promote inclusive social work practice. The views of disabled children and their families, and disabled adults, will be shown to be central to understanding some of the barriers to inclusion that disabled children face in their daily lives. The chapter will be based on the Children Act 1989 *Guidance and Regulations, Volume 6: Children with Disabilities; Children Act 2004, Aiming High for Disabled Children: Better Support for Families* (DfES, 2007b) and the *National Service Framework Standard 8 for disabled children and young people and those with complex health needs.*

The first part of the chapter will focus on the different models of disability and an explanation of the social model of disability before considering some of the definitions of disability and terminology which you will encounter. The views of disabled people about the use of language and acceptable terminology will be considered.

There will be an opportunity for you to think about some of the issues associated with pre-natal testing and diagnosis of disability. Case examples will help you apply your knowledge to developing skills in communication with disabled children and their families.

Assessment will be considered in relation to the *Together from the Start* guidance (DoH, 2003, www.rightfromthestart.org.uk and www.espp.org.uk) and *Early Support Professional Guidance* (DoH/DfES, 2004, as previous websites). Multi-agency working and the importance for families of effective key working services will be explored (CCNUK Key working standards). Holistic assessments that include housing, as well as education and supports such as short-breaks, will be considered (DoH, 2000b). There will be an exploration of the vulnerability of disabled children (who are more likely to be abused than non-disabled children) and how to work to safeguard disabled children from abuse. Transition to adulthood is an important time for disabled young people and their families. The focus will be on the need to plan with disabled teenagers, their families and communities to ensure that our disabled young people develop valued opportunities as adults in education, employment, housing, leisure and relationships (*Aiming High for Disabled Children: Better Support for Families*, 2007b).

Models of disability

There are different models explaining disability which have changed over time and in different societies as attitudes to disability have changed. Models of disability are influenced by wider views in society, so the importance of religious explanations, which were once central, have declined in our increasingly secular society. The two main models of disability are the individual model (medical model) and the social model. When working with disabled children, it is important that a child is seen as a child first rather than a disabled child, whatever your preferred model of disability. This does not, however, mean that disabled children do not have particular health needs associated with their impairment that must also be met.

> *Ensuring equality of opportunity does not mean that all children are treated the same. It does mean understanding and working sensitively and knowledgeably with diversity.*

> *(DoH/DfEE/Home Office, 2000, paragraph 1.4)*

It is important to listen to the views of disabled children about what is important to them. Young people say they want to:

- be listened to when decisions are made about their lives;

- have friends of the same age or who share similar experiences;

- do the same things as other children and young people of their age – shopping, going to the cinema, clubbing, going to youth and sport clubs, playing football, etc.;

- have the opportunity to be involved in out-of-school activities;

- be safe from harassment and bullying;

- have control of spending money, and have enough money to enjoy life;

- live in a society where they don't face prejudice.

(NSF for Children Standard 8, 2004, page 8)

Medical model

The medical model is part of the individual model of disability, which locates the disability within the person, concentrating on the impairment. This view of disability tends to portray the disabled person as tragic or someone who is superhuman and has overcome obstacles (Oliver, 1983). The focus is on the impairment and prevention and cure, or rehabilitation and care. It may lead to provision of adaptations to enable the disabled person to 'fit in' to society with individual impairments seen as the cause of people's difficulties in functioning, rather than addressing the barriers to inclusion that disabled people face.

ACTIVITY **6.1**

Can you think of examples of the medical model and how the focus on the individual and 'cure or care' might have influenced services for disabled people?

COMMENT

You may have thought about disabled children who have been provided with artificial limbs to make them seem non-disabled, or children who are wheelchair users spending long periods of time in physiotherapy during school time at the expense of their academic work. You may want to keep some notes to help you think about different ways in which disabled children are seen within the medical model. It is also important to recognise that disabled children may not have equality of access to medical care such as a community dentist or primary health care (Russell, 1995). Better Care, Better Lives was published by the government (DoH, 2008) as part of an attempt to improve palliative care for children with life limiting conditions.

Social model

The social model was developed by disabled people who identified the barriers to their inclusion in a society which discriminates against disabled people (Oliver, 1990, 2011; Swain et al., 1993). Disabled children are marginalised and segregated from society in leisure, education and opportunities that non-disabled children take for granted (Marchant, 2001b). Historically, disabled children have been educated in segregated 'special' schools and separated from their peers in their communities.

ACTIVITY **6.2**

Think about a disabled child you know. In what ways is the life of this child different from that of non-disabled children?

COMMENT

You may find that you had difficulty thinking of a disabled child because of the way that disabled children are marginalised in our society. Did you identify barriers to inclusion in terms of accessible play facilities, separate education or resourced provision/units in mainstream schools and accessible transport facilities?

You may also have identified the way that attitudes to disability may cause barriers to inclusion. Disabled children may not be invited to play at friends' houses or participate in the activities that non-disabled children take for granted.

Social-psychological model

The social-psychological model of disability highlights the importance of the experience of the disabled person, emphasises that disabled people should be listened to and recognises the way that some experiences of oppression may be internalised in ways that are not conscious (Marks, 1999a). Research with disabled children has identified that they see disability as only one aspect of their identity and in some situations other aspects may be more important, e.g. gender or ethnicity (Watson et al., 1999).

Definitions of disability

Definitions of disability have changed over time according to different views of disability, and this is reflected in the language in different pieces of legislation. You will find that the definitions you encounter will vary; some may seem out-dated, particularly in older legislation such as the Chronically Sick and Disabled Person's Act. It is important to be aware of the power of language and the views of disabled people themselves (Barnes, 1992). Some people prefer the term *disabled person* because it identifies the way that people are disabled by society. Other people prefer *person with disabilities*, as it concentrates on the person first. People with learning disabilities often say they prefer the term learning difficulties (People First, London and Thames) although this has sometimes led to confusion with the term *specific learning difficulties,* which is used in the Education Act 1981 to refer to dyslexia. The government uses the term *learning disabilities* in the *Valuing People* White Paper

(2001d). People First say *Label Jars not People*. I shall use the terms *disabled children* or *children with disabilities* within this chapter. We need to recognise the importance of language and the fact that this is developing. We need to listen to, and take account of, the views of disabled people themselves. It is important that we see disabled children as children first and develop services to ensure that they have the same rights as non-disabled children.

ACTIVITY 6.3

Think about some of the ways that disabled children are portrayed in the media. How might that influence your perception of the abilities of disabled children?

NB: You might want to collect magazine and newspaper articles and make notes about television or radio programmes you have watched or listened to.

COMMENT

Did you find that disabled children are rarely portrayed in the media? If they are it may be a token disabled child, rather than a central character in the programme. Were disabled children portrayed positively, or did you find that the disabled children were seen as evoking pity? You may also want to look at children's books and consider how disabled children feature in books or whether they are largely absent. How might this affect the self-esteem of disabled children?

Diagnosis

Research summary

Estimates of the numbers of disabled children in the UK vary, and this is partly due to different definitions of disability. The Equality Act 2010 defines a disabled person as having: *A physical or mental impairment which has a substantial and long-term adverse effect on his or her ability to carry out normal day-to-day activities*. Using this definition, the Prime Minister's Strategy Unit (2005) estimates that there are approximately 770,000 disabled children under 16 in Great Britain, which is 7 per cent of the child population. What is clear is that there is an increased incidence of children with severe and complex disabilities as well as increasing numbers of children who are being diagnosed with autistic spectrum disorders. The reasons for this are due to a number of factors including improved medical care leading to the survival of more pre-term babies and children who have experienced severe trauma and illness. In addition, children with complex disabilities are surviving and living longer with improved medical treatment and the availability of assistive technology. The NSF for Children, Young People and Maternity Services recognises that the majority of disabled children live with their families. Marchant (2001b) points out that everyone working with children should be working with disabled children sometimes, as 1.5 to 5 per cent of children are disabled (DoH, 1998a; OPCS, 1986).There are more disabled children in social class V than in social class I, and there is a link between disability and poverty in household income. The cost of bringing up a child with a disability is approximately three times the cost for a non-disabled child (Baldwin, 1985; Dobson and Middleton, 1998).

Mothers of disabled children are less likely to be in employment, and only one in 13 disabled children receives regular support from their local authority (Contact a Family, 2011).

Right from the Start is guidance based on a template developed by Scope working with parents of disabled children, disabled people and voluntary organisations. It is a framework for professionals to develop good practice in communicating with parents about diagnosis of disability. The Good Practice Framework covers all areas to do with the communication of the diagnosis, including who should be present and the next steps in terms of practical help and information (www.rightfromthestart.org.uk).

ACTIVITY 6.4

You are asked to be present at a discussion with parents, which will inform them of the diagnosis of disability for their child. What things might be important to you, as a professional, to consider in preparing for this meeting?

COMMENT

You might have recognised that many children do not receive a diagnosis as a young baby in hospital, but parents may become concerned that their child is not developing in the way that they had expected. Parents say that what is important to them is that their child is seen as important. 'Valuing the child' can be done by: showing respect for the child, using the child's name, talking positively about the child and avoiding making predictions, keeping the baby or the child with the parents wherever possible to share the diagnosis. Respect for parents and families is also important and developing partnership with parents at this stage is crucial for positive relationships to develop with professionals who may continue to be involved in their child's life.

Perl Kingsley describes the experience of diagnosis of disability as similar to a journey: where parents have planned a trip to Italy but find themselves touching down in Holland instead. Their plans had included visits to the Coliseum, Michelangelo's David and the gondolas in Venice. It was not what they had planned when they set out on their journey, but as they look around they find that Holland has windmills and tulips and Rembrandts, too. The trip is different to what they had expected but just as beautiful (printed in DIAL – Disablement Information and Advice Line; www.dialuk.info). Randall and Parker (1999) also deal with this complex and emotionally sensitive search for a diagnosis.

Assessment

> *Children and young people who are disabled or who have complex health needs receive co-ordinated, high-quality child and family-centred services which are based on assessed needs, which promote social inclusion and, where possible, which enable them and their families to live ordinary lives.*
>
> *(NSF for Children Standard 8, 2004, page 5)*

The Early Support Programme (www.espp.org.uk) is putting into practice the principles outlined in the government guidance document Together From the Start, which was published in May 2003. Right from the Start (see page 112) identified the way that families with disabled children may experience numerous assessments by different professionals, adding to the stress that families may already be experiencing. The *Early Support Programme Professional Guidance* (2004, page 44) states that:

> *Effective, joint multi-agency assessment in the early years means:*
>
> * *Co-ordinating action, particularly where different aspects of a child's situation need to be assessed by different people.*
> * *Responding to a family's need to get reliable information as quickly as possible and learn from more than one perspective at a time.*
> * *Ensuring that initial assessment leads to action and prompt provision of information and practical help.*

Disabled children have a right to assessments as 'children in need' under section 17 of the Children Act 1989. Social workers need, at present, to follow the guidance in the *Framework for the Assessment of Children in Need and their Families*, 2000. This includes the child's development, the family's needs and capacities, as well as environmental factors such as housing. The initial and/or core assessments can be used as the basis for the development of the Family Service Plan, agreed by the family and agencies working with them (see Chapter 3).

In addition, the assessment should take into account the needs of parents and carers: *The assessment of a disabled child must address the needs of the parent carers. Recognising the needs of parent carers is a core component in agreeing services which will promote the welfare of the disabled child* (Assessing Children in Need and their Families: Practice Guidance, Section 3.6, DoH, 2000).

CASE STUDY

Will Adams is a two-year-old child who was born with a rare syndrome resulting in complex disabilities including dual sensory loss (hearing and visual impairment) and congenital heart problems, which meant that Will had several operations at a very young age. His mother gave up employment to become a full-time carer to Will. Her health visitor has asked social services to complete an assessment for Will and his family as she is concerned that Will's mother is physically and emotionally exhausted.

(By permission of Kirklees Parent Carer Forum)

ACTIVITY 6.5

As the social worker responsible for undertaking the assessment for Will and his family, in your opinion:

* *What are the issues?*
* *Who else might you involve in the assessment?*
* *What plans might you consider?*

You will have recognised that Will requires a holistic assessment that takes into account a range of issues which include his health needs, housing and leisure activities, as well as education and social services' support. You may also have thought about the different professionals who may be involved with Will and his family. These could include the GP, health visitor, paediatrician, speech therapist, portage worker, physiotherapist and occupational therapist. Will may attend tertiary health care centres because of the complexity of his health needs, resulting in numerous appointments and assessments. You may have suggested that Will and his family should have a key worker to facilitate the maze of services involved with them. You may also wish to undertake a carer's assessment for Will's mum under the Carers and Disabled Children Act 2001 and Carers (Equal Opportunities) Act 2004, to identify what support she may need in her caring role.

Communication

Nothing about us without us.

This quotation from the disabled people's movement is an important reminder of the need to ensure participation for disabled children. Disabled people have argued for inclusion, not only in society as a whole, but in fundamental decisions about their lives. Non-disabled children have frequently found themselves excluded from important decisions in their lives, but disabled children may still be routinely excluded from important meetings such as education or social services reviews. Disabled children have given examples of the ways in which they have been excluded by not having their views sought (Marchant, 2001b; Morris, 1998b). Social workers and other professionals working with disabled children need to ensure that they routinely involve children in the assessment and decision-making process.

ACTIVITY **6.6**

You have been asked to work with a child who has a learning disability or a communication impairment. What would you do to find out their wishes?

COMMENT

Good communication skills are important in communicating with all children, not just disabled children. You may have thought about being child-centred and taking the child's age and interests into account. Children may be more relaxed in environments that are familiar to them. Good listening skills, being prepared to take extra time or use play skills are all important. Do not be frightened to ask a child to repeat themselves if you have not understood. If a child does not use verbal communication you will need to ensure that you observe carefully their non-verbal communication, which may include gestures, facial expression, body language or behaviour. Use a carer, friend or someone who knows the child well to help if you are uncertain of their communication. Some children may use alternative methods of communication, which may include BSL (British Sign Language) or Makaton (a form of sign language used to augment verbal communication) or symbols. All children can communicate; we need to be aware of the barriers which affect their participation.

Key working

My child isn't split into three pieces.

> (National Service Framework Standard 8: Key worker standards CCNUK)

Parents of disabled children have identified the benefits for them of having a key worker to assist them to deal with the complex network of services with which they are involved. As children grow and develop their needs change and so the process of assessments and reviews may be ongoing, involving education and housing as well as health and social services. Parents who have had the benefit of a key worker report satisfaction with the support that they received through having a named worker who was able to help them co-ordinate services.

> *A key worker or lead professional is both a source of support for the families of disabled children and a link by which other services are accessed and used effectively. They have responsibility for working together with the family and with professionals from their own and other services and for ensuring delivery of the plan for the child and family. Workers performing this role may come from a number of different agencies, depending on the particular needs of the child.*
>
> (*Together from the Start, page 87 (www.espp.org.uk)*)

Aiming High for Disabled Children (2007b) recognised the importance of joined up services for disabled children and their families. It included a pilot programme of Individual Budgets, to enable more choice and flexible packages of support.

Safeguarding disabled children

Children with disabilities have the same rights to protection as all children, but research indicates that disabled children are more vulnerable to abuse than non-disabled children (Westcott and Cross, 1996), and yet they are less likely to be represented in the child protection system (Morris,1995, 1998a, 1999a; The Safeguarding Disabled Children Practice Guidance DCSF, 2009).

ACTIVITY *6.7*

Consider some of the reasons why disabled children may be particularly vulnerable to abuse.

COMMENT

You may have identified the way that disabled children are marginalised in society and tend to be more isolated from their communities. You may also have considered some of the ways in which services are provided to disabled children and their families, leading to disabled children being cared for by more adults than non-disabled children in residential or 'special' schools away from their families. You may also have thought about the need for personal assistance, which may increase the vulnerability of disabled children to abuse.

RESEARCH SUMMARY

There are important issues to consider in relation to the vulnerability of disabled children to abuse:

- *social attitudes towards disability;*

- *special treatment of disabled children;*

- *denial of sexuality for disabled people.*

(Marchant, 2001b)

Social attitudes toward disability have led to the attitude that as disabled children are 'tragic' nobody would abuse a disabled child. Paradoxically, the alternative stereotype that a disabled child is not 'perfect' has led to assumptions that abuse may matter less (Westcott and Cross, 1996). The way that disabled children are marginalised in society may increase their vulnerability to abuse: they may be more isolated, be more dependent and have less control over their lives (Marchant, 2001b). The way that support services are provided to disabled children and their families may also increase their vulnerability, with more adults caring for them than non-disabled children and periods of time spent in respite or residential settings, without the usual safeguards for children living away from their families (Morris, 1995). Research has indicated that disabled children in residential education or respite placements may not be treated as looked-after children and not be afforded the safeguards of the Children Act (Russell, 1995; Platts et al., 1996). The denial of the sexuality of disabled people may lead to a lack of sex education for disabled children, increasing their vulnerability (Marchant, 2001b). Social workers need to be alert to the increased risk and reduced access to protection when working with disabled children (The Safeguarding Disabled Children Practice Guidance, DCSF, 2009).

Leisure

Disabled children may not experience the same leisure opportunities as non-disabled children because of barriers to participation. Parents from the Kirklees Parent Carer Forum (workshop with social work students, University of Leeds, 2005) explained that it is difficult for their children to participate in activities that many non-disabled children take for granted. Playgrounds may not be accessible for children with mobility impairments, a child with a hearing impairment may need a communicator, or lack of accessible transport may mean that a parent has to take a child to leisure activities. Some parents explain that their children are simply not invited to friends' houses to play, because of distance from friends' homes when children attend special schools, inaccessible houses, or lack of personal assistants to enable them to participate (Marchant, 2001b).

The Disability Discrimination Act 1995 included leisure activities in its remit. These examples from parents highlight the importance of inclusion for disabled children and emphasise that leisure opportunities don't just happen for disabled children in the way that they do for non-disabled children; disabled children may be excluded from society by acts of omission as well as commission. This also applies to services, which may act as if disabled children are invisible.

Short breaks

Social services have a duty to publicise services for disabled children, but many families describe accessing services as a 'battle' to get the supports that they need for their disabled children. Christine Lenehan, Director of the Council for Disabled Children (2004), identifies the way that parents may become *warring parents* as they struggle to access services. The challenge is to develop services that value the child and work in partnership with parents as children's needs change. Of particular concern is the need to ensure that services are accessible to families where there is more than one child with a disability and to families from ethnic communities (Shah, 1995).

Traditionally, services have offered respite to families with disabled children. The use of the term 'respite' suggests that disabled children are a burden and the service is for families, rather than the child. A study of the needs of children with learning disabilities and complex health needs (Platts et al., 1996) found that for parents to benefit from a short break they needed to know that their children were happy. Parents valued the opportunity to have a flexible service which included babysitting, day time activities, care in the family home or overnight stays. Families from ethnic communities appreciated flexible short breaks with families who knew their children well. One Asian parent commented that she would be unable to go out in the holidays with her children without the short-break carer as she had two children who used wheelchairs. She particularly valued this support within the home, which enabled them to do the things that many families take for granted. Short breaks are valued by families but should also be child-centred for the child, parents and other siblings to benefit. One parent at a parent workshop (Russell, 1995) commented that her child was no longer a shadow in someone else's eyes when her child was able to have short breaks with another family.

The importance of short breaks for families and for their children was recognised in the disabled children's review by the government. *Aiming High for Disabled Children: Better Support for Families* included a specific grant of £280 million for short breaks for the period 2008–2011. From April 2011, Regulations on Breaks for Carers of Disabled Children have required local authorities to provide a range of services for disabled children. This is to include services inside and outside the home, including evenings, weekends and holidays.

Housing

Housing is an area that needs to be included in assessments. Oldman and Beresford (1998) identified the importance of housing for disabled children and their families. Nine out of ten families who were interviewed for their research reported at least one housing need, with many reporting multiple needs. Many families described the difficulties of space for their children. This was not just space for children with mobility difficulties to move around in their wheelchairs, but included space for equipment, adequate space for children with challenging behaviours or sleep problems and for their brothers and sisters.

Disabled children want to be able to use the kitchen and communal areas of the family home as well as accessing the garden. Many families report lack of adaptations and delays in the provision of equipment exacerbating the strains of caring for disabled children. Although there is some financial support available, the limitations of the Disabled Facilities Grant may mean that families are unable to afford the necessary adaptations, particularly for children with profound and complex needs (Beresford, 2006).

Education

Historically, disabled children have been educated in segregated special schools. Under the 1944 Education Act, children with learning disabilities were described as ineducable. It was not until 1971 that children with learning disabilities became entitled to education, but this was in special schools according to the diagnosis of disability. The 1978 Warnock Committee advocated the integration of disabled children into mainstream schools and integration was promoted under the 1981 Education Act. The proviso was that this should be in accordance with the efficient use of resources and as long as it did not affect the education of other pupils. However, one of the benefits of inclusive education is the opportunity for non-disabled children to learn from their disabled peers. The 1996 Education Act continued the policy of integration but many disabled children continue to be educated in special schools rather than included in their local community schools. Not all disabled children will have special educational needs, but for many children they will have a formal assessment process where the LEA is considering a Statement of Special Educational Needs (Special Educational Needs and Disability Act 2001). Social workers will be expected to contribute reports as part of the assessment process. Some children may be educated at residential special schools and these children should be regarded as looked-after children with the protection and safeguards of the Children Act 1989. The supervision provided by social services varies between local authorities, and Morris (1998a) found that many children were not consulted. The White Paper, *Care Matters: Time for Change* (2007), recognised the importance of consultation and the involvement of disabled young people, and discussed the looked-after children status for disabled children.

The SEN and Disabilities Green Paper 2011 sets out a vision for special educational needs and disability, including a new single assessment process and education, health and care plan by 2014, and the option of a personal budget. A real choice is to be offered of mainstream or special school.

Transition

Children with a Statement of Special Educational Needs should have an Annual Review. The Review following a disabled child's 14th birthday is known as the Transition Review as plans should start being formulated with them for their future. At each subsequent review, the Transition Plan should be considered and amendments made if necessary. This should be the basis for future planning and should include areas such as social services support, housing and education. *The Valuing People* White Paper (2001) for people with learning disabilities prioritised transition as a time for Person Centred Planning. Person

Centred Plans focus on the person who is being planned with, their friends and family, identifying core components for Essential Life Style Plans and PATHS (Planning Alternative Tomorrows with Hope) (O'Brien, 2002). Morris (1999a) describes the experiences of disabled young people at transition as *hurtling into the void*. Her research recommends good practice guidelines for services working with disabled young people to promote positive futures. The difficulties faced by disabled young people at transition were recognised in the government review of services for disabled children, and *Aiming High for Disabled Children* included £19 million for a Transition Support Programme modelled on the Early Support Programme.

If we are really going to develop an inclusive society which values people, then creative assessments, working in partnership with disabled young people and their families, must work towards achieving 'alternative tomorrows' today.

FURTHER READING

Marchant, R (2001) Working with disabled children, in Foley et al. (eds) (2001) *Children in Society: Contemporary Theory, Policy and Practice*. Basingstoke: Palgrave.

This chapter gives a useful overview of a range of issues for social workers working with children with disabilities.

Morris, J (1999) *Hurtling into the Void: Transition to Adulthood for Young People with Complex Health and Support Needs*. Brighton: JRF Pavilion.

This book will be helpful to all students working with disabled young people at transition.

Shah, R (1995) *The Silent Minority. Children with Disabilities in Asian Families*. Derby: National Children's Bureau.

This book helps social work students recognise the oppression faced by disabled children and their families from black and minority ethnic families.

Westcott, H and Cross, M (1996) *This Far and No Further: Towards Ending the Abuse of Disabled Children*. Birmingham: Venture Press.

This is particularly relevant for all professionals working with disabled children to enable them to work towards safeguarding children from abuse.

Useful contacts

Contact a Family, 170 Tottenham Court Road, London W1 0HA

Council for Disabled Children, 8 Wakley St, London EC1V 7QE

Resources and professional guidance

Department of Health (2000) Assessing Children in Need and their Families: Practice Guidance. Chapter 3: Assessing the needs of disabled children and their families.

Department for Education and Employment (2001) SEN Code of Practice.

Contact a Family (2004) *Working with families affected by a disability or health condition from pregnancy to pre-school*.

Contact a Family (2004) *Parent participation: improving services for disabled children*. Parents' guide.

Contact a Family and Council for Disabled Children (2004) Professionals' Guide.

www.ccnuk.org.uk

www.c4eo.org.uk/themes/disabledchildren/positiveactivities/

www.contactafamily.co.uk

www.councilfordisabledchildren.org.uk

www.education.gov.uk

www.doh.gov.uk

www.espp.org.uk

www.jrf.co.uk

www.rightfromthestart.org.uk

www.sharedcarenetwork.org.uk

Chapter 7

Substitute care for children

Maureen O' Loughlin and Steve O' Loughlin

This chapter will help you to develop the following capabilities from the **Professional Capabilities Framework:**
- **Professionalism**
Identify and behave as a professional social worker committed to professional development.
- **Knowledge**
Apply knowledge of social sciences, law and social work practice theory.
- **Judgement**
Use judgement and authority to intervene with individuals, families and communities to promote independence, provide support and prevent harm, neglect and abuse.
- **Critical reflection and analysis**
Apply critical reflection and analysis to inform and provide a rationale for professional decision-making.

It will also introduce you to the following academic standards as set out in the 2008 social work subject benchmark statement:
5.1.1. Social work services and service users
5.5 Problem solving skills
    5.5.2 Gathering information
    5.5.3 Analysis and synthesis
    5.5.4 Intervention and evaluation

Introduction

Substitute care is provided by local authorities, voluntary, private and independent agencies. These agencies provide accommodation for children in a number of different ways. This chapter will introduce and discuss the different types of substitute care which are available to children including:

- fostering;

- adoption;

- residential care.

Children are cared for in the Looked-After Children System (LAC) in different ways and for different reasons, which include:

- short breaks: children being cared for as part of a package of support, for example, a child with disabilities (Children Act 1989, sections 17 and 20);

- accommodation: children being cared for as part of an agreement with parents or those with parental responsibility, or if a child has been abandoned or there is no one who has parental responsibility for them (Children Act 1989, section 20);

- care and related orders: children who are the subject of care or interim care orders; placement for adoption orders or emergency protection or police protection orders;

- offending: children and young people on remand or subject to some orders made by the youth court.

An analysis of children looked after at 31 March between the years 2007 and 2011 is shown in Table 7.1. The table shows the ages, gender, category of need and ethnic origin of children and young people for these years. The statistics show that there are more males than females and that there are peaks in ages (10 to 15), which is worth reflecting on in terms of the life course and your knowledge of child development. It is also worth noting the number of children in the 1 to 4 category.

What factors do you think might cause these peaks?

As you will see, Table 7.1 also gives information about ethnicity and category of need including disability. The percentage of children and young people who started to be looked after in the year ending 31 March 2011 who were White British has increased since 2007, there have been falls in the numbers of Black and Black British looked-after children, slight increases in children of mixed heritage but a greater proportion of children from Asian and British Asian backgrounds than previously.

Table 7.1 Children looked after at 31 March by gender, age at 31 March, category of need, and ethnic origin[1,2,3]
Years ending 31 March 2007 to 2011
Coverage: England

						rates per 10,000 children under 18 years				
	2007	2008	2009	2010	2011					
All children looked after at 31 March	59,970	59,360	60,890	64,410	65,520					
Rates per 10,000 children under 18 years[4]	55	54	55	58	59					

	numbers					percentages				
	2007	2008	2009	2010	2011	2007	2008	2009	2010	2011
All children looked after at 31 March	59,970	59,360	60,890	64,410	65,520	100	100	100	100	100
Gender	59,970	59,360	60,890	64,410	65,520	100	100	100	100	100
Male	33,390	33,380	34,580	36,150	36,470	56	56	57	56	56
Female	26,580	25,990	26,310	28,260	29,050	44	44	43	44	44

Table 7.1 Continued

	numbers					percentages				
	2007	2008	2009	2010	2011	2007	2008	2009	2010	2011
Age at 31 March (year)	59,970	59,360	60,890	64,410	65,520	*100*	*100*	*100*	*100*	*100*
Under 1	2,990	2,900	3,260	3,720	3,660	*5*	*5*	*5*	*6*	*6*
1 to 4	8,740	9,020	9,440	10,840	12,020	*15*	*15*	*16*	*17*	*18*
5 to 9	10,930	10,380	10,470	11,200	11,830	*18*	*17*	*17*	*17*	*18*
10 to 15	25,500	24,900	24,890	24,930	24,160	*43*	*42*	*41*	*39*	*37*
16 and over	11,810	12,160	12,820	13,710	13,860	*20*	*20*	*21*	*21*	*21*
Category of need[5]	59,970	59,360	60.890	64,410	65,520	*100*	*100*	*100*	*100*	*100*
Abuse or neglect	37,270	36,750	37,160	39,290	40,410	*62*	*62*	*61*	*61*	*62*
Child's disability	2,330	2,290	2,210	2,180	2,150	*4*	*4*	*4*	*3*	*3*
Parent's illness or disability	2,970	2,750	2,700	2,820	2,720	*5*	*5*	*4*	*4*	*4*
Family in acute stress	4,730	4,910	5,320	5,800	5,880	*8*	*8*	*9*	*9*	*9*
Family dysfunction	6,320	6,330	6,840	8,020	8,930	*11*	*11*	*11*	*12*	*14*
Socially unacceptable behaviour	1,270	1,170	1,220	1,290	1,230	*2*	*2*	*2*	*2*	*2*
Low income	110	130	140	170	160	*–*	*–*	*–*	*–*	*–*
Absent parenting	4,970	5,040	5,310	4,830	4,050	*8*	*8*	*9*	*7*	*6*
Ethnic origin	59,970	59,360	60,890	64,410	65,520	*100*	*100*	*100*	*100*	*100*
White	46,410	45,580	46,200	48,990	50,340	*77*	*77*	*76*	*76*	*77*
White British	44,590	43,810	44,510	47,170	48,480	*74*	*74*	*73*	*73*	*74*
White Irish	410	420	390	390	370	*1*	*1*	*1*	*1*	*1*
Traveller of Irish Heritage[6]	.	.	20	30	30	.	.	*–*	*–*	*–*
Gypsy/Roma[6]	.	.	30	50	80	.	.	*–*	*–*	*–*
Any other White background	1,410	1,360	1,250	1,350	1,390	*2*	*2*	*2*	*2*	*2*
Mixed	5,310	5,220	5,260	5,590	5,620	*9*	*9*	*9*	*9*	*9*
White and Black Caribbean	2,130	2,100	2,080	2,190	2,150	*4*	*4*	*3*	*3*	*3*
White and Black African	490	490	490	530	600	*1*	*1*	*1*	*1*	*1*
White and Asian	850	820	810	910	950	*1*	*1*	*1*	*1*	*1*
Any other mixed background	1,840	1,810	1,870	1,960	1,920	*3*	*3*	*3*	*3*	*3*
Asian or Asian British	2,330	2,780	3,190	3,380	3,090	*4*	*5*	*5*	*5*	*6*
Indian	300	300	300	320	300	*–*	*1*	*–*	*–*	*–*
Pakistani	640	660	670	740	770	*1*	*1*	*1*	*1*	*1*
Bangladeshi	270	310	350	410	420	*–*	*1*	*1*	*1*	*1*
Any other Asian background	1,120	1,510	1,880	1,920	1,610	*2*	*3*	*3*	*3*	*2*
Black or Black British	4,720	4,450	4,400	4,570	4,520	*8*	*7*	*7*	*7*	*7*
Caribbean	1,640	1,600	1,570	1,660	1,640	*3*	*3*	*3*	*3*	*2*
African	2,320	2,150	2,090	2,110	2,050	*4*	*4*	*3*	*3*	*3*
Any other Black background	750	710	740	800	840	*1*	*1*	*1*	*1*	*1*
Other ethnic groups	1,190	1,330	1,690	1,700	1,530	*2*	*2*	*3*	*3*	*2*
Chinese	120	130	140	130	110	*–*	*–*	*–*	*–*	*–*
Any other ethnic group	1,070	1,200	1,550	1,570	1,420	*2*	*2*	*3*	*2*	*2*
Other	.	.	.	180	410	.	.	.	*–*	*1*
Refused[6]	.	.	.	10	30	.	.	.	*–*	*–*
Information not yet available[6]	.	.	.	170	390	.	.	.	*–*	*1*

1. Numbers have been rounded to the nearest 10. Percentages have been rounded to the nearest whole number.
2. Figures exclude children looked after under an agreed series of short term placements.
3. Historical data may differ from older publications. This is mainly due to the implementation of amendments and corrections sent by some local authorities after the publication date of previous materials.
4. The rates per 10,000 children under 18 years have been derived using the mid-year population estimates for 2010 provided by the Office for National Statistics.
5. The most applicable category of the eight "Need Codes" at the time the child started to be looked after rather than necessarily the entire reason they are looked after.
6. Ethnic origin classification collected for the first time in 2009.

. Not applicable.
– Negligible. Percentage below 0.5%

Age and gender clearly impact on the relative numbers of children and young people in the LAC system. There would also seem to have been an impact following the death of Peter Connelly. However, although research in the past has shown that black and minority ethnic children were increasingly over-represented, this would seem to be changing. There remains though little information with regard to the experience of children with disabilities in the LAC system (Barn, 1993; Ince, 1998a; Morris, 1998; Kirton, 2000; Flynn, 2002). These statistics are useful for providing a basis for planning appropriate provision, and considering developing trends in the LAC system.

Children who are looked after

No matter how a child enters the looked-after system the local authority has responsibilities towards that child. These include a duty to safeguard and promote their welfare (Children Act 1989, section 22 (3)) and a duty to promote their well-being in the Children Act 2008, section 7). These duties should encompass all areas of a child's life and underline the importance of the responsibility of the corporate parent in ensuring that all a child's needs are met, for example, educational, religious, cultural, etc.

CASE STUDY

Kylie is placed in a residential children's home. She is going out at night and will not say where. She is reluctant to go to school, and the home is not providing her with an appropriate diet or care for her hair or skin. Is the local authority fulfilling its duty as a corporate parent?

Table 7.2 gives information on the types of placements experienced as well as types of court orders, age and gender. The table shows that some children who are the subject of full or interim care orders are living with parents but because of the orders they are still part of the looked-after system.

Table 7.2 Children looked after at 31 March by placement[1,2,3]
Years ending 31 March 2007 to 2011
Coverage: England

										numbers and percentages	
	number					percentages					
Placement at 31 March	2007	2008	2009	2010	2011	2007	2008	2009	2010	2011
All children looked after at 31 March	59,970	59,360	60,890	64,410	65,520	*100*	*100*	*100*	*100*	*100*
Foster placements	42,030	41,930	43,870	46,840	48,530	*70*	*71*	*72*	*73*	*74*
Foster placement inside Council boundary										
With relative or friend	5,100	4,990	4,930	5,280	5,350	*9*	*8*	*8*	*8*	*8*
With other foster carer provided										
by Council	19,920	19,580	19,910	20,540	21,370	*33*	*33*	*33*	*32*	*33*
arranged through agency[4]	2,370	2,740	3,330	4,030	4,460	*4*	*5*	*5*	*6*	*7*
Foster placement outside Council boundary										
With relative or friend	1,910	1,890	1,940	2,070	2,080	*3*	*3*	*3*	*3*	*3*
With other foster carer provided by										
Council	5,300	5,220	5,780	6,010	6,060	*9*	*9*	*9*	*9*	*9*
arranged through agency[4]	7,440	7,520	7,990	8,910	9,210	*12*	*13*	*13*	*14*	*14*

Table 7.2 Continued

numbers and percentages

Placement at 31 March	number					percentages				
	2007	2008	2009	2010	2011	2007	2008	2009	2010	2011
Placed for adoption	2,720	2,860	2,690	2,500	2,450	5	5	4	4	4
Placed for adoption with placement order with current foster carer (under S21 AA 2002)	170	190	190	230	180	–	–	–	–	–
Placed for adoption with placement order not with current foster carer (under S21 AA 2002)	1,680	1,960	2,150	2,050	2,070	3	3	4	3	3
Placement with parents	5,110	4,580	4,170	4,230	3,970	9	8	7	7	6
Other placement in the community	1,720	1,910	2,060	2,430	2,460	3	3	3	4	4
Living independently	1,720	1,910	2,060	2,420	2,460	3	3	3	4	4
Residential employment	x	x	x	10	x	x	x	x	–	x
Secure units, children's homes and hostels	6,460	6,220	6,090	6,170	5,890	11	10	10	10	9
Secure unit inside Council boundary	30	20	20	20	20	–	–	–	–	–
Secure unit outside Council boundary[5]	170	160	190	180	140	–	–	–	–	–
Homes and hostels subject to Children's Homes regulations										
inside Council boundary	2,890	2,900	2,730	2,630	2,610	5	5	4	4	4
outside Council boundary	2,290	2,120	2,150	2,340	2,230	4	4	4	4	3
Homes and hostels *not* subject to Children's Homes regulations	1,090	1,020	1,000	1,000	880	2	2	2	2	1
Other residential settings	590	570	740	1,000	1,050	1	1	1	2	2
Residential care homes	230	250	360	550	640	–	–	1	1	1
NHS Trust providing medical/nursing care	70	80	90	110	110	–	–	–	–	–
Family centre or mother and baby unit	140	100	150	200	170	–	–	–	–	–
Young offenders institution or prison	150	140	150	140	130	–	–	–	–	–
Residential schools	1,090	1,080	1,040	1,030	970	2	2	2	2	1
Missing – Absent for more than 24 hours from agreed placement	150	130	120	110	110	–	–	–	–	–
In refuge (section 51 of Children's Act, 1989)	x	x	x	x	x	x	x	x	x	x
Whereabouts known (not in refuge)	30	40	30	30	30	–	–	–	–	–
Whereabouts unknown	120	100	90	80	80	–	–	–	–	–
Other placement	90	70	100	90	90	–	–	–	–	–
Number of placements during the year[6]	59,970	59,360	60,890	64,410	65,520	100	100	100	100	100
1	38,890	38,710	40,400	42,230	43,870	65	65	66	66	67
2	13,390	13,620	13,720	14,870	14,650	22	23	23	23	22
3 or more	7,590	7,030	6,770	7,300	7,000	13	12	11	11	11

1. Numbers have been rounded to the nearest 10. Percentages have been rounded to the nearest whole number.
2. Figures exclude children looked after under an agreed series of short-term placements.
3. Historical data may differ from older publications. This is mainly due to the implementation of amendments and corrections sent by some local authorities after the publication date of previous materials.
4. This category includes placement provider codes "Other Local Authority provision", "private provision" and "voluntary/third sector provision" for 2009, 2010 and 2011.
5. There are currently only 16 secure units operating in England therefore most placements will inevitably be outside the council boundary.
6. Where a child is subsequently placed for adoption with their existing foster carers, then this is not counted as a placement change.

x Figures not shown in order to protect confidentiality.
– Negligible. Percentage below 0.5%

The local authority should also try to find out what the wishes and feelings of the child, their parents or those with parental responsibility and anyone else who has a reasonable interest in the child, are so that these can be taken into account both in terms of day-to-day living and also in longer-term planning. A person with reasonable interest in a child could be a relative (aunt, uncle, grandparent etc.) or a non-relative (close family friend).

The prime factors for consideration are their importance to the child and their level of involvement with them. When decisions are made about reasonable interest, the amount of meaningful contact a person has had with the child will be of particular importance. The Children Act 1989 gives an expectation that due regard must be given to the child's wishes and feelings but this must take into account their age and level of understanding as well as their religion, race, culture and language (Children Act 1989, section 22 (4) and (5)). This can be an area of tension as social workers have an overriding duty to put the welfare of the child or young person first (Children Act 1989, section 1).

ACTIVITY **7.1**

What do you think due regard *means? How do you think a child's age and understand-ing might affect this? Would the level of due regard be different for a child of 4, a young person of 12, or a 16-year-old with learning difficulties? What would influence your answer?*

COMMENT

The age and level of understanding of the child or young person are of particular relevance but in the context of their particular situation, for example, if there are allegations of abuse or high levels of neglect which are impacting on health and well-being. For example Kylie, who is aged 12 and has learning disabilities, wants to go home to live. Her stepfather is alleged to have sexually abused her. In these circum-stances as a social worker what would you have to put first, Kylie's wishes or her welfare? If the same situation arose with Tariq who is four and has been physically injured in the care of his parents, would your dilemma be easier to resolve?

Care planning

Once a child is being looked after the local authority has to make a care plan, in con-sultation with the child and their parents, which has to be reviewed on a regular basis. The plan must be prepared before a child is placed or, if this is not practicable, within ten working days. A plan for permanence must be considered from the beginning of a child's placement (Care Planning, Placement and Case Review Regulations 2010), though if a child is subject to care proceedings this will be finalised in the court arena. These regu-lations increase the role of the independent reviewing officer who already had a duty to monitor care plans and take an active problem-solving role on behalf of the child. As part of their role they will need to ensure that consideration is given to plans for permanence for the child at an early stage of being looked after to ensure that they are not allowed to remain in the system through lack of planning and drift.

They have a further duty to refer children's cases to the Children and Families Courts Advisory and Support Service (CAFCASS) for legal action on behalf of the child to be con-sidered. This provision has been introduced to help address the issue of detrimental delay in decision-making for children (Parker, 1999; Lowe and Murch, 1999). There are pre-scribed minimum intervals for reviews, although additional reviews can be convened in response to circumstances or on the request of a child or parent:

- within 20 working days of a child becoming looked-after;

- not more than three months after the first review;

- not more than six months after the previous review.

Before holding reviews the responsible authority (the local authority or the voluntary agency that is accommodating the child) must consult with, and seek the views of, a number of people including the child, their parent/s or anyone else with parental responsibility, foster carer, residential staff, health visitor, GP. All these people should be invited to the review, attending for as much of it as is thought appropriate. They will also be notified of the results of the review and any decisions taken.

Looked-after children have to receive a health assessment, which may include a physical examination, at specified intervals (every six months for children under five and 12 months for those over five). Children who are of sufficient age and understanding may refuse to co-operate with medical examinations. This may result in dilemmas and conflicts for the social worker which are not easily resolved (Fostering Services (England) Regulations 2011). Each responsible authority should have written procedures for reviews but these may not always help to resolve dilemmas. Venues are supposed to be chosen in consultation with children, parents and carers, though this may not help if there is conflict between their views not only about place but also about who should attend. Social workers need to think about who will offer support to children and parents during the review as their needs and views may be very different.

The next activity will help you to begin to have an understanding of the dilemmas involved in the review process.

ACTIVITY 7.2

Kylie is attending her review with her social worker. Her stepfather has been invited – she does not want him there, but her mother will not attend without him. Kylie is also due to have her annual health assessment, this time with a physical examination as she has been having frequent stomach pains. She has, however, refused to co-operate with this. What are the dilemmas in this situation for the social worker and the independent reviewing officer? How might they be resolved?

COMMENT

Kylie should be consulted about her review, as should her mother. This difference in views raises dilemmas, which may not be able to be resolved and may necessitate the review having to be split to enable everyone to attend. At the same time it also raises the dilemma of Kylie's wishes being overridden, possibly because she is a young person with learning difficulties.

You will need to think about Kylie's right to refuse an examination balanced against her interests if she has a medical problem that needs attention. There may be ways she would agree if she had some control over what was happening, for example, some choice of examiner and possibly venue. Time would be needed to help her work through her anxieties to see if they could be resolved.

Fostering

This section will discuss and consider the different types of fostering available to children and the processes involved in the provision of foster care. Fostering, formerly called *boarding out*, has existed informally for many years. However it is only since the Monckton Report, 1945 and the Curtis Report, 1946, which were both concerned with the care of children living away from home, that the need for quality controls and supervision was recognised. The Monckton Report was particularly influential as it was an inquiry into the death of a child, Dennis O'Neill (a 13-year-old boy) who was starved and beaten to death by his foster father. The subsequent Children Act 1948 envisaged children living with ordinary families as opposed to living in residential care or with carers under informal arrangements, which offered few safeguards for their welfare. Fostering has developed since that time.

This section will discuss and consider the different types of fostering currently available to children and the processes involved in the provision of foster care. Fostering services are provided by a variety of agencies including local authorities and voluntary (not for profit) organisations. Over recent years a growing number of independent fostering agencies (IFAs) have developed, providing services through business agreements. Local authorities can make arrangements for its fostering services in respect of a child being delegated to an independent fostering agency (IFA) if that is the most effective way of achieving a placement for a child. This is happening more and more frequently as local authorities struggle to provide sufficient foster carers. These arrangements are regulated and should ensure that all independent agencies have a manager who is registered with Ofsted. The manager must ensure that the welfare of children is safeguarded and promoted at all times (Fostering Services (England) Regulations 2011).

What is fostering?

In simple terms fostering relates to the care of children within a family environment by people who are not their parents or those with parental responsibility. This short definition hides a complex set of relationships which can be considered in five categories, although one survey found 47 different classifications among local authorities (Waterhouse, 1997).

The five categories are:

- short-term foster care;
- permanent foster care;
- connected person foster care;
- concurrent foster care;
- private foster care.

The first four categories are types of fostering which apply to children in the looked-after system and will be discussed further below. Private fostering is an arrangement between the families concerned and although covered by the Children Act 1989 under section 66 little was known about it, with limited research being carried out in this area (Wilson et al., 2004). Private fostering is an area though of considerable concern, particularly since the case of Victoria Climbié who was privately fostered. There have been changes post Climbié which seek to offer more protection to privately fostered children; section 44 of the Children Act 2004 introduced national minimum standards for private fostering arrangements. Placements are now subject to regulation through the Children (Private Arrangements for Fostering) Regulations 2005. Replacement practice guidance (also introduced in 2005) strengthens and enhances the previous Children Act 1989 guidance by seeking to focus the attention of local authorities on private fostering by requiring them to be more proactive. Many now have dedicated workers for private fostering; however, the scope of their role does seem to vary from authority to authority.

What provision for monitoring and supporting private fostering arrangements is there in your local area? Do these arrangements comply with the practice guidance?

Short-term foster care
This provides a service for the many children who enter the looked-after system for a short time. There were around 32,000 short-term fostered children in 2000–2001 at any one time, with a similar number leaving the system (DoH, 2001a). More recent statistics (DoE, 2011b) no longer provide this total so comparisons are difficult. However, as there is little difference in other categories, similarities may well remain. Among the children who left the looked-after system just under 44 per cent had less than 12 weeks in the system; a further 18 per cent had six months. Of the children who remain in the LAC system, 65 per cent who have been looked after for more than six months are likely to stay in the system for more than four years (DoH, 1999a). Short-term fostering is used for a variety of purposes, for example:

- in an emergency to safeguard a young child of three months who has fractures where there are no apparent medical reasons or satisfactory explanations;

- where a parent has been admitted to hospital in an emergency and there is no one to care for the child;

- when a parent of a baby is being assessed to see if their parenting is of a safe standard;

- where a young person has been remanded to the care of the local authority pending trial for offences.

Permanent foster care
Permanent-foster care provides children who, for whatever reason, either cannot live with their parents or be placed for adoption, with continuity of care throughout their remaining childhood. Adoption is not appropriate for all children and young people: they may have significant relationships within their birth families, or they may wish for permanence but without severing legal relationships. Special Guardianship Orders (which gives Special Guardians parental responsibility and the ability to make decisions about children in most areas of their lives, whether their parents agree or not) are an option available to long-term foster carers. These orders remove children from the looked-after system but do not sever their legal relationship with their birth family. However, they do give them security, and their carers parental responsibility, in their placement.

Connected person foster care

This is provided for looked-after children by relatives and friends, without having parental responsibility for the child. Children who are subject to care (full or interim) orders can be placed with relatives or friends after a full assessment under the 2011 regulations. There is provision to place with connected persons on an interim basis for a maximum of 16 weeks with the possibility of one extension for a further eight weeks. Children's Services must be satisfied it is 'necessary' to place a child prior to full assessment. Support for kinship carers has been variable, as research (Hunt et al., 2007) affirmed. However, as connected person carers are now assessed as foster carers, allowances and support should be comparable. Some service providers offer a specialist service for connected carers in recognition of the difference between them and non-connected foster carers. Special Guardianship is also an option for connected person carers where it is felt by the courts to be appropriate.

Concurrent foster care

These placements have provided a limited resource within the UK though there is discussion of increasing provision to support the speedy placement of young children for adoption. In these placements a child is placed with foster carers who are both approved foster carers and approved adopters. The child is usually the subject of court proceedings where there are ongoing assessments and efforts to try to return the child to their parents. However, if these are not successful then the foster carers, as approved adopters, can apply to adopt the child. There are high expectations of foster carers in these situations. They must have a positive approach to the assessment processes, which are likely to involve frequent contact, while maintaining a commitment to the child as a potentially permanent family member. Such situations require a high level of support for the carers if they are to fulfil these roles, which are potentially in conflict.

Regulations

Fostering placements for looked-after children are provided by local authorities, independent fostering organisations and voluntary organisations under section 59 of the Children Act 1989. Fostering provision is made subject to the Fostering Service (England) Regulations 2011 and the National Minimum Fostering Standards 2011 (in addition to those for private fostering mentioned above). The regulations cover all aspects of fostering including the conduct of agencies as well as the assessment, approval and support of foster carers. The minimum standards are qualitative, but intended to be measurable and are grouped in eight areas as follows:

- statement of purpose;
- fitness to carry on or manage a fostering service;
- management of a fostering service;
- securing and promoting welfare;
- recruiting, checking, managing, supporting and training staff and foster carers;
- records;
- fitness of premises;
- financial requirements.

The legal basis for fostering is found in the Children Act 1989, but this has been further developed by subsequent policy and further legislation. The Quality Protects 1998 (DoH, 1998b) and Choice Protects 2003 (DoH, 2003a) initiatives, the Care Standards Act 2000, the Children (Leaving Care) Act 2000 and the DfEE/DoH *Guidance on the Education of Children and Young People in Public Care* and the *National Minimum Standards for Foster Care* (DfE, 2011) have the underlying purpose of promoting and safeguarding the welfare of children and young people as well as an emphasis on their involvement in decisions which affect them.

The process of fostering

Fostering begins with the initial contact with prospective carers and involves assessment, approval, referral, matching, support and review processes. See Figure 7.1 below for an illustration of these processes.

The assessment and approval of foster carers

All foster carers (including connected carers), apart from those who are fostering privately, go through a process which both assesses and prepares them to foster. Some agencies use the Fostering Network's assessment package, others might use the British Association of Adoption and Fostering's Prospective Foster Carers report (Form F) or Connected Person report (Form C), others devise their own, however all cover the same essential areas. The majority of agencies employ specialist, experienced workers to undertake these tasks.

Both fostering and adoption assessments consider whether applicants have the 'competence' to meet the needs of children through processes which although not identical are similar: see Figures 7.1 and 7.3. 'Competence' is assessed in the following areas:

- **Caring for children:** this would include providing a good standard of physical and emotional care to children who will have experienced loss and who are likely to have been harmed as well as ensuring they receive appropriate education and health care.

- **Providing a safe and caring environment:** this would include providing a safe physical environment and keeping children safe from harm outside the home.

- **Working as part of a team:** this would include the ability to keep information confidential, to work with other professional people and the child's family whether directly or indirectly through contact.

- **Carers' own past history and development:** this would include looking at past experiences and how they impact on carers now, what they have learnt from these experiences and how they might impact on their ability to care for a child.

In addition to the competence assessment, fostering and adoption assessments undertake statutory checks with a number of agencies including the police, the health authority and social services as well as a full medical examination. For further information see www.baaf.org.uk and www.fostering.net.

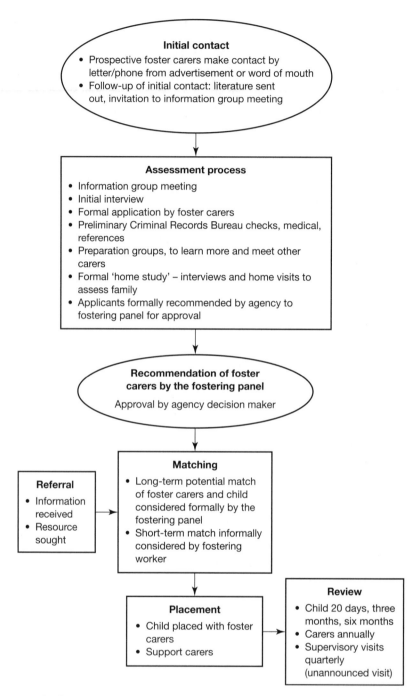

Figure 7.1 *The fostering process*

All the information about prospective foster carers is presented to a fostering panel (see Figure 7.2), which has to make a recommendation to the agency as to whether or not the applicant(s) should be approved as a carer(s). The panel has to have a minimum of five members: one must be independent, one must be a social worker with three years relevant experience and there must be three other members. There is no longer a

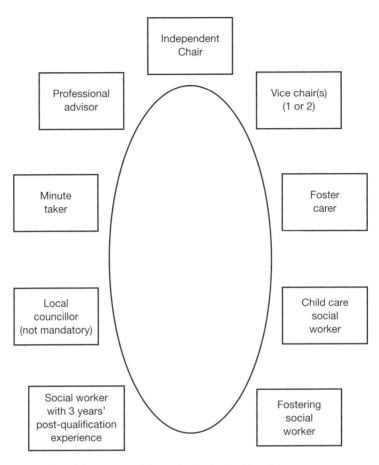

Figure 7.2 An example of the composition of a Fostering Panel

requirement to have an elected member representative. As with adoption panels all recommendations are considered by a decision-maker (a senior manager) within the agency for final approval. Agency decision-makers (ADM) normally agree with the panel's decision although this is not always the case. If the ADM is minded not to approve foster carers then they can apply to the Independent Reviewing Mechanism (IRM) for a hearing by an independent panel, which will then make recommendations to the ADM, which again s/he can either accept or reject giving reasons why. Foster carers also have access to the IRM if they disagree with a decision regarding their terms of approval: the number, ages and gender of the children they can care for. This process has been available to applicants for adoption since 2004 and was introduced for foster carers in 2009. Further information about panel functions is contained in the Fostering Service (England) Regulations 2011 and the Independent Review of Determinations (Adoption and Fostering) Regulations 2009 (also see Borthwick and Lord, 2011).

The following case study, which has already been introduced to you in previous chapters, will now be used to highlight the various processes you may be involved in as a social worker in a fostering team.

CASE STUDY

A referral has been made for foster care for three children: Kylie Cole, aged 12, who is African Caribbean/White and has learning disabilities; Tariq Khan, aged three, African Caribbean/Asian; and Nadia Khan, aged one, African Caribbean/Asian. Donna Green, aged 26, is living with her partner Ahmed Khan, the father of the two youngest children. The eldest child, Kylie, has contact with her father, Alan Cole, aged 28. The reason for the referral is the neglect of Kylie; subsequently there are allegations of sexual abuse. Both younger children are found to be neglected, with later injuries found on Nadia (fractures). This case study will enable you to consider the processes of fostering by working through the activities below.

The referral process

This can be thought of as the collation of key information in order to obtain a service or resource, which in this instance is a foster home. Activity 7.3 will help you to understand the referral process.

ACTIVITY 7.3

What information do you think is needed when a referral is received for foster care? Is there a minimum amount of information that you would need to help you to place the children with suitable foster carers?

COMMENT

The information received should include the full names of the children, ages and dates of birth, current address; ethnic, racial and religious background; details of any school or nurseries attending; general practitioner (GP); details of parents and other carer or person with whom the children has contact.

What about diet, any allergies, medication needed? Would this subsequent information be easy to obtain and from whom would you obtain the information? How would you obtain this information? Who do you think would best provide this sort of detail about a child's life? Ideally, you would obtain information from parents, relatives, friends, or carers, however other professionals such as health visitors, GPs and teachers may also be useful sources.

ACTIVITY 7.4

Look back at the case study and consider the following points.

Do you think Kylie has been neglected? If she has, how might this affect the kind of foster placement that will best meet her needs, and indeed the needs of the other children? Can all of the three children's needs be met in one foster placement? Do you think that there are sufficient resources available to enable you to place all three children together?

These are complex issues, which may require further assessment and consultation with other professionals. Iwaniec (1995) provides a good introduction to the identification, assessment and intervention and treatment of the emotionally abused and neglected child. Iwaniec defines neglect as: the passive ignoring of a child's emotional needs, a lack of attention and stimulation, parental unavailability to care, supervise, guide, teach and protect *(1995, page 5). She gives a helpful account of how to identify emotional abuse and neglect including such issues as non-organic failure to thrive, the failure to grow and develop healthily. It refers to children whose weight, height and general development are significantly below the expected norms (see Chapter 4 for further discussion).*

The matching process

This can be thought of as assembling or linking two sets of information with each other in order to make a placement decision, which is beneficial to both the child(ren) and carers. The information about the child(ren) which is contained on the referral is matched or linked with the information about the foster carers.

ACTIVITY **7.5**

What information might you need to know about the foster family before you place all of these children with them?

COMMENT

The information that you might need to know would include the following:

- *Which foster carers have vacancies?*

- *How many children are they approved for and what is the age range of the child or children that they are approved for?*

- *What experience do the carers have of caring for children?*

- *Can the children share a bedroom or is there a need for separate bedroom accommodation?*

- *Do the foster carers share the children's ethnic, racial and religious background?*

- *Some estimate of the length of time the foster placement is needed would also be helpful.*

- *Is the foster placement in a geographical area that is easily accessible for family, friends and relatives and school or nursery?*

- *How will the placements of the children affect the foster carer's own children and their position within the foster family?*

- *Finally, would the order of this list be different if the foster placement was being requested on a Monday as opposed to a Friday afternoon?*

Continued

Each fostering agency would have a centrally held information resource, which you would need to access. This could be through a duty social worker but practice will vary from agency to agency. Subject to there being appropriate carers available, you would then contact the fostering social worker or the carers directly to obtain the information needed and then decide whether to place the children. The realities of practice mean that there may be little choice or that children may be placed, in emergency, with carers who do not match their needs. Systems that operate out of office hours will again vary from agency to agency, for example, some are covered by emergency duty teams who cover all provisions whereas others have on-call social workers and/or 'buddy' foster carers.

The support process

As the fostering social worker your task is to support the foster carers. This involves sharing the burden by giving additional assistance in the form of physical, financial and psychological support. The support starts by sharing the initial information from the referral. Support for the carers continues with a discussion with the foster carers of the children's needs and the provision of any financial or physical support that the foster carer may need. Providing psychological support involves thinking about the needs of others, including their feelings and emotions, and offering appropriate assistance.

ACTIVITY **7.6**

How important is this support to the foster carer? What impact would having three extra people staying with you have on your family? Think about what the foster carers might need immediately in order to care for a one-year-old, a three-year-old and a twelve-year-old.

COMMENT

The first considerations may well be around practicalities, for example, who would provide the money to buy nappies, clothes, appropriate food, some toys, appropriate bedding, buggies, cot, etc.? Who would you expect to obtain these items? If the carer, would the carer's transport be adequate? Will the carers have the time? How would the eldest child get to school? How would the carer manage to take their own children to school as well as the foster children? If the children are separated and placed in different foster homes are the carers given each other's contact numbers? How much ongoing support will be required to ensure that the children's basic needs continue to be met? As well as dealing with the day-to-day care of the children the foster carers also need to be encouraged to keep a record of any changes in the children's behaviour. If you are supporting them well you will need to ensure that they have the means to record this information. Finally, how much support should foster carers be given? Is 9 a.m. to 5 p.m. adequate or should they receive 24-hour support and, if this is the case, should that support be shared between their fostering agency and a network of other carers? In any case, should foster carers be paid properly for the work they do or should they continue to receive an allowance?

Continued

COMMENT *continued*

Being able to offer appropriate support involves having the knowledge to know when to intervene, the skill to know how to intervene, and an awareness of the reason why you are intervening.

The review process

This involves examining the previous process and the care that the children are currently receiving. The views of the children and others should be sought and recorded as part of the review process. Decisions are made regarding whether the foster placement should continue or alternative care provision be sought. The safety and well-being of the children is paramount and the review should address whether the behaviour of the child gives any cause for concern, such as sexualised or aggressive behaviour towards self or others. The review should be chaired by an independent reviewing officer as outlined in the Care Planning, Placement and Case Review Regulations 2010, and also take into account the statutory guidance which was issued in 2011. The legislation relating to independent reviewing officers was introduced by section 118 of the Adoption and Children Act 2002. The review will also consider if there has there been any improvement or deterioration in the children's behaviour or conduct. When has this occurred?

We hope that by working through some of the questions you have been able to imagine that you are the fostering social worker and indeed the foster carer. We also hope that you have managed to analyse the processes involved and think about how much time, energy and effort might be devoted to the different parts of the process. Finally, and most importantly, the next activity will help you to think about how you might feel as one of the children in the process.

ACTIVITY **7.7**

How would you feel if you were suddenly transported to live with people you did not know, in a place that was unfamiliar, where all of the certainties you knew before no longer existed? How would you be?

COMMENT

The healing process begins with the recognition of pain and hurt and the re-establishment of routines that give meaning, purpose and pleasure to life, and the long-term provision of care, patience, stability, understanding and love, which the potential stability of fostering and the permanence of adoption can provide.

RESEARCH SUMMARY

Innovative, Tried and Tested: A Review of Good Practice in Fostering (Sellick and Howell, 2003) provides a helpful summary of key areas that children, carers, social workers and agencies identify as important key messages for good practice.

Key messages

- Many fostering agencies are using research evidence to make recruitment effective: for example, local recruitment schemes, word of mouth and brief articles in the local press achieve success.

- There is innovative training practice, consistent with research evidence, about what carers say that they want: managing contacts, dealing with children's behaviour, and supporting children's education.

- Information and communication technology (ICT) is playing an increasingly important role in key areas: training, information and user evaluation.

- Agencies are developing a wide range of retention schemes, for example, loyalty payments, 'buddying' arrangements, stress management and services for carers' own children.

- Some agencies are providing carers with career choices within or connected to fostering. The benefits include retaining carers, using their skills flexibly and increasing their job satisfaction.

- Partnership working and commissioning enables many agencies to improve the availability of both general and specialised placements.

- There is evidence of the growing development of specialist placements for children with complex and special needs, some of which have been researched and evaluated.

- Many agencies now offer additional services to help the children placed; foster carers themselves are satisfied when children and young people they care for receive them.

- Fostered children and young people are consulted quite often; however, their opinions are rarely communicated to senior managers or elected members to inform policy.

- Foster carers participate in the evaluation of many aspects of fostering services.

- Parents and other relatives of fostered children are given few opportunities to participate in shaping fostering services.

(Sellick and Howell, 2003)

Adoption

Adoption as an informal arrangement has existed for many years, but its history in law is much shorter. Prior to the first adoption act, the Adoption of Children Act 1926, birth parents could legally demand the return of their children even though they had been cared for in another family for many years. This Act was the first to allow for the transfer of rights and obligations in respect of a child from birth parents to adopters, and also gave courts the power to dispense with the agreement of birth parents in some circumstances. Subsequent legislation followed which built on this Act until the current legislation was introduced by the Adoption and Children Act 2002.

Adoption is the legal transfer of parental responsibility from birth parent(s) to adoptive parent(s). This is the only process which permanently removes parental responsibility from the birth parent(s) and gives it to another parent(s). Adoption also has the effect of removing parental responsibility from local authorities. Adoption can be through agreement, for example, for a baby whose parent is unable to care for them, or through compulsion against the wishes of the birth parent, usually where a child has been made the subject of a care order. Adoption procedures take place under the Adoption and Children Act 2002 (ACA 2002) which was fully implemented in December 2005 (some parts of the Act had already been implemented piecemeal over the preceding years). The ACA 2002 was drafted following the Quality Protects initiative (DoH, 1998b), and the Performance and Innovation Unit Report in 2000. Both of these publications considered reforms to adoption, although there had already been a previous adoption bill published in 1993. The previous law was felt to be out of step with the Children Act 1989, and there were concerns that there were children waiting for adoption and that too many applicants were unsuccessful.

ACA 2002 has changed the process of adoption by introducing placement orders which are required before a child can be placed for adoption without parental consent. It has also made adoption accessible to couples who are not married and those who have civil partnerships. Adoption continues to be available to single people and to step-parents.

Table 7.3 Looked-after children adopted during the years ending 31 March by gender, age at adoption, ethnic origin, category of need, final legal status, duration of final period of care and age on starting final period of care, 2003–2007[1,2]

England										numbers and percentages
	number					percentages				
	2003	2004	2005	2006	2007	2003	2004	2005	2006	2007
All looked-after children[1]	61,200	61,200	61,000	60,300	60,000					
All Children looked after adopted[1]	3,500	3,800	3,800	3,700	3,300	100	100	100	100	100
Gender	3,500	3,800	3,800	3,700	3,300	100	100	100	100	100
Male	1,900	1,900	1,900	1,900	1,700	53	51	51	51	50
Female	1,700	1,900	1,800	1,800	1,600	47	49	49	49	50
Age at adoption (years)	3,500	3,800	3,800	3,700	3,300	100	100	100	100	100
Under 1	220	220	210	200	150	6	6	6	5	5
1 to 4	2,200	2,200	2,300	2,400	2,100	62	58	62	64	64
5 to 9	960	1,100	1,100	950	880	27	30	28	26	27
10 to 15	180	210	160	180	160	5	6	4	5	5
16 and over	10	20	20	20	10	0	0	0	0	0
Average age (yrs: months)	4:4	4:5	4:2	4:1	4:2					
Ethnic origin	3,500	3,800	3,800	3,700	3,300	100	100	100	100	100
White	3,100	3,200	3,200	3,200	2,800	87	86	86	85	85
Mixed	290	330	350	380	340	8	9	9	10	10
Asian or Asian British	40	50	50	50	60	1	1	1	1	2
Black or Black British	90	100	80	90	90	2	3	2	2	3
Other ethnic groups	40	50	40	30	30	1	1	1	1	1
Category of need[3]	3,500	3,800	3,800	3,700	3,300	100	100	100	100	100
Abuse or neglect	2,600	2,800	2,800	2,700	2,400	75	74	74	74	74
Child's disability	30	30	30	20	20	1	1	1	1	1
Parent's illness or disability	200	160	190	180	160	6	4	5	5	5
Family in acute distress	170	230	220	230	160	5	6	6	6	5
Family dysfunction	290	290	340	310	310	8	8	9	8	9

139

Table 7.3 Continued

England										numbers and percentages
	number					percentages				
	2003	2004	2005	2006	2007	2003	2004	2005	2006	2007
Category of need[3]										
Socially unacceptable behaviour	10	–	–	10	–	0	–	–	0	–
Low income	0	–	–	10	–	0	–	–	0	–
Absent parenting	210	260	200	190	190	6	7	5	5	6
Final legal status	3,500	3,800	3,800	3,700	3,300	100	100	100	100	100
Freed for adoption[4]	1,500	1,700	1,900	1,900	1,200	42	44	49	51	38
Placement Order[5]	X	X	X	20	630	X	X	X	0	19
Care order	1,700	1,700	1,600	1,500	1,200	48	46	42	41	36
Voluntary agreement (S20)	350	370	340	280	230	10	10	9	8	7
Duration of final period of care[6]	3,500	3,800	3,800	3,700	3,300	100	100	100	100	100
Under 1 year	250	260	260	240	170	7	7	7	6	5
1 year to under 2 years	1,200	1,300	1,400	1,400	1,200	35	33	36	38	36
2 years to under 3 years	960	1,100	1,100	1,100	980	27	28	30	30	30
3 years and over	1,100	1,200	1,000	950	970	31	32	27	26	29
Average duration (yrs: mths)	2:9	2:8	2:7	2:7	2:8					
Age on starting final period of care (years)[6]	3,500	3,800	3,800	3,700	3,300	100	100	100	100	100
Under 1	2,000	2,000	2,100	2,100	1,900	56	53	56	57	58
1		440	470	470	470	370	13	12	13	13
2		380	400	400	340	360	11	11	11	9
3	280	310	300	270	250	8	8	8	7	8
4 and over	450	580	500	510	420	13	15	13	14	13
Average age (yrs: mths)	1:7	1:8	1:7	1:7	1:6					

1. Source: SSDA903 return on children looked after.
2. Historical data may differ from older publications. This is mainly due to the implementation of amendments and corrections sent by some local authorities after the publication date of previous materials.
3. The most applicable category of the eight "Need Codes" (i.e. the reason why the child is receiving social services) at the time the child was taken into care rather than necessarily the reason they are looked after.
4. No new applications for freeing orders may be made on or after 30 December 2005.
5. Placement orders came into force on 30 December 2005.
6. "Period of care" refers to a continuous period of being looked after, which may include more than one placement or legal status.

In spite of the introduction of ACA 2002 there continues to be a decrease in the numbers of children looked after who have been placed for adoption in 2006 and 2007 (see Table 6.2). Some of the decrease may have been caused by the use of Special Guardianship orders but there may also be other factors which are impacting, including the economic downturn. The government has expressed concern about the delay in placing children for adoption and the length of time that assessments can take. The action plan for adoption attempts to address these issues: work is ongoing to try to speed up the process and increase the resource of prospective adopters available.

The process of adoption

Adoption, like fostering, begins with the initial contact with prospective carers and involves assessment, approval, referral, matching, support and review processes (see Figure 7.3 for an illustration of these processes).

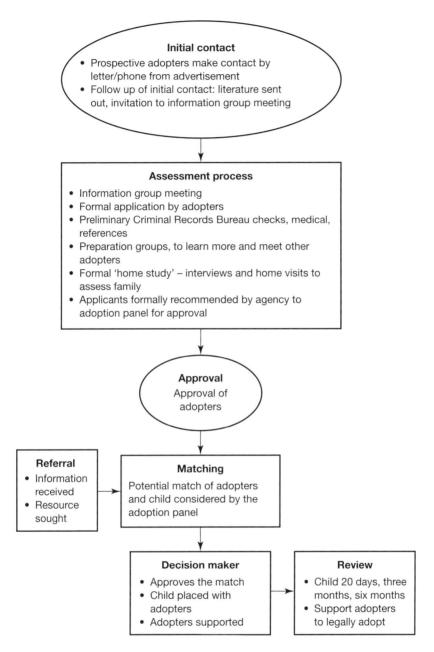

Figure 7.3 *The adoption process*

Adoption also involves the permanent transfer of parental responsibility to an adoptive parent or parents. As you will have seen in Chapter 4, Kylie, Tariq and Nadia came into the looked-after system following allegations of abuse. They have now been made the subject of care orders and have been placed in foster care. The task for the social worker is to meet the needs of each individual child. Adoption can be thought of as permanent substitute care and is a way of achieving a more stable, secure life for a child. It is a way of severing the birth parental responsibilities and creating a new legal adoptive parental responsibility. Adoption involves making difficult decisions. In this instance the decision is made to separate Kylie from her younger siblings.

Vera Fahlberg provides an excellent guide to the child's experience in care and the management of their journey in *A Child's Journey through Placement* (2004).

The referral process

This begins with a decision that Tariq's and Nadia's needs would be best met by being placed for adoption together, following the section 47 investigation and court proceedings discussed in Chapter 4. Tariq and Nadia are then referred to the adoption agencies as children who need adoptive parents. Information about each child is assembled using the Child's Permanence Report (CPR). This is a method of collating extensive information about the child and their family including development, life history, medical details, education, family details, any harm experienced and special needs. Following the implementation of ACA 2002 there is some variation in format but the information should be the same. A similar process is undertaken for adoptive parents: the information is prepared using the British Association of Adoption and Fostering's Prospective Adopters report (PAR). The children's social worker would prepare the documentation for Tariq and Nadia, the adoption worker for the adoptive parent(s).

Consider the following:

- What issues might the children's social worker face when collecting information about the children if the parents are not in agreement with the plan for adoption?

- If the parents are co-operating with the plan, how reliable is the information which they are giving you?

- Is there any influential involvement from relatives that might assist the information gathering process or slow it down?

- Are there any legal considerations that need to be taken into account?

- How would things be different if consent to the adoption was given?

- How would things be different if consent was withheld?

- How would you check the accuracy of the information?

The matching process

For adoption this can be thought of as assembling or linking two sets of information with each other in order to make a placement decision, which is beneficial to both the children and adopters. Before this linking can occur the children, Tariq and Nadia, have to be recommended as suitable for adoption by an adoption panel, although the government have expressed the intention of removing this responsibility from the panel and leaving it solely with the courts. The panel must consist of at least five members with no upper limit but it should not be so large as to be unmanageable or intimidating to prospective adopters. The panel includes:

- an independent chair person;

- one or two vice chairs (panel members);

- one or two suitably qualified social workers with three years relevant post-qualifying experience;

- the agency medical advisor;

- enough members who between them have the necessary experience and expertise. The quorum for a panel is five which must include the chair or vice chair, one social worker

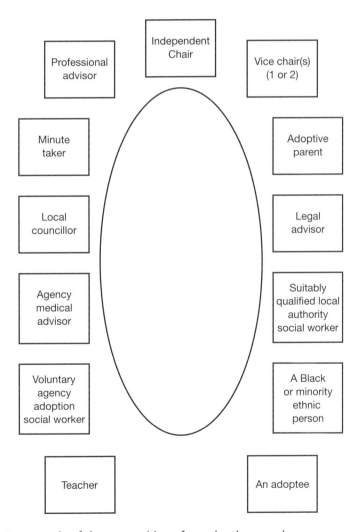

Figure 7.4 An example of the composition of an adoption panel

with relevant experience and one member of the panel who must be independent. If the panel cannot agree the chair has the casting vote.

A typical example of an adoption panel is represented in Figure 7.4.

The adoption panel will also have a legal advisor who provides advice on all the legal aspects of applications from prospective adopters, current children recommended for placement for adoption and the matching process. There will also be a professional advisor from the agency to provide advice on practice and procedure. Adoption panels, as with fostering panels, make recommendations, which also have to be confirmed by the agency decision-maker. Prospective adopters, like foster carers, have recourse to the IRM for a hearing *de novo* (anew) if they are not approved by the agency decision maker. The IRM also provides a hearing when adoption agencies refuse to disclose information from adoption files.

As well as recommending that children should be placed for adoption and adopters as suitable adoptive parents, adoption panels also recommend approval of the match between the approved adoptive parents and children who should be placed for adoption. The process of matching is much more rigorous and complex than for fostering, as you would expect when attempting to ensure that the adopters will be able to meet the needs of the child for life. Panels have to consider some complex and controversial issues. These may be grouped as follows:

- Issues about the child's birth family, such as mental illness, which the adopters may well have some difficulty accepting.

- The wishes and feelings of the birth family about the type of adoptive family the child should be placed with might be unrealistic.

- The child's current understanding of, and feelings about, the past and about what is planned might not have been known fully due to the child's age and level of understanding.

- Identity issues are sometimes in conflict with attachment issues.

- Is a same race placement more important than being able to make an attachment to a carer?

- How accepting or otherwise are the adopters of:

  - abuse and neglect issues, behavioural issues
  - health and disability issues
  - education issues
  - contact issues
  - the needs of siblings
  - other children in the new family
  - any financial issues and their own feelings and expectations.

Many of these issues should have already been explored in general with the prospective adopters during the assessment. The social workers for the child and the adopters (usually two different people, possibly from different agencies) will explore how the children's needs can be met, focusing on the relevant issues in more depth prior to the match going to the adoption panel. The panel will consider all the information about the child and the prospective adoptive family as well as a report detailing why this is felt to be an appropriate match and what support will be offered following placement. A fuller account is given of these issues in Lord and Cullen (2006); Byrne (2000) also offers helpful advice on linking children with new families prior to placement. The panel considers the support plan and can offer advice about any aspect of this including contact, financial support, therapeutic input and the delegation of parental responsibility, which occurs in restricted form when the child is placed with the prospective adopters.

ACTIVITY 7.8

Can adopters attend the panels in the agencies? What factors do you think may prevent adopters from attendance at the panel?

COMMENT

All agencies should facilitate prospective adopters attending panels. Many provide information about the process and membership to help prepare people for the experience, though it can still be a stressful experience for them.

Think about what 'criteria of suitability' the adoption panel might use when recommending that Tariq and Nadia should be placed for adoption. The panel will offer advice to the child's social worker about applying for a placement order (to enable the child to be placed with prospective adopters), contact arrangements with birth families and any matching criteria which might be relevant. The adoptive parents also have to be approved as suitable adopters. The panel considers age, health, parenting capacity/ potential, ethnic/racial/cultural background, religion and motivation. What else do you think might be included?

Do you think space, time, energy and commitment from the adopters are just as important?

The support process

Generally, three periods of support can be identified within the process: pre-approval, pre-adoption and post-adoption. The pre-approval phase includes the period of initial assessment of suitability. The pre-adoption stage includes the period from approval by the adoption panel to the granting of an adoption order, and the post-adoption period includes the period after an adoption order has been granted. Adopters should receive support during the assessment process or pre-approval phase. What form do you think this support might take? Usually adopters are either encouraged to continue with the process or they are discouraged from continuing. The pre-adoption phase is usually characterised by intensive activity. The adopters have been approved, they have also been matched to a child by the adoption panel and the child has usually been placed. Adopters at this stage are surrounded by people, the adoption worker, the child's social worker, health visitors, all of whom are generally wanting to be helpful. What core skills, knowledge and values would you have used up to this point?

You will have used your preparatory skills to communicate verbally and in writing with many of the above people. You will have used your relationship building skills to form an open, honest and trusting relationship with the prospective adopters. You will have used your assessment skills to determine the suitability of the prospective adopters and explored the risks and benefits of the match. You will have used your knowledge of child protection to inform, assess and clarify the prospective adopters' expectations of an adopted child. You will have valued the contributions of the prospective adopters and helped them to understand the value and usefulness of their positive and negative life experiences.

Other types of support have been offered to adopters, including help with contact with birth families as well as supporting adopted children to enable them to obtain access to their birth records.

The Adoption and Children Act 2002 has addressed some of the issues around the variable provision of support services by requiring an adoption support plan for all placements. This should mean some improvement in the services provided for adoptive families. There does however remain a central problem because although all adopters are entitled to an assessment of need for their children (a duty under the Act) there is only a power to pro-vide services, leaving this at the discretion of the local authority.

The review process

During this process you might want to consider how Tariq and Nadia have settled since being placed with their adoptive parents. What specific factors would you want to exam-ine? Have the children established a routine? Have they begun to make an attachment to their new carers and have they begun to detach themselves from their previous carers? Do they sleep well or are they awake during the night? Are they eating well? How are Tariq and Nadia getting on together? Do you as the adoption worker share the social worker's assessment? Is there any contact with any siblings? A decision was made to separate Kylie from her siblings, Tariq and Nadia. Kylie has been placed in residential care. A brief discus-sion of this form of substitute care will be outlined.

Residential care

The majority of children in the LAC system are placed in foster care or for adoption. However, around 10 per cent of children are cared for in residential settings. This percent-age has remained virtually static for the last five years (see Table 7.2 above) though there has been an increase in 'other residential' numbers. Residential care is provided by local authorities and voluntary and independent agencies. All residential homes for children must be registered and inspected by Ofsted through its review processes.

Over the course of many years there have been concerns about the abuse of power in residential children's homes (Levy and Kahan, 1991; Warner, 1992). Further and more recent concerns have led to a number of inquiries, including that of Utting, 1991 and Waterhouse, 2000, which considered the safeguarding of children living away from home and the scandal of abuse in children's homes in Wales respectively. These inquiries identified the need to ensure that children could be safely cared for in residential care by promoting minimum standards and ensuring appropriate staffing. Additional national occupational standards were introduced for managers in residential childcare (Topss, 2003), to try to ensure all children's homes met the requirements of the National Minimum Care Standards for Children's Homes 2001 (DoH, 2001b) and the Children's Homes Regulations 2001 (DoH, 2001a). The most recent Children's Homes: National Minimum Standards (2011) provide statutory guidance to ensure that local authorities as providers and commissioners of children's homes focus on securing positive welfare, health and education outcomes for children and young people and on reducing risks to their safety and welfare.

RESEARCH SUMMARY

Unsworth (2004), in her review of how care services provide information in relation to National Minimum Standards of care homes in England, found that there were still disparities between homes. Nineteen per cent (representing about 280 homes) did not meet the standard required to provide information; the majority (59 per cent) almost met it; 21 per cent did meet it; and 2 per cent exceeded it. She also found that where there was good practice there was no significant difference by provider type and that only one region was significantly worse than the rest. Good practice in children's homes is shown through user service guides, in easy to understand and appropriate language, which are actually used. It is further indicated by service user involvement in creating statements of purpose and guides and the use of appropriate formats.

All these sought and seek to ensure that children and young people receive appropriate and safe care by addressing a wide range of issues. These range from requiring each home to have a statement of purpose, placement plans for children and regular reviews on privacy, personal appearance and the provision and preparation of meals. All areas of a child's life have a minimum standard which homes are assessed against. In theory this should mean that a child or young person should have their needs met in a similar way wherever they are in England.

Some of the concerns that have arisen about residential care and indeed children in the looked-after system generally have been the inability of children and young people to be listened to and heard. Efforts are being made to address this in different ways, and to build on the Children Act 1989, which has clear statements on ascertaining the child's wishes and feelings.

Complaints procedures for children and young people were introduced by the 2001 Act to provide a formal process for service users to either complain or express their views. These have been updated by the Advocacy Services and Representations Procedure (Children) (Amendment) Regulations 2004 to try to ensure that children and young people are listened to when they wish to formally express a view or make a complaint and that they have access to an independent advocate to support them if they wish.

Residential care can be used for a number of purposes including short-term care for children with disabilities. The majority of residential provision is for young people with challenging behaviour for whom foster care is either not appropriate or has not been successful (Colton et al., 2001).

CASE STUDY

Kylie is unable to remain in her foster home. Her behaviour has become very challenging; she has started to steal money from the foster carers and has assaulted their 12-year-old son. She has also begun to stay out at night and has been seen with a man who is thought to deal in drugs and act as a pimp for young girls. You need to find Kylie an alternative placement. How will you go about this and what will influence you?

COMMENT

All children's homes should have a statement of purpose, which may be a good starting point in your discussions with Kylie. The minimum standards may also be useful as would any inspection reports about the home. You will need to find out Kylie's views, taking them into account while balancing them with her welfare and best interests.

Homes are staffed by teams of people who provide care for the children and young people. The majority of homes have rotas with staff working shifts, information being shared through change-over meetings or by daily logs of events. Issues can arise if teams do not take the same approach with service users, which can result in inconsistent care. Young people can also find it difficult to relate to teams and struggle if their key worker is not available when they need them. Conversely, others prefer this setting because it is less like family life, as for example in a foster home. In addition to the average sized eight-bed home larger units do exist. Some provide secure accommodation for young people who are considered to be putting themselves at risk and have been placed there by court order. These units also accommodate young people who are either on remand for, or have been convicted of, serious criminal offences. For further discussion see Johns, 2011, Chapter 6.

CHAPTER SUMMARY

This chapter will help you to meet the subject benchmark 3.2.2, which requires you to develop problem-solving skills. You have been introduced to the concept of substitute care for children and young people. The chapter has outlined the structure which underlies the provision of services and has considered the processes involved in them. The chapter has also given you the opportunity of beginning to work through and reflect upon the complexities and dilemmas that arise in successful substitute care for children.

Cockburn, V (ed.) (2000) *It's Mad That's All: A Collection of Poems About Being Looked After*. London: Foster Carers Association.

Poems from young people in the looked-after system in which young people express their feelings about all aspects of life.

Fahlberg, V (2004) *A Child's Journey Through Placement*. London: British Association for Adoption and Fostering.

A classic text on the experience of children in the looked-after system which includes child development, separation and loss, attachment and direct work with children.

Salter, A N (2004) *The Adopters' Handbook: Information, Resources and Services for Adoptive Parents*. London: British Association for Adoption and Fostering.

Sellick, C and Howell, D (2003) *Innovative, Tried and Tested: A Review of Good Practice in Fostering*. London: Social Care Institute for Excellence.

This text describes good innovative practice in fostering in the context of findings from research.

Smith, F, Stewart, R and Conroy Harris, A (2011) *Adoption Now*. London: British Association for Adoption and Fostering.

Smith, F, Brann, C and Conroy Harris, A (2011) *Fostering Now*. London: British Association for Adoption and Fostering.

These are both useful handbooks of law, regulations, guidance and standards, which can be used as handy references.

Conclusion

This book has sought to introduce you to social work practice with children and families through discussion of the context of the work and how that work can be carried out. We have done this by focusing on differing aspects of practice and by introducing a case study to highlight social workers' involvement with children and families as a basis for further exploration.

Chapter 1 introduced you to some of the issues and dilemmas that you will face when working with children and families. This chapter will have assisted your understanding and appreciation of how values and ethics influence social work practice with children and families. This is a complex area of work which requires much personal self-evaluation and reflection, and this chapter will have helped you to begin that process. The activities in the chapter were designed to get you to think about how personal, professional, agency and societal values can influence social work practice with children and families. As you have worked through the activities we also hope that you have been able to make the links between the Professional Capabilities Framework that social workers need to meet in order to demonstrate professional competence. In addition, we also hope that you have been able to identify the social processes that can lead to marginalisation, isolation and exclusion, which in turn lead to families needing support. This chapter also sought to start you thinking about developing your problem-solving skills by taking account of the impact of discrimination: personal, professional, agency and societal. Thinking about how values and ethics impact on your practice will also help you to develop a solid value base which will, we hope, help you to become a reflective, anti-oppressive and empowering practitioner.

Chapter 2, in considering the historical and policy context as a starting point for practice with children and families, offers a context to the work, giving you a sense of how working with children and families has changed over time. This chapter provides a foundation for working within the Professional Capabilities Framework, particularly relating to knowledge, rights and justice, as well as an introduction to some of the issues which have arisen, for example, within child death inquiries and the treatment of children in the looked-after system. Finally, the chapter tried to help you consider the more recent changes in social work with children and families and those which are to come.

Chapter 3 further developed your foundation for working within the Professional Capabilities Framework by introducing you to ideas around supportive and preventative social work. These ideas have become embodied in government policies, such as Homestart and Sure Start, the promotion of Family Centres and the developments encompassed in Every Child Matters. Definitions of family support were discussed to help gain an understanding of how the concept has developed over time. The chapter also considered the characteristics of family support and related areas of social work practice, together with how needs are defined and the importance of the assessment process. The chapter then raised your awareness of the need for the planning and reviewing of any intervention in ways that are sensitive to the individual circumstances of children and their families.

Additionally, the chapter provided you with case examples of family support interventions for different problems and outcomes to enable you to relate the theory to practice examples. These discussions provide a sound basis for developing your social work practice and meeting the relevant quality assurance benchmarks. Finally, this chapter highlighted the importance of this work and acknowledged how early intervention can prevent situations deteriorating to the point where there is little option but to take a much more interventionist approach.

Chapter 4 provided a foundation for meeting all the Professional Capabilities Framework by focusing on the skills and knowledge needed by social workers to work effectively with children and families within the safeguarding children arena. It outlined the categories and definitions of child abuse before introducing you to the issues being addressed by safeguarding children practitioners throughout the country, particularly the impact of domestic violence, drug and alcohol problems and mental illness/distress on children. The chapter then highlighted current legislation, policies, guidance, methods of intervention and the framework for assessing children and families, using examples from practice in relation to the Cole/Green family to enhance your understanding. You were then introduced to the developments and changes in legislation, guidance and the assessment framework following the implementation of the Children Act 2004 and Every Child Matters. Finally, the chapter helped you to consider safeguarding children as a high profile area of social work practice and what causes concerns about children's welfare. The chapter also highlighted the dilemmas of safeguarding children from harm, for example, by their parent/s and protecting the privacy and respect for family life from over-zealous state intervention, while you as a social worker consistently put the interests of the child first.

Chapter 5 introduced you to direct work with children and young people, setting the context for exploring young people's views and the role of the social worker in that task, helping you to meet the Professional Capabilities Framework in the areas of professionalism, diversity, knowledge and judgement. The planning and process of direct work was discussed, together with practical ways to approach and relate to children and young people. This chapter considered four different groups of children and young people to highlight the differences, as well as the similarities, that need to be considered by practitioners when planning their work. The importance of direct work with children and the skills it needs was highlighted, as it can often be overlooked when workers are focusing on safeguarding or struggling to provide a service. There was recognition of the need to ensure that the wishes and views of children and young people are listened to and respected, even though they cannot always be followed.

Chapter 6 led you into a discussion of a particular area of practice and reinforced the idea that as a social worker you need to focus on seeing and working with the child rather than the disability. This chapter provided you with a basis for meeting the Professional Capabilities Framework in values and ethics, diversity, knowledge and judgement by helping you consider some of the issues facing children with disabilities and their families. It will have also helped you to develop your understanding, knowledge and skills to enable you to work effectively to support children with disabilities within their communities. Different models of disability were explored with emphasis on the social model to help you promote inclusive social work practice. The chapter also emphasised the centrality of the views of children with disabilities and their families, and disabled adults, to aid your understanding of some of the barriers to inclusion that disabled children face in their daily lives. Finally, the chapter considered the differing services offered to children with disabilities and their families, including the important areas of education and transition.

The final chapter in the book considered the care of children who are living away from their birth families by discussing the looked-after children system and by reviewing the three main areas of substitute care. This chapter again provided a foundation for meeting the Professional Capabilities Framework in the areas of values and ethics, diversity, knowledge and judgement. You were introduced to the principles of adoption, fostering and residential care within the current legal and social policy context. The processes of adoption and fostering were outlined using case study material to highlight the skills you will need, especially in assessment. The chapter also discussed residential provision as the other area of substitute care, again using case material to highlight principles, procedures and processes. The chapter highlighted the importance of the review process for all children within the looked-after children system by providing you with details and discussion as a basis for developing your practice.

Working with children and their families incorporates many aspects of social work practice; this book focuses on six of these key areas. Through the use of case studies and other exercises you should have gained an understanding of family support, safeguarding children, direct work with children and young people, and the particular challenges working with children with disabilities and children in the looked-after system. The book has begun your introduction to the skills and knowledge you will need to develop in working with children and families, and provides a foundation for you to build on in your future career.

Work with children and families is challenging but can be very rewarding. You will be practising as a social worker at a time of change when there are exciting opportunities for significant improvements in the whole arena. We wish you well as you continue on your journey.

Appendix 1 Professional capabilities framework

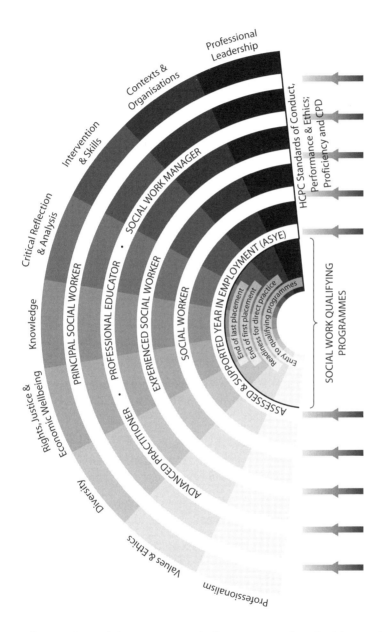

Professional Capabilities Framework diagram reproduced with permission of The College of Social Work

See page xiv for the full list of standards.

Appendix 2 Subject benchmark for social work

5 Subject knowledge, understanding and skills

Subject knowledge and understanding

5.1 During their degree studies in social work, honours graduates should acquire, critically evaluate, apply and integrate knowledge and understanding in the following five core areas of study.

5.1.1

Social work services, service users and carers, which include:

- the social processes (associated with, for example, poverty, migration, unemployment, poor health, disablement, lack of education and other sources of disadvantage) that lead to marginalisation, isolation and exclusion, and their impact on the demand for social work services

- explanations of the links between definitional processes contributing to social differences (for example, social class, gender, ethnic differences, age, sexuality and religious belief) to the problems of inequality and differential need faced by service users

- the nature of social work services in a diverse society (with particular reference to concepts such as prejudice, interpersonal, institutional and structural discrimination, empowerment and anti-discriminatory practices)

- the nature and validity of different definitions of, and explanations for, the characteristics and circumstances of service users and the services required by them, drawing on knowledge from research, practice experience, and from service users and carers

- the focus on outcomes, such as promoting the well-being of young people and their families, and promoting dignity, choice and independence for adults receiving services

- the relationship between agency policies, legal requirements and professional boundaries in shaping the nature of services provided in interdisciplinary contexts and the issues associated with working across professional boundaries and within different disciplinary groups.

5.1.2

The service delivery context, which includes:

- the location of contemporary social work within historical, comparative and global perspectives, including European and international contexts

- the changing demography and cultures of communities in which social workers will be practising

- the complex relationships between public, social and political philosophies, policies and priorities and the organisation and practice of social work, including the contested nature of these

- the issues and trends in modern public and social policy and their relationship to contemporary practice and service delivery in social work

- the significance of legislative and legal frameworks and service delivery standards (including the nature of legal authority, the application of legislation in practice, statutory accountability and tensions between statute, policy and practice)

- the current range and appropriateness of statutory, voluntary and private agencies providing community-based, day-care, residential and other services and the organisational systems inherent within these

- the significance of interrelationships with other related services, including housing, health, income maintenance and criminal justice (where not an integral social service)

- the contribution of different approaches to management, leadership and quality in public and independent human services

- the development of personalised services, individual budgets and direct payments

- the implications of modern information and communications technology (ICT) for both the provision and receipt of services.

5.1.3

Values and ethics, which include:

- the nature, historical evolution and application of social work values

- the moral concepts of rights, responsibility, freedom, authority and power inherent in the practice of social workers as moral and statutory agents

- the complex relationships between justice, care and control in social welfare and the practical and ethical implications of these, including roles as statutory agents and in upholding the law in respect of discrimination

- aspects of philosophical ethics relevant to the understanding and resolution of value dilemmas and conflicts in both interpersonal and professional contexts

- the conceptual links between codes defining ethical practice, the regulation of professional conduct and the management of potential conflicts generated by the codes held by different professional groups.

5.1.4

Social work theory, which includes:

- research-based concepts and critical explanations from social work theory and other disciplines that contribute to the knowledge base of social work, including their distinctive epistemological status and application to practice

- the relevance of sociological perspectives to understanding societal and structural influences on human behaviour at individual, group and community levels

- the relevance of psychological, physical and physiological perspectives to understanding personal and social development and functioning

- social science theories explaining group and organisational behaviour, adaptation and change

- models and methods of assessment, including factors underpinning the selection and testing of relevant information, the nature of professional judgement and the processes of risk assessment and decision-making

- approaches and methods of intervention in a range of settings, including factors guiding the choice and evaluation of these

- user-led perspectives

- knowledge and critical appraisal of relevant social research and evaluation methodologies, and the evidence base for social work.

5.1.5

The nature of social work practice, which includes:

- the characteristics of practice in a range of community-based and organisational settings within statutory, voluntary and private sectors, and the factors influencing changes and developments in practice within these contexts

- the nature and characteristics of skills associated with effective practice, both direct and indirect, with a range of service-users and in a variety of settings

- the processes that facilitate and support service user choice and independence

- the factors and processes that facilitate effective interdisciplinary, interprofessional and interagency collaboration and partnership

- the place of theoretical perspectives and evidence from international research in assessment and decision-making processes in social work practice

- the integration of theoretical perspectives and evidence from international research into the design and implementation of effective social work intervention, with a wide range of service users, carers and others

- the processes of reflection and evaluation, including familiarity with the range of approaches for evaluating service and welfare outcomes, and their significance for the development of practice and the practitioner.

Subject-specific skills and other skills

5.2 As an applied subject at honours degree level, social work necessarily involves the development of skills that may be of value in many situations (for example, analytical thinking, building relationships, working as a member of an organisation, intervention, evaluation and reflection). Some of these skills are specific to social work but many are also widely transferable. What helps to define the specific nature of these skills in a social work context are:

- the context in which they are applied and assessed (eg, communication skills in practice with people with sensory impairments or assessment skills in an interprofessional setting)

- the relative weighting given to such skills within social work practice (eg, the central importance of problem-solving skills within complex human situations)

- the specific purpose of skill development (eg, the acquisition of research skills in order to build a repertoire of research-based practice)

- a requirement to integrate a range of skills (ie, not simply to demonstrate these in an isolated and incremental manner).

5.3 All social work honours graduates should show the ability to reflect on and learn from the exercise of their skills. They should understand the significance of the concepts of continuing professional development and lifelong learning, and accept responsibility for their own continuing development.

5.4 Social work honours graduates should acquire and integrate skills in the following five core areas.

Problem-solving skills

5.5 These are sub-divided into four areas.

5.5.1

Managing problem-solving activities: honours graduates in social work should be able to plan problem-solving activities, ie to:

- think logically, systematically, critically and reflectively

- apply ethical principles and practices critically in planning problem-solving activities

- plan a sequence of actions to achieve specified objectives, making use of research, theory and other forms of evidence

- manage processes of change, drawing on research, theory and other forms of evidence.

5.5.2

Gathering information: honours graduates in social work should be able to:

- gather information from a wide range of sources and by a variety of methods, for a range of purposes. These methods should include electronic searches, reviews of relevant literature, policy and procedures, face-to-face interviews, written and telephone contact with individuals and groups

- take into account differences of viewpoint in gathering information and critically assess the reliability and relevance of the information gathered

- assimilate and disseminate relevant information in reports and case records.

5.5.3

Analysis and synthesis: honours graduates in social work should be able to analyse and synthesise knowledge gathered for problem-solving purposes, ie to:

- assess human situations, taking into account a variety of factors (including the views of participants, theoretical concepts, research evidence, legislation and organisational policies and procedures)

- analyse information gathered, weighing competing evidence and modifying their viewpoint in light of new information, then relate this information to a particular task, situation or problem

- consider specific factors relevant to social work practice (such as risk, rights, cultural differences and linguistic sensitivities, responsibilities to protect vulnerable individuals and legal obligations)

- assess the merits of contrasting theories, explanations, research, policies and procedures

- synthesise knowledge and sustain reasoned argument

- employ a critical understanding of human agency at the macro (societal), mezzo (organisational and community) and micro (inter and intrapersonal) levels

- critically analyse and take account of the impact of inequality and discrimination in work with people in particular contexts and problem situations.

5.5.4

Intervention and evaluation: honours graduates in social work should be able to use their knowledge of a range of interventions and evaluation processes selectively to:

- build and sustain purposeful relationships with people and organisations in community-based, and interprofessional contexts

- make decisions, set goals and construct specific plans to achieve these, taking into account relevant factors including ethical guidelines

- negotiate goals and plans with others, analysing and addressing in a creative manner human, organisational and structural impediments to change

- implement plans through a variety of systematic processes that include working in partnership

- undertake practice in a manner that promotes the well-being and protects the safety of all parties

- engage effectively in conflict resolution

- support service users to take decisions and access services, with the social worker as navigator, advocate and supporter

- manage the complex dynamics of dependency and, in some settings, provide direct care and personal support in everyday living situations

- meet deadlines and comply with external definitions of a task

- plan, implement and critically review processes and outcomes

- bring work to an effective conclusion, taking into account the implications for all involved

- monitor situations, review processes and evaluate outcomes

- use and evaluate methods of intervention critically and reflectively.

Communication skills

5.6 Honours graduates in social work should be able to communicate clearly, accurately and precisely (in an appropriate medium) with individuals and groups in a range of formal and informal situations, ie to:

- make effective contact with individuals and organisations for a range of objectives, by verbal, paper-based and electronic means

- clarify and negotiate the purpose of such contacts and the boundaries of their involvement

- listen actively to others, engage appropriately with the life experiences of service users, understand accurately their viewpoint and overcome personal prejudices to respond appropriately to a range of complex personal and interpersonal situations

- use both verbal and non-verbal cues to guide interpretation

- identify and use opportunities for purposeful and supportive communication with service users within their everyday living situations

- follow and develop an argument and evaluate the viewpoints of, and evidence presented by, others

- write accurately and clearly in styles adapted to the audience, purpose and context of the communication

- use advocacy skills to promote others' rights, interests and needs

- present conclusions verbally and on paper, in a structured form, appropriate to the audience for which these have been prepared

- make effective preparation for, and lead meetings in a productive way

- communicate effectively across potential barriers resulting from differences (for example, in culture, language and age).

Skills in working with others

5.7 Honours graduates in social work should be able to work effectively with others, ie to:

- involve users of social work services in ways that increase their resources, capacity and power to influence factors affecting their lives

- consult actively with others, including service users and carers, who hold relevant information or expertise

- act cooperatively with others, liaising and negotiating across differences such as organisational and professional boundaries and differences of identity or language

- develop effective helping relationships and partnerships with other individuals, groups and organisations that facilitate change

- act with others to increase social justice by identifying and responding to prejudice, institutional discrimination and structural inequality

- act within a framework of multiple accountability (for example, to agencies, the public, service users, carers and others)

- challenge others when necessary, in ways that are most likely to produce positive outcomes.

Skills in personal and professional development

5.8 Honours graduates in social work should be able to:

- advance their own learning and understanding with a degree of independence

- reflect on and modify their behaviour in the light of experience

- identify and keep under review their own personal and professional boundaries

- manage uncertainty, change and stress in work situations

- handle inter and intrapersonal conflict constructively

- understand and manage changing situations and respond in a flexible manner

- challenge unacceptable practices in a responsible manner

- take responsibility for their own further and continuing acquisition and use of knowledge and skills

- use research critically and effectively to sustain and develop their practice.

ICT and numerical skills

5.9 Honours graduates in social work should be able to use ICT methods and techniques to support their learning and their practice. In particular, they should demonstrate the ability to:

- use ICT effectively for professional communication, data storage and retrieval and information searching

- use ICT in working with people who use services

- demonstrate sufficient familiarity with statistical techniques to enable effective use of research in practice

- integrate appropriate use of ICT to enhance skills in problem-solving in the four areas set out in paragraph 6.2

- apply numerical skills to financial and budgetary responsibilities

- have a critical understanding of the social impact of ICT, including an awareness of the impact of the 'digital divide'.

7 Benchmark standards

7.1 Given the essentially applied nature of social work and the co-terminosity of the degree and the professional award, students must demonstrate that they have met the standards specified in relation to **both** academic and practice capabilities. These standards relate to subject-specific knowledge, understanding and skills (including key skills inherent in the concept of 'graduateness'). Qualifying students will be expected to meet each of these standards in accordance with the specific standards set by the relevant country (see section 2).

Typical graduate

7.2 Levels of attainment will vary along a continuum from the threshold to excellence. This level represents that of typical students graduating with an honours degree in social work.

Knowledge and understanding

7.3 On graduating with an honours degree in social work, students should be able to demonstrate:

- a sound understanding of the five core areas of knowledge and understanding relevant to social work, as detailed in paragraph 5.1, including their application to practice and service delivery

- an ability to use this knowledge and understanding in an integrated way, in specific practice contexts

- an ability to use this knowledge and understanding to engage in effective relationships with service users and carers

- appraisal of previous learning and experience and ability to incorporate this into their future learning and practice

- acknowledgement and understanding of the potential and limitations of social work as a practice-based discipline to effect individual and social change

- an ability to use research and enquiry techniques with reflective awareness, to collect, analyse and interpret relevant information

- a developed capacity for the critical evaluation of knowledge and evidence from a range of sources.

Subject-specific and other skills

7.4 On graduating with an honours degree in social work, students should be able to demonstrate a developed capacity to:

- apply creatively a repertoire of core skills as detailed in section 5

- communicate effectively with service users and carers, and with other professionals

- integrate clear understanding of ethical issues and codes of values, and practice with their interventions in specific situations

- consistently exercise an appropriate level of autonomy and initiative in individual decision-making within the context of supervisory, collaborative, ethical and organisational requirements

- demonstrate habits of critical reflection on their performance and take responsibility for modifying action in light of this.

Bibliography

Adoption and Children Act (2002) London: The Stationery Office.

Aldgate, J and Simmonds, J (eds) (1988) *Direct Work with Children. A Guide for Social Work Practitioners.* London: Batsford.

Aldgate, J and Tunstill, J (1995) *Making Sense of Section 17: Implementing Services for Children in Need Within the Children Act 1989.* London: HMSO.

Allen, G (2011) *Early Intervention: The Next Steps. An Independent Report to Her Majesty's Government.* London: The Stationery Office.

Allen, N (2007) *Making Sense of the New Adoption Law.* Lyme Regis: Russell House Publications.

Anderson, H and Goolishian, H (1992) The client is the expert: A not-knowing approach to therapy. In McNamee, S and Bergen, K (eds) (1992) *Therapy as Social Construction.* Newbury Park, CA: Sage.

Audit Commission (1994) *Seen But Not Heard: Co-ordinating Community Child Health and Social Services for Children in Need.* London: HMSO.

Badinter, E (1981) *The Myth of Motherhood: An Historical View of the Maternal Instinct.* New York: Macmillan.

Baker, A and Duncan, S (1985) Child sexual abuse: a study of prevalence in Great Britain. *Journal of Child Abuse and Neglect*, 9: 457–467.

Baldwin, S (1985) *The Costs of Caring: Families with Disabled Children.* London: Routledge and Kegan Paul.

Bannister, A (2003) *Creative Therapies with Traumatized Children.* London and Philadelphia: Jessica Kingsley.

Barker, R (ed) (2009) *Making Sense of Every Child Matters. Multi-professional Practice Guidance.* Bristol: Policy Press.

Barker, J and Hodes, D (2007) *The Child in Mind: A Child Protection Handbook,* Third Edition. London: Routledge.

Barn, R (ed.) (1993) *Working with Black Children and Adolescents in Need.* London: British Association for Adoption and Fostering.

Barnes, C (1992) *Disabling Imagery and the Media.* Halifax: British Council of Disabled People/ Ryburn Publishing.

Batmanghelidjh, C (2008) at www.kidsco.org.uk

Beckett, C (2007) *Child Protection: An Introduction,* Second Edition. London: Sage.

Beckett, C and Maynard, A (2005) *Values and Ethics in Social Work.* London: Sage.

Bell, M and Wilson, K (eds) (2003) *Practitioner's Guide to Working With Families.* Hampshire: Palgrave Macmillan.

Bellhouse, B, Fuller, A, Johnson, G and Taylor, N (2005) *Managing the Difficult Emotions*. London: Paul Chapman Publishing.

Beresford, B (1995) Expert Opinions: A Survey of Parents Caring For a Severely Disabled Child. Bristol: The Policy Press.

Beresford, B (2002) Preventing the social exclusion of disabled children in McNeish, D, Newman, T and Roberts, H (2002) *What Works for Children?* Buckingham: Open University Press.

Beresford, B (2006) *Housing and Disabled Children: A review of Policy Levers and Opportunities*. York: Joseph Rowntree Foundation.

Beresford, B and Oldman, C (2002) *Housing Matters: National Evidence Relating to Disabled Children and Their Housing*. Bristol: The Policy Press.

Berlins, M (2008) If a 16 year old cannot buy cigarettes, surely they should not be allowed anywhere near a Polling Booth, *Guardian*, 29.10.08.

Betts, B and Ahmad, A (2003) *My Life Story*, CD Rom. Orkney: Information Plus.

Birmingham Safeguarding Children Board (2010) Serious Case Review: Khyra Ishaq. Birmingham: Birmingham Safeguarding Board. Available at www.lscbbirmingham.org.uk/downloads/Case+14.pdf (accessed 30 May 2012).

Booth, C (1889) *The Life and Labour of the People of London*. London: Macmillan.

Borthwick, S and Lord, J (2011) *Effective Fostering Panels*. London: British Association for Adoption and Fostering.

Brammer, A (2002) *Social Work Law*. Harlow: Longman.

Brammer, A (2010) *Social Work Law*, Third Edition. Harlow: Pearson Education.

Brandon, M, Schofield, G and Trinder, L (1998) *Social Work With Children*. London: Palgrave Macmillan.

Brandon, M, Belderson, P, Warren, C, Howe, D, Gardner, R, Dodsworth, J and Black, J (2008) Analysing child deaths and serious injury through abuse and neglect: what can we learn? A biennial analysis of serious case reviews 2003–2005. DCSF Research Review 023. London: DCSF (available at www.education.gov.uk/publications/eOrderingDownload/DCSF-RR023.pdf) (accessed 30 May 2012).

Brandon, M, Howe, A, Dagley, V, Salter, C, Warren, C and Black, C (2006) *Evaluating the CAF and Lead Professional Guidance and Implementation in 2005–06*. Research Report RR740. Nottingham, Department for Education and Skills.

Brandon, M, Sidebotham, P, Bailey, S and Belderson, P (2010) *A Study of the Recommendations Arising From Serious Case Reviews 2009-2010*. London: Department for Education. Available at www.education.gov.uk/publications/eOrderingDownload/DFE-RR157.pdf (accessed 30 May 2012).

Brandon, M and Thoburn, J (2008) Safeguarding children in the UK: A longitudinal study of services to children suffering or likely to suffer significant harm. *Child and Family Social Work*, 13: 365–377.

Buckley, B (2003) *Children's Communication Skills. From Birth to Five Years*. London and New York: Routledge.

Butler, I and Williamson, H (1994) *Children Speak: Children, Trauma and Social Work.* London: Longman.

Butt, J (1998) Are we being served? *Community Care*, 24–25.

Butt, J and Box, L (1998a) *Family Centred: A Study of the Use of Family Centres by Asian Families.* London: Race Equality Unit.

Butt, J and Box, L (1998b) Engage and provide. *Community Care*, 22–23.

Byrne, S (2000) *Linking and Introductions: Helping Children Join Adoptive Families.* London: British Association for Adoption and Fostering.

Bywater, J and Jones, R (2007) *Sexuality and Social Work.* Exeter: Learning Matters.

Camis, J (2006) *My Life and Me.* London: British Association for Adoption and Fostering.

Carers and Disabled Children Act (2000) London: The Stationery Office.

Cattanach, A (1992) *Play Therapy with Abused Children.* London and Philadelphia: Jessica Kingsley.

Centre for Excellence and Outcomes in Children and Young People's Services (2010) *Knowledge Review 1: Effective Practice to Protect Children Living in 'Highly Resistant' Families,* available at www.c4eo.org.uk (accessed 30 May 2012).

Chand, A (2000) Over-representation of black children in the child protection system. *Journal of Child and Family Social Work*, 5: 67–77.

Children Act (1948). London: Her Majesty's Stationery Office.

Children Act (1989). London: Her Majesty's Stationery Office.

Children Act (2004). London: The Stationery Office.

Children (Leaving Care) Act (2000). London: The Stationery Office.

Clark, A (2005) Listening to and involving young children: a review of research and practice. *Early Child Development and Care,* 175 (6): 489–505.

Clark, C L (2000) *Social Work Ethics: Politics, Principles and Practice.* Basingstoke: Macmillan.

Cleaver, H, Unell, I and Aldgate, J (2007) *Children's Needs – Parenting Capacity: The Impact of Parental Mental Illness, Problem Alcohol and Drug Use, and Domestic Violence on Children's Development.* London: The Stationery Office.

Cleaver, H and Walker, S with Meadows, P (2004) *Assessing Children's Needs and Circumstances: The Impact of the Assessment Framework.* London: Jessica Kingsley.

Colton, M, Drury, C and Williams, M (1995) *Children in Need. Family Support Under the Children Act 1989.* Aldershot: Avebury.

Colton, M, Sanders, R and Williams, M (2001) *An Introduction to Working With Children.* Basingstoke: Palgrave.

Connolly, M, Crichton-Hill, Y and Ward, T (2006) *Culture and Child Protection: Reflexive Responses.* London: Jessica Kingsley.

Corby, B (2006) *Child Abuse: Towards a Knowledge Base,* Third Edition. Buckingham: Open University Press.

Crawford, K and Walker, J (2010) *Social Work and Human Development*. Exeter: Learning Matters.

Curtis Committee (1946) *Report of the Care of Children Committee*, Cmnd 6922. London: HMSO.

Daniel, B, Wassell, S and Gilligan, R (2010) *Child Development for Child Care and Protection Workers*, Second Edition. London: Jessica Kingsley.

DCSF (Department for Children, Schools and Families) (2007) *The Children's Plan*. London: The Stationery Office.

DCSF (Department for Children, Schools and Families) (2008) *Staying Safe: Action Plan*. London: DCSF.

DCSF (2009) *Safeguarding Disabled Children Practice Guidance*. London: DCSF.

DCSF (Department for Children, Schools and Families) (2010b) *Working Together to Safeguard Children: A Guide to Interagency Working to Safeguard and Promote the Welfare of Children*. London: The Stationery Office.

De Mause, L (1976) *The History of Childhood*. London: Souvenir Press.

Department for Work and Pensions (2004) *Family Resources Survey 2002–03*. Available at www.dwp.gov.uk (accessed 30 May 2012).

DfE (Department for Education) (2010a) *Haringey Local Safeguarding Children Board: Serious Case Review*. London: DfE.

DfE (Department for Education) (2011a) *National Minimum Standards for Foster Care 2011*. London: The Stationery Office.

DfE (Department for Education) (2011b) *Children Looked After by Local Authorities in England*, FR21/ 2011. London: The Stationery Office.

DfEE (Department for Education and Employment) (2000) *Guidance on the Education of Children and Young People in Public Care*. London: The Stationery Office.

DfES (Department for Education and Skills) (2001) *Learning to Listen: Core Principles for the Involvement of Children and Young People*. London: The Stationery Office.

DfES (Department for Education and Skills) (2002) *Children Act Report 2002*. London: The Stationery Office.

DfES (Department for Education and Skills) (2004) *Every Child Matters: Change for Children*. London: The Stationery Office.

DfES (Department for Education and Skills) (2007a) *Aiming High for Children: Supporting Families*. London: The Stationery Office.

DfES (Department for Education and Skills) (2007b) *Aiming High for Disabled Children: Better Support for Families*. London: The Stationery Office.

DfES (Department for Education and Skills) (2007c) *Care Matters: Time For Change*. London: The Stationery Office.

DHSS (Department of Health and Social Security) (1974) *The Report of the Committee of Inquiry into the Care and Supervision Provided in Relation to Maria Colwell*. London: HMSO.

DHSS (Department of Health and Social Security) (1988) *The Report of the Inquiry into Child Abuse in Cleveland* (Butler-Sloss inquiry). London: HMSO.

Dixon, J, Schnelder, V, Lloyd, C, Reeves, A, White, C, Tomaszewski, W, Green, R and Ireland, E (2010) *Monitoring and Evaluation of Family Interventions*, Research Brief DFE-RR044. London: Department for Education. Available at www.education.gov.uk/publications/ eOrderingDownload/DFE-RR044.pdf (accessed 30 May 2012).

Dobson, B and Middleton, S (1998) *Paying to Care: the Cost of Childhood Disability*. York: York Publishing Services.

DoH (Department of Health) (1988) *Protecting Children. A Guide for Social Workers Undertaking a Comprehensive Assessment (the Orange Book)*. London: HMSO.

DoH (Department of Health) (1993) *Adoption: The Future*, Cmnd 2288. London: HMSO.

DoH (Department of Health) (1995a) *Child Protection: Messages From Research*. London: HMSO.

DoH (Department of Health) (1995b) *The Challenge of Partnership in Child Protection. Practice Guide*. London: HMSO.

DoH (Department of Health) (1996) *Reporting to Court Under the Children Act 1989: A Handbook for Social Services*. London: HMSO.

DoH (Department of Health) (1998a) *Disabled Children: Directions for Their Future Care*. London: The Stationery Office.

DoH (Department of Health) (1998b) *Quality Protects*. London: The Stationery Office.

DoH (Department of Health) (1999a) *Children in the Looked After System*. London: The Stationery Office.

DoH (Department of Health) (1999b) *Opportunity For All: Tackling Poverty and Social Exclusion*. London. The Stationery Office.

DoH (Department of Health) (2000a) *Assessing Children in Need. Practice Guidance*. London: The Stationery Office.

DoH (Department of Health) (2000b) *Framework for the Assessment of Children in Need and Their Families*. London: The Stationery Office.

DoH (Department of Health) (2000c) *Carers and Disabled Children Act*.

DoH (Department of Health) (2000d) *Lost in Care (the Waterhouse Report)*. London: The Stationery Office.

DoH (Department of Health) (2001a) *Children's Homes Regulations*. London: The Stationery Office.

DoH (Department of Health) (2001b) *National Minimum Care Standards for Children's Homes*. London: The Stationery Office.

DoH (Department of Health) (2001c) *The Children Act Now: Messages from Research*. London: The Stationery Office.

DoH (Department of Health) (2001d) *Valuing People. A New Strategy for Learning Disability for the 21st Century*. London: The Stationery Office.

DoH (Department of Health) (2002) *Safeguarding Children in Whom Illness is Fabricated or Induced*. London: Department of Health Publications.

DoH (Department of Health) (2003a) *Choice Protects*. London: The Stationery Office.

DoH (Department of Health) (2003b) *Safeguarding Children.* London: The Stationery Office.

DoH (Department of Health) (2003c) *Together from the Start.* Available at www.dh.gov.uk (accessed 30 May 2012)

DoH (Department of Health) (2004*) National Service Framework for Children, Young People and Maternity Services,* Core Standards. London: Department of Health.

DoH (Department of Health) (2008) *Better Care, Better Lives.* London: COI.

DoH (Department of Health) (2011) *The Family Nurse Partnership in England.* Available at www. dh.gov.uk/publications (accessed 30 May 2012)

DoH (Department of Health) and the Home Office (2003) *The Victoria Climbié Inquiry: Report of an Inquiry by Lord Laming.* London: The Stationery Office.

DoH/DfES (Department of Health/Department for Education and Skills) (2004) *Early Support Professional Guidance.* Available at www.education.gov.uk (accessed 30 May 2012)

Douglas, A and Philpot, T (1998) *Caring and Coping.* London: Routledge.

Doyle, C (1997) *Working with Abused Children,* Second Edition. Basingstoke: Macmillan.

Doyle, C (2006) *Working With Abused Children,* Third Edition. Basingstoke: Palgrave Macmillan.

Fahlberg, V (2004) *A Child's Journey Through Placement.* London: British Association for Adoption and Fostering.

Falkov, A (1996) *Fatal Child Abuse and Parental Psychiatric Disorder.* London: Department of Health.

Family Justice Review (2011) *Streamlining the System: Final Report.* Available at www.justice. gov.uk/downloads/publications/policy/moj/family-justice-review-final-report

Featherstone, B (2004) *Family Life and Family Support.* Basingstoke: Palgrave Macmillan.

Ferguson, H (1990) Rethinking child protection practices: a case for history, cited in the Violence Against Children Study Group, *Taking Child Abuse Seriously.* London: Unwin Hyman.

Ferguson, H (2005) Blame culture in child protection. *Guardian,* 16.01.2005.

Ferguson, H (2011) *Child Protection Practice.* Basingstoke: Palgrave Macmillan.

Fitton, P (2000) *Listen to Me. Communicating the Needs of People with Profound Intellectual and Multiple Disabilities.* London: Jessica Kingsley.

Flynn, R (2002) *Short Breaks: Providing Better Access and More Choice for Black Disabled Children and Their Parents.* Bristol: Policy Press.

Fox-Harding, L (1991) *Perspectives in Child Care Policy.* Harlow: Longman.

Franklin, B and Parton, N (1991) *Social Work, the Media and Public Relations.* London: Routledge.

Frost, N (2003) Understanding family support: theories, concepts and issues in Frost, N, Lloyd, A and Jeffrey, L (2003) *The RHP Companion to Family Support.* Lyme Regis: Russell House Publishing.

Frost, N and Stein, M (1989) *The Politics of Child Welfare: Inequality, Power and Change.* Hemel Hempstead: Harvester Wheatsheaf.

Frost, N, Lloyd, A and Jeffrey, L (2003) *The RHP Companion to Family Support*. Lyme Regis: Russell House Publishing.

Garrat, D, Roche, J and Tucker, S (2007) *Changing Experiences of Youth*. London: Open University/Sage.

Geldard, K and Geldard, D (2002) *Counselling Children. A Practical Introduction*. London, Thousand Oaks, New Delhi: Sage.

General Social Care Council (2002) *Codes of Practice for Social Care Workers and Employers*. London: GSCC.

Golding, K S, Dent, H R, Nissim, R and Stott, L (eds) (2006) *Thinking Psychologically About Children Who Are Looked After and Adopted: Space for Reflection*. Chichester: Wiley Blackwell.

Gordon, L (1989) Heroes of Their Own Lives: The Politics and History of Family Violence. London: Virago – cited in Corby, B (2006) *Child Abuse: Towards a Knowledge Base*, Third Edition. Buckingham: Open University Press.

Greco, V, Sloper, P and Barton, K (2004) Care co-ordination and key worker services for disabled children in the UK. *Research Works 2004–01*. York: Social Policy Research Unit, University of York.

Hamilton, C (2005) *Working with Young People: Legal Responsibility and Liability*. Colchester: Children's Legal Centre.

Hearn, B (1995) *Child and Family Support and Protection: A Practical Approach*. London: National Children's Bureau.

Hill, N (2004) Childcare strategy fails minority families. *Guardian*, 08.12.2004.

HM Treasury Spending Review (2002) Available online at www.hm-treasury.gov.uk/spending_review_02_key_documents.htm (accessed 30 May 2012)

Holman, B (1987) Family Centres. *Children and Society*, 2: 157–173.

Holman, B (1988) *Putting Families First. Prevention and Child Care*. Basingstoke: Macmillan.

Home Office (1998) *Supporting Families: A Consultation Document*. London: The Stationery Office.

Horwath, J (ed.) (2001) *The Child's World: Assessing Need in Children*. London: Jessica Kingsley.

Horwath, J (2007) *Child Neglect: Identification and Assessment*. Basingstoke: Palgrave Macmillan.

Horwath, J (ed.) (2010) *The Child's World. Assessing Children in Need*, Second Edition. London: Jessica Kingsley.

Human Rights Act (1998). London: The Stationery Office.

Hunt, J, Waterhouse, S and Lutman, E (2007) *Keeping Them in the Family: Outcomes for Abused and Neglected Children Placed with Family or Friends Carers Through Care Proceedings*. Oxford: University of Oxford/DfES.

Ince, L (1998) *Making It Alone: A Study of the Care Experiences of Young Black People*. London: British Association for Adoption and Fostering.

Iwaniec, D (1995) *The Emotionally Abused and Neglected Child: Identification, Assessment and Intervention*. Chichester: John Wiley.

Jewett, C (1997) *Helping Children Cope with Separation and Loss*, Revised Edition. London: Free Association Books and British Association for Adoption and Fostering.

Johns, R (2011) *Using the Law in Social Work*, Fifth Edition. Exeter: Learning Matters.

Johnson, P (1990) *Child Abuse: Understanding the Problem*. Marlborough: Crowood Press.

Jones, D P H (1997) 'Treatment of the child and the family where child abuse or neglect has occurred' in Helfer, R, Kempe, R and Krugman, R (1997) *The Battered Child*. Chicago, IL: Chicago University Press.

Jones, D P H (2003) *Communicating with Vulnerable Children. A Guide for Practitioners*. London: Gaskell.

Kirton, D (2000) *Race, Ethnicity and Adoption*. Buckingham: Open University Press.

Koprowska, J (2008) *Communication and Interpersonal Skills in Social Work*. Exeter: Learning Matters.

Koris, J (1987) Health visitor involvement in a family centre. *Health Visitor*, 60: 43–44.

Laming, H (2009) *The Protection of Children in England: A Progress Report* (HC 330), London: TSO. Available at www.education.gov.uk/publications/eOrderingDownload/HC-330.pdf (accessed 30 May 2012)

Lenehan, C (2004) Speech at *Early Support Programme* launch, Manchester.

Levy, A and Kahan, B (1991) *The Pindown Experience and the Protection of Children: The Report of the Staffordshire Child Care Enquiry 1990*. Stafford: Staffordshire County Council.

Lindon, J (2003) *Child Protection*, Second Edition. Bristol: Hodder Arnold.

Lloyd, N and Rafferty, A (2006) *Black and Ethnic Minority Families and Sure Start Findings from Local Education Reports*. London: Birkbeck College.

Local Safeguarding Children Board Haringey (2009) *Serious Case Review Executive Summary*. Available at www.haringeylscb.org/executive_summary_peter_final.pdf (accessed 30 May 2012)

London Borough of Brent (1985) *A Child in Trust. The Report of the Panel of Inquiry into the Circumstances Surrounding the Death of Jasmine Beckford*. London: London Borough of Brent.

Lord, J and Cullen, D (2006) *Effective Panels: Guidance on Regulations, Process and Good Practice in Adoption and Permanence Panels*. London: British Association for Adoption and Fostering.

Lowe, N and Murch, M (1999) *The Plan for the Child: Adoption or Long-Term Fostering*. London: British Association for Adoption and Fostering.

Makins, V (1997) *Not Just a Nursery ... Multi-Agency Early Years Centres in Action*. London: National Children's Bureau.

Marchant, R (2001a) The assessment of children with complex needs, in Horwath, J (2010) *The Child's World. Assessing Children in Need*. London: Jessica Kingsley.

Marchant, R (2001b) Working with disabled children, in Foley, P, Roche, J and Tucker, S (eds) (2001) *Children in Society: Contemporary Theory, Policy and Practice*. Palgrave: Basingstoke.

Marchant, R (2008) Working with disabled children who live away from home some or all of the time, in Luckock, B and Lefevre, M (eds) (2008) *Direct Work: Social Work with Children and Young People in Care*. London: British Association for Adoption and Fostering.

Marchant, R and Gordon, R (2001) *Two Way Street: Communicating with Disabled Children and Young People,* DVD/video and handbook. London: Triangle/NSPCC.

Marks, D (1999a) Dimensions of oppression: theorising the embodied subject. *Disability and Society*, 14 (5): 611–626.

Marsh, P and Crow, G (1997) *Family Group Conferences in Child Welfare*. Oxford: Blackwell.

Middleton, L (1996) *Making a Difference: Social Work with Disabled Children*. Birmingham: Venture Press.

Millam, R (2002) *Anti-Discriminatory Practice*. London: Continuum.

Ministry of Justice (2011) *Family Justice Review: Final Report.* Available at www.justice.gov.uk/publications/policy/moj/2011/family-justice-review-final.pdf

Morris, J (1995) *Gone Missing? A Research and Policy Review of Disabled Children Living Away From their Families*. London: Who Cares? Trust.

Morris, J (1998a) *Still Missing? Vol. 2 Disabled Children and the Children Act.* London: Who Cares? Trust.

Morris, J (1998b) *Don't Leave Us Out: Involving Children and Young People With Communication Impairments*. York: York Publishing Services.

Morris, J (1999a) *Hurtling into the Void: Transition to Adulthood for Young People with 'Complex Health and Support Needs'.* Brighton: JRF Pavilion.

Morris, J (1999b) *Transition to Adulthood for Young Disabled People with 'complex health and support needs'.* JRF: York Publishing Services.

Morris, J (2005) *Children on the Edge of Care. Human Rights and the Children Act.* York: JRF/York Publishing Services.

Munro, E (1999) Common errors in reasoning in child protection. *Journal of Child Abuse and Neglect,* 23 (8): 745–758.

Munro, E (2002) *Effective Child Protection*. London and Thousand Oaks, CA: Sage.

Munro, E (2008) *Effective Child Protection*, Second Edition. London and Thousand Oaks, CA: Sage.

Munro, E (2010) *The Munro Review of Child Protection. Part One: A Systems Analysis.* London: Department for Education.

Munro, E (2011) *The Munro Review of Child Protection* (final report), May 2011. London: The Stationery Office.

Murphy, M (2004) *Developing Collaborative Relationships in Interagency Child Protection Work.* Lyme Regis: Russell House Publications.

National Audit Office (2006) *Sure Start Children's Centres*. London: The Stationery Office.

NESS (2010) *The Impact of Sure Start Local Programmes on 5 Year Old Children and their Families,* Research Brief DFE-RB067. Available at www.ness.bbk.ac.uk/impact/documents (accessed 11 October 2011).

O'Brien, J (2002) *Person Centred Planning.* Toronto: Inclusion Press.

Office of Disability Issues (2006) *Improving the Life Chances of Disabled People: The First Annual Report from the Office of Disability Issues.* London: Office of Disability Issues.

O'Hagan, K (2006) *Identifying Emotional and Psychological Abuse,* Buckingham: Open University Press.

Oldman, C and Beresford, B (1998) *Homes Unfit for Children.* Basingstoke: Polity Press.

Oliver, M (1983) *Social Work with Disabled People.* Basingstoke: Macmillan.

Oliver, M (1990) *The Politics of Disablement.* Basingstoke: Macmillan.

Oliver, M (2011) *Social Work with Disabled People.* Basingstoke: Macmillan.

OPCS (Office of Population and Censuses and Surveys) (1986) *Surveys of Disability in Great Britain, Reports 1–6.* London: HMSO.

O'Sullivan, T (2011) *Decision Making in Social Work.* Basingstoke: Palgrave Macmillan.

Parker, R (ed.) (1999) *Adoption Now: Messages From Research.* London: Department of Health.

Parrot, L (2007) *Values and Ethics in Social Work Practice.* Exeter: Learning Matters.

Parton, N (2001) Protecting children: a socio-historical analysis, cited in Wilson, K and James, A (eds) *The Child Protection Handbook.* London: Balliere Tindall.

Parton, N (2009), Statutory children's social work in England. *Child and Family Social Work,* 2009, 14: 68–78.

Parton, N (2011) Child protection and safeguarding: changing and competing conceptions of risk and their implications for social work. *British Journal of Social Work,* 41 (5): 854–875.

Performance and Innovation Unit (2000) *Prime Minister's Review of Adoption.* London: The Cabinet Office.

Platts, H, Hughes, J, Lenehan, C and Morris, S (1996) *We Miss Her When She Goes Away: Respite Services for Children with Learning Disabilities and Complex Health Needs.* Manchester: NDT.

Plummer, D (2001) *Helping Children to Build Self-Esteem. A Photocopiable Activities Book.* London and Philadelphia: Jessica Kingsley.

Plummer, D (2006) *The Adventures of the Little Tin Tortoise. A Self-Esteem Story with Activities for Teachers, Parents and Carers.* London and Philadelphia: Jessica Kingsley.

Prime Minister's Strategy Unit (2005) *Improving the Life Chances of Disabled People.* Joint publication with Department for Work and Pensions, Department of Health, Department for Education and Skills, Office of the Deputy Prime Minister. Available at http://webarchive. nationalarchives.gov.uk/+/http://www.cabinetoffice.gov.uk/media/cabinetoffice/strategy/assets/disability.pdf (accessed 30 May 2012)

Professional Capabilities Framework (2012) Available at www.education.gov.uk/swrb/a0074240/professional-standards-for-social-workers-in-England (accessed 30 May 2012)

Quinton, D (2004) *Supporting Parents. Messages from Research.* London: Jessica Kingsley.

Randall, P and Parker, J (1999*) Supporting the Families of Children with Autism.* Chichester: John Wiley.

Report of the Home Office Advisory Group on Video Evidence (1989) London: HMSO.

Respect Task Force (2006) *Respect Action Plan.* London: Home Office.

Rinaldi, C (2001) A pedagogy of listening: a perspective of listening from Reggio Emilia, Italy. *Children in Europe*, 1: 2–5.

Rose, R and Philpot, T (2005) *The Child's Own Story. Life Story Work With Traumatized Children.* London and Philadelphia: Jessica Kingsley.

Rose, W (1994) An overview of the developments of services – the relationship between protection and family support and the intentions of the Children Act 1989, Sief Conference, September.

Rowntree, S (1901) *Poverty: A Study in Town Life.* London: Macmillan.

Russell, P (1995) *Positive Choices. Services for Children with Disabilities Living Away from Home.* London: National Children's Bureau.

Russell, P (1996) Listening to children with disabilities and special educational needs, in Davie, R, Upton, G and Varma, V (1996) *The Voice of the Child. A Handbook for Professionals.* London: Falmer Press.

Scott, J and Ward, H (eds) (2005) *Safeguarding and Promoting the Well-Being of Children, Families and Communities.* London: Jessica Kingsley.

Seden, J, Sinclair, R, Robbins, D and Pont, C (2001) *Studies Informing the Framework for the Assessment of Children in Need and Their Families.* London: The Stationery Office

Seebohm Report (1968) *Report of the Committee on Local Authority and Allied Personal Services,* Cmnd 3703. London: HMSO.

Seedhouse, D (2005) *Values-Based Decisionmaking For The Caring Professions: The Fundamentals of Ethical Decisionmaking.* Chichester: Wiley.

Sellick, C and Howell, D (2003) *Innovative, Tried and Tested: A Review of Good Practice in Fostering.* London: Social Care Institute for Excellence.

SEU (Social Exclusion Unit) Taskforce (2007a) *Reaching Out: Progress on Social Exclusion.* London: The Cabinet Office.

SEU (Social Exclusion Unit) Taskforce (2007b) *Families at Risk Review: Background Analysis.* London: The Cabinet Office.

SEU (Social Exclusion Unit) Taskforce (2008) *Reaching Out: Think Family.* London: The Cabinet Office.

Shah, R (1995) *The Silent Minority. Children With Disabilities in Asian Families.* Derby: National Children's Bureau.

Sinclair, R and Carr-Hill, R (1997) *The Categorisation of Children in Need.* London: National Children's Bureau.

Smith, F, Brann, C and Conroy Harris, A (2011) *Fostering Now.* London: British Association for Adoption and Fostering.

Smith, F, Stewart, R and Conroy Harris, A (2011) *Adoption Now.* London: British Association for Adoption and Fostering.

Smith, R (2008) *Social Work with Young People.* Cambridge: Polity Press.

Stallard, P (2002) *Think Good – Feel Good.* Chichester: John Wiley and Sons Ltd.

Statutory Instrument (1991) *No. 895: Review of Children's Cases Regulations (1991)* (repealed). London: The Stationery Office.

Statutory Instrument (2004) *No. 1419: Review of Children's Cases (2004) (Amendment) England Regulations* (repealed). London: The Stationery Office.

Statutory Instrument (2010) *No. 959: Care Planning, Placement and Case Review Regulations 2010.* London: The Stationery Office

Statutory Instrument (2011) Fostering Services (England) Regulations 2011 S1 2011/581

Stones, C (1994) *Focus on Families. Family Centres in Action.* Basingstoke: Macmillan.

Swain, J, Finkelstein, V, French, S and Oliver, M (eds) (1993) *Disabling Barriers – Enabling Environments.* London: Sage.

The Advocacy Services and Representations Procedure (Children) (Amendment) Regulations (2004) SI719. London: The Stationery Office.

Thomas, C and Beckford, V with Lowe, N and Murch, M (1999) *Adopted Children Speaking.* London: British Association for Adoption and Fostering.

Topss UK Partnership (2003) *National Occupational Standards for Managers in Residential Care.* Leeds: Topss UK Partnership.

Tunstill, J and Aldgate, J (2000) *Services for Children in Need: From Policy to Practice.* London: The Stationery Office.

Tunstill J, Aldgate J and Hughes M (2007) *Improving Children's Services Networks. Lessons from Family Centres.* London and Philadelphia: Jessica Kingsley.

Tunstill, J, Hughes, M *et al* (2004) Family support at the centre: family centres, services and networks, in Quinton, D (2004) *Supporting Parents. Messages From Research.* London: Jessica Kingsley.

Tunstill, J, Meadows, P Allnock, D and McLeod, A (2002) *Sure Start National Evaluation.* Nottingham: Department for Education and Skills.

UNICEF (2006) The Convention on the Rights of the Child. Available at www.unicef.org/crc (accessed 30 May 2012).

UNICEF (2007) *Child Poverty in Perspective: An Overview of Child Well-Being in Rich Countries.* Available at www.unicef-irc.org/publications445 (accessed 30 May 2012).

Unsworth, L (2004) *Choice, Power, Performance: The Need for Information on Care Services in England.* London: The Stationery Office

Utting, W (1991) *Children in the Public Care: A Review of Residential Child Care.* London: HMSO.

Van der Gaag, A (2008) *Health Professions Council, Standards of Conduct, Performance and Ethics.* Available at www.hpc-uk.org/aboutregistration/standards (accessed 30 May 2012).

Walker, S and Beckett, C (2011) *Social Work Assessment and Intervention,* Second Edition. Lyme Regis: Russell House Publishing.

Warner, N (1992) *Choosing with Care (The Warner Report).* London: HMSO.

Warren, C (1998) Family centres and their role in community development. *Family Support Network Newsletter* (13): 14–20.

Waterhouse, R (2000) *Lost in Care: Report of the Tribunal of Inquiry into the Abuse of Children in Care in the Former County Council Areas of Gwynedd and Clwyd Since 1974.* London: Department of Health.

Waterhouse, S (1997) *The Organisation of Fostering Services.* London: NFCA.

Watson, N, Shakespeare, T, Cunningham-Burley, S and Barnes, C (1999) *Life as a Disabled Child: A Qualitative Study of Young People's Experiences and Perspectives. Final Report of an ESRC-Funded Study.* Edinburgh: University of Edinburgh.

Westcott, H and Cross, M (1996) *This Far and No Further: Towards Ending The Abuse of Disabled Children.* Birmingham: Venture Press.

Whalley, M (1994) *Learning to Be Strong: Setting Up a Neighbourhood Service for Under-5s and Their Families.* London: Hodder and Stoughton.

Wheal, A (2004) *Adolescence: Positive approaches for Working with Young People,* Second Edition. Devon: Russell House Publishing.

Wilson, K, Kendrick, P and Ryan, V (1992) *Play Therapy. A Non-Directive Approach for Children and Adolescents.* London, Philadelphia: Bailliere Tindall.

Wilson, K, Sinclair, I, Taylor, C, Pithouse, A and Sellick, C (2004) *Fostering Success: An Exploration of the Research Literature in Foster Care.* London: Social Care Institute for Excellence.

Wooley, P V and Evans, W A (1955) The significance of skeletal lesion in infants resembling those of traumatic origin. *Journal of the American Medical Association,* 158 (7).

Websites

www.baaf.org.uk
www.ccnuk.org.uk
www.contactafamily.co.uk
www.councilfordisabledchildren.org.uk
www.dfe.gov.uk
www.direct.gov.uk/en/parents/preschooldevelopmentandlearning/
nurseriesplaygroupsreceptionclasses/dg_173054
www.doh.gov.uk
www.education.gov.uk
www.education.gov.uk/childrenand young people/families/a00205069/action-plan-for-adoption-tackling-delay
www.espp.org.uk
www.fostering.net
www.jrf.org.uk
www.nwtdt.com
www.rightfromthestart.org.uk
www.sharedcarenetwork.co.uk

Index

Added to a page number 't' denotes a table.